PRAISE FOR *MAD CITY: THE TRUE STORY OF THE CAMPUS MURDERS THAT AMERICA FORGOT*

An Amazon Charts most-read book

"Arntfield presents his murder case as 'perhaps the greatest story never told in American history, at least the history of American crime.'"
—*New York Times Book Review*

"All of the stories are fascinating, especially the aspects of criminal profiling in them . . . Fans of TV shows like *Criminal Minds* and *CSI*, especially, will be intrigued."
—*Kirkus Reviews*

"Thrilling . . . Ranks among the most important books to rise from the dust of the true-crime explosion."
—M. William Phelps, host of *Dark Minds* and *New York Times* bestselling true-crime author

"Written by the internationally renowned criminologist and criminal humanist Michael Arntfield, this book is remarkable in several ways—it provides deep, penetrating insight into the nature of the criminal mind via an eclectic approach, and it sheds light on the kinds of internal pathologies that guide the behavior of many criminals. This is required reading for experts and the general public alike. A truly great read."
—Marcel Danesi, PhD, director of the Program in Semiotics and Communication Theory and professor of linguistic anthropology at the University of Toronto

"Arntfield's ability to dig deep on case details in the story of one woman's quest to catch a killer is truly inspiring. A must-read for anyone interested in true crime."

—Karla Tolstoy, host of *Stand Up, Speak Up*

"Arntfield is a tireless cold case investigator, armed with a razor-sharp mind and even sharper prose. In *Mad City*, he makes all the right connections—a fascinating work of true crime and popular criminology."

—Lee Mellor, author of *Cold North Killers* and *Rampage*

MONSTER CITY

MONSTER CITY

CITY

MURDER, MUSIC, AND
MAYHEM IN
NASHVILLE'S DARK AGE

MICHAEL
ARNTFIELD

Little
a

Published by Little A, New York
www.apub.com

Amazon, the Amazon logo, and Little A are trademarks of Amazon.com, Inc., or its affiliates.

ISBN-13: 9781503952881 (hardcover)
ISBN-10: 1503952886 (hardcover)
ISBN-13: 9781503954359 (paperback)
ISBN-10: 1503954358 (paperback)

Cover design by Faceout Studio, Derek Thornton

Printed in the United States of America

First edition

In loving memory of my mother

CONTENTS

Prologue

The Nashville Sound

"When I hear music, I fear no danger. I am invulnerable. I see no foe."

—Henry David Thoreau, "Winter"

March 7, 1994

The only record in the jukebox that didn't qualify as what they were still curiously calling "new" country was a prehistoric-looking vinyl .45 single by Bill Deal and the Rhondels. He'd flipped through the repertoire twice—and then thrice—and was dead sure of the fact. He was equally sure that he *hated* country music, both old and new alike. He had figured that out long before he came back to Nashville.

But, after all, he hadn't returned to Music City for the pedal steels, fiddles, or line dances. Nor had he come back for the BBQ chicken, Daisy Dukes, Commodores, or any of the reasons others had come or would again. He'd come for the hunt, for the sport of it all. He was awake now. His eyes were open. When it was all over, they would use newfangled terms like *activated psychopath* and *malignant narcissist* to try to capture the essence of his malevolence—to clinically classify and quantify his pure evil.

In the meantime it dawned on him that the revamped country motif and ensuing city renaissance had spawned a Nashville that was markedly different from how he first remembered it. Music City had changed; it had undergone a makeover as unexpected as it was extreme. By the spring of '94, his evil odysseys had sent him to all kinds of locales. They had squired him from one coast to another, up Tornado Alley and back down again. But they had now taken him back to the South—back to his preferred hunting ground. His home turf. It was where he knew that his prey would eventually come to him. He knew his victims would inevitably come, as they had before, to Music City in search of the Nashville sound. He'd done his homework: He listened to people. He studied them like scientists study specimens in a cage or a terrarium, from the outside looking in. After all, he wasn't like them, not like other people. But he'd gotten good at pretending—at least for a little while.

He'd inevitably fooled just about everyone. He'd fooled the hack judge who let him walk out on bail after his first murder. He'd fooled his marquee lawyer, who still thought he might somehow be innocent of the horrors for which he'd already been accused and would be again soon. He'd even fooled his own kids. He'd fooled all the customers and staff—*especially* the staff—back at his computer store that had turned into a license to print money. It was a good store. It was an even better cover. The customers who came and went were the same people from whom he'd learned the most—the regular Nashvillians he studied to discover what made them tick. To find out what made them scared.

But there was one person he couldn't fool. It was the one cop who'd caught him—the same cop who'd solved his first murder and who'd locked him up for as long as he could. But not long enough. He even knew the cop's name. That name was Pat Postiglione. It was the name of the man who, before long, would be onto him once more—who'd be watching his every move. Pat was the man. Pat knew that he would soon be compelled to kill again—what he was capable of.

In the meantime the monster couldn't help but wonder what made Pat tick, how he was able to see the things that other cops couldn't or wouldn't see. He especially wondered how Pat had managed to solve the last murder so quickly—especially after he'd burned the body. Burned it badly and cruelly. He also wondered how he'd need to switch things up this time around, even if just to throw Pat a curveball. One thing he knew for certain was that he'd picked the location of his next murder more wisely. It was a dive bar with a stage and mic—a place subsumed in the Nashville sound. It was pitch-perfect.

He knew that the Nashville sound was the driving force behind the city's undeniable revival and what was drawing fresh meat there from all over America. He also knew the "sound" wasn't just a sound at all. It wasn't just a certain timbre or studio gimmick. It was more of an ethos, one that marked the dawn of a new era—the harbinger of a new genre and a new generation all at once.

By summertime all the local hot spots—Broadway, the Opry, Printers Alley, the Bluebird, the Country Music Hall of Fame—would be full of aspiring star-lets and guests at bachelorette parties chasing the sound. They'd all be wall-to-wall with Southern belles and other ingénues with their guards down—girls either too naïve or too polite to not get into a stranger's car. He'd already killed once for thrills and just to scratch the itch. Now he was getting a taste for it. Now on open mic night at the latest dive bar in his sights, he'd merely have to sit and wait. He scanned the scene of his current death trap for the next contestant.

As a Michelob clock behind the bar read 7:02 p.m. in blue neon, the mon-ster was deep in thought and pondering his first move. His eyes widened as he took in the panorama of the bar in search of suitable prey. To his right, a lifer at Bridgestone crash-landed an empty tumbler glass on the bar and nodded for another. To his left, a kid in a Tennessee State U jacket slouched in a pri-vate booth littered with happy-hour debris. He gabbed on a Motorola "brick" proto–cell phone and took Arena Football League bets. Across the room, a Germantown cougar with white eyeliner talked dirty to a gadfly from the Gulch and flogged her demo tape. To their left, a rube replete with camouflage rum-maged for change while sizing up a row of arcade machines collecting dust: *Defender, Centipede, Paperboy, After Burner*. A trio of Alabama debutantes with mile-high hair huddled near the door while guzzling Zimas and fighting over a battered pack of Winstons; a good old boy from McMinn County KO'd the mirror in the men's room when he didn't like what he saw. It was at that moment that the monster caught a glimpse of the main entrance. That's when *they* walked in.

The man walking in front was barely a man in the literal or legal sense. He was more of a kid—maybe midtwenties, at most—and was slinging a new Yamaha six-string acoustic. Unlike most of the poseurs to come to Nashville, this particular contestant had not only the obligatory "Achy Breaky" mullet but also a high-priced guitar case to round out the ensemble—to confirm that he'd arrived that night in search of stardom and wanted to look the part. He was a kid out of his league with no antennae up, completely unprepared for what would come next. He was lost in a fantasy—a new country dream about to become a nightmare.

It was then that the barkeep stepped up to a mic on the modest stage at the back of the room. It was then that he announced the start of amateur talent night. It was then that the monster's plan began to take shape. It was then that the plan coalesced from nothing into something. Soon it would be his everything. It would be his dénouement. It would be his punctuation mark on Music City.

As the kid with the guitar mounted the stage, a pair of Roper boots less than a day outside the store gave him away as an out-of-towner playing with house money—maybe a trust fund, maybe an inheritance—and trying his luck for a few months until the well went dry. Alongside the kid, *she* was a platinum blonde with pin-up panache. She also had a gleam in her eye and an innocent naïveté about her. She'd believe anything anyone told her; she'd do anything to stand by her man. They were picture-perfect. They were perfect targets.

The monster watched as the Stagecoach Lounge's sound guy tipped his Stetson to the kid with new boots while he unclasped the newly bought department-store case. It was then that the girl by his side began lathering him with praise and encouragement. The aspiring entertainer had arrived right on cue; he would be the first to take the stage that night. The warm-up routine would also leave the watching monster just enough time—time enough at last— to be with the girl alone and to seal the deal. Time enough to lay the trap. The night was still young. So were they.

As the kid stepped to the mic amid some tepid applause, his hands trembled as he formed a basic C chord for the first strum. He checked tuning; he turned some pegs for show—he looked around and feigned conviction. All the while he stared through some bad stage lights refracted by secondhand smoke while desperately seeking the girl he'd come with—his biggest fan. He soon found her seated only a few feet into the crowd. He looked at the girl as she looked back at him. She rocked back and forth with genuine excitement, screaming "Go, Robb!" with gusto.

Now, at last, the first of the monster's unwitting prey had a name. It would be all he needed to butter her up, to make his entrée and reel her in. They had never even seen him coming. For reasons that no one would ever really know, the road had taken the wide-eyed young couple from San Diego to, of all Nashville bars, that particular bar on the first and, ultimately, last day they'd ever spend in Music City. Their last night on earth.

It was only once Robb started clumsily building the chords of what sounded like the latest Toby Keith single that it all began to unfold as the monster had planned—as he had predicted. In no time flat—before even sitting down—he had flipped the girl a fake smile after she caught his eye by chance. A minute later he flipped her an equally fake biz card. The card and the antics alike were meant to spell *Music Row Big Shot* in living color. He told her what she wanted to hear—what she *needed* to hear. He told her that Robb wasn't just channeling Toby Keith, he was the *next* Toby Keith. He said that Robb had mastered the right sound—that he had *that* Nashville sound. He told her that he knew things. He knew people.

In Nashville in March of '94, it was the oldest trick in the book, but it was good enough. She smiled back and said her name was Kelli. She hadn't a clue in the world that she was now on a clock—that she had no more than two hours to live. Like those who'd come before them and those yet to follow, Robb and Kelli Phillips's road to Nashville was a one-way trip. This time, the monster would give Pat more than he bargained for—a case that would truly test his mettle. He felt as though he and the cop were perhaps even starting to develop a repartee through murder. Like James Moriarty and Sherlock Holmes, he was the criminal genius, and Pat was the sleuth—the necessary adversary who both dogged and inspired him. His dramatic foil.

One way or another, the monster knew he'd started something—something even bigger than himself. Beneath the bright lights, a sinkhole was about to open up beneath Music City to reveal a darkened recess—an abyss from which other odious and unfathomable things would soon come crawling. The monster was, after all, much like his next victim, only the opening act. The feature attraction would soon be on his way.

Part I

The Vandyland Murders

"Everyone who has ever built anywhere a 'new heaven' first found the power thereto in his own hell."

—Friedrich Nietzsche, *On the Genealogy of Morals*

Chapter 1

Innocence Lost

They called it the "rural purge." It was in the fall of '71 when the network suits at all three major broadcasters—NBC, ABC, CBS—made it clear they were cutting the cord on the flyover states. Especially the South. Especially Tennessee. That same fall season, the execs in corner offices summarily jettisoned all things countrified, the same shows that had been their bread and butter since the golden age of television. Serialized Westerns, heartland dramas, and rural-themed comedies and variety series were the hardest hit. Viewers had grown weary, they thought, of wholesome entertainment and longed for more provocative and gritty urban content—for series that allowed them to protract the same violence and human misery they watched on the evening news into their living rooms every night as prime-time entertainment. In a sense the suits were right. The world had changed, and television had failed to keep pace. America was now more *Streets of San Francisco* than it was *Green Acres*.

But the rural purge was more than just a cabal of studio honchos in LA redrawing lines on the national television map. The choice to permanently pull the plug on nostalgic and good-natured television content—America's proverbial window into the modern world—was symbolic of a larger change, a new revolution on both sides of the Mason–Dixon line. It was a seismic shift in the nation's collective mood and awareness, a tilt toward the belief that such old-time sentiments were outmoded at best, corny at worst. The belief among cynics of the day was that an era of innocence had ended, or perhaps never even existed in the first place. For the most part, those same cynics were right.

The city of Nashville, as the Tennessee state capital and America's beloved Music City, at once bore the brunt of the rural purge and the perceived end of this same innocence. Many variety shows as well as country-and-western-themed series had been shot on location there from time immemorial. The then still popular *Johnny Cash Show*, filmed at the iconic Grand Ole Opry, was among the first musical variety series to meet the axe. Others soon followed, including the intentionally campy and always tedious *Hee Haw*, which defied the odds and later managed to hobble along in the endless purgatory of syndication for another two decades. It would be nearly another ten years before TNN—The Nashville Network—rode the wave of mainstream popularity that was "new" country and put the city back on the television map. In the meantime Music City was to do some purging of its own. It was the beginning of the end.

What no one had bothered to notice at the time was that the network-television cycle for 1971–72 had also kick-started another trend. Beginning with a slow burn that would last for the next two decades and beyond, Nashville's annual murder rate would eventually creep up by over 60 percent. It would prove to be a staggering increase for what had historically been a safe, stable, and predictably low-crime city, at least by the standards of the South, where crime had always been higher than the national average. The city had long been a tourist trap where unwieldy mechanical bulls and the price of drinks at the honkytonks off Lower Broadway had been the greatest perils that locals and visitors alike were apt to face. But the seventies brought forth change. At first that change was subtle and insidious. Soon, however, there was a noticeable spike, coinciding with television's rural-themed purge, in overall violent crime across the whole city. Although it was an increase also seen in other American municipalities, Nashville's rise was surpassed only by traditionally and notoriously notable locales such as Miami, Chicago, and New York, the latter at that time a drug-infested dystopia with over ten times the population of Music City. But amid this new era of violence, it seemed one Nashville institution would remain unscathed. The locals called it Vandyland.

Vanderbilt University was founded in 1873 by the famed shipping-and-railroad magnate Cornelius Vanderbilt. The "Commodore," as he was known, ponied up the initial million dollars (worth about twenty million today) in needed seed money despite never having himself been to Nashville. He had hoped that the endowment sent via New York City would serve as a goodwill gesture—a seven-figure olive branch—to ease tensions between the North and the South following the Civil War. Before long, the Commodore's donation would in fact turn Vanderbilt University into one of the most prestigious and distinctive private universities in the world and arguably the leading medical center in America. On the heels of that same endowment used to purchase the seventy-five acres of prime land, located in present-day Midtown, other money—both old and new—soon followed. The Vanderbilt campus, or Vandy, as it soon became affectionately known, later expanded beyond its original core. Before long it also included the abundant woodland known as Sacred Grove, which was then followed by expansion along all areas of West End Avenue and 21st Avenue. In due course the entire area surrounding the lush and manicured campus—Greek Row, expansive medical and athletic complexes, stately homes replete with ivy—became collectively known as Vandyland. The name stuck.

The original seventy-five-acre Vanderbilt campus as it appeared to the first students arriving there in the fall of 1875. Courtesy of Haines Photo Co.

Vandyland has a zip code and can be found on a map but also has a certain immaterial value, a certain ethos of timeless sophistication and imagination—an old-money respectability that can't be faked. Vandyland, like many parts of Nashville, has an otherworldly quality to it, one that can lead you to not only let your hair down but also your guard. Living and working within Vandyland was and remains like being immersed in a protective bubble—like existing under a specially designed and utopian dome. It's a place where you are protected from the outside, and bad things are not supposed to happen. It was always supposed to be perfect by design—not to mention perfectly safe. That's precisely why what happened overnight on February 2, 1975, was so unbelievable. How it served as a portent of things yet to come. Why it changed everything.

Chapter 2

STALKED

The winter of 1975 started like most winters in Nashville, at least weather-wise. The same humid subtropical climate that brings out the rattlers and Jurassic-sized insects in the summertime means sunny and generally mild days in the winter. It also means—both then and now—that so much as a single freezing rainfall or inch of powder snow shuts down the entire city as though it were the storm of the century. There had already been a couple of these Tennessee-style "snow days" by February of '75. Snow days that had sent the inhabitants of Vandyland into disaster-prep mode, picking the shelves of nearby markets clean and battening down the hatches, much to the amusement of anyone hailing from New England or the Midwest—anyone in town who'd seen and survived *real* winter storms before.

But the night of Saturday, February 1, had been milder than usual, and nineteen-year-old Sarah "Sally" Des Prez had decided to blow off her usual week-end duties as a part-time supervisor at her Vandyland dorm on the north side of the campus. Sarah was a freshman student and the daughter of a prominent physician at the illustrious Vanderbilt Medical Center. She was also an interminable free spirit who chose to move out of her family's palatial home in the city's Green Hills enclave and into the fold of Vanderbilt upon matriculating there in the fall of '74. Once there, she inevitably made new friends and quickly immersed herself in the nearby party scene, all the more lively since the Tennessee drinking age had been lowered to eighteen in 1964. And so it was that Sarah chose that balmy night of February 1 to go on a date with another Commodore freshman named George Hudson, known as Tram around campus.

The young pair started out the evening by catching the early show of Sidney Lumet's *Murder on the Orient Express*, starring Albert Finney as Hercule Poirot, the quirky detective. From there the couple hit up the city's Church Street bar known as Mississippi Whiskers, a now-defunct live-music joint near the Baptist hospital in Midtown. Defying the cautionary adage that nothing good ever happens after midnight, Sarah and Tram stayed well past closing time and caught annoyed looks from staff putting chairs on tables before deciding to then hit up an after-party at the Sigma Alpha Epsilon fraternity house. A massive and imposing medieval-looking structure with two crenelated towers, known as the Vanderbilt Castle, the frat house was a customary after-hours melting pot full of every college stereotype imaginable. It routinely looked like a casting call for any teenage angst film ever made, a setting that would foreshadow future films like *Animal House* and nearly every 1980s John Hughes coming-of-age movie. But, like those same nostalgic movies, the place was also betrayed by a more stark reality. Described in a 2013 *Bloomberg News* hit piece as being the deadliest fraternity in America due to a spate of hazing and alcohol-related deaths— negative publicity that would begin a campaign, in 2018, to ban fraternities from Tennessee altogether—the Vanderbilt chapter of SAE would, in the spring of '75, also have an initial indirect connection to what would become the first of Music City's most terrifying sex slayings. For decades, the case would also live in infamy as one of Nashville's most vexing cold cases. Some said it would never be solved. Most liked to pretend it never happened in the first place.

After watching Sarah throw up at least once at the SAE bender that night, the chivalrous Tram squired his date back home to her walk-up apartment in an old house on 20th Avenue South in Midtown. Worse for wear, Sarah, after letting herself into the small one-bedroom unit where she lived alone, made it clear the date was over at that point, offering Tram an earnest "good night" and nothing more. He saw her off at the door just before 2:00 a.m. That was the last time she was seen alive—the last words she is known to have spoken. Had Tram entered the apartment, a much different future might have unfolded for Vandyland and the entirety of Music City. Perhaps Sarah would have lived, or perhaps she and Tram would both be dead. Either way, a divergent course would have been charted. Whatever the case, someone was already inside the apartment waiting for Sarah's date to end. He was waiting for her to come home.

Within the next twelve hours—by the evening of Sunday, February 2—a cold front had moved back into Music City. A heavy winter rain drummed on the hood of Officer Thales Finchum's black-and-white Chevy Caprice when he caught the radio call to attend a third-floor apartment at 911 20th Avenue. The call that shot over the police band just after 11:00 p.m. sent the grizzled career street cop with the Nashville Metro PD to attend what the dispatcher described as a "female 10-64"—the dead body of a woman. It was Sarah Des Prez.

After not getting an answer on the telephone over the course of that same afternoon and on into the evening, Sarah's father and her brother Roger, a respected doctor himself, sensed trouble and drove over to her apartment, where they found the door locked. Flummoxed and filled with dread for reasons they could only chalk up to protector instinct, they used a second latchkey Sarah's father had made, to immediately make entry to the modest unit. While frantically calling out Sarah's name, they arrived at the open door to her bedroom to find her—motionless and cold to the touch—lying prone in her bed, naked from the waist down. Her face and neck were badly bruised and battered. Her attacker had sexually assaulted and strangled her to death after first pounding her face in with a severe beating. The scene read to Sarah's grief-stricken family—and to Officer Finchum's instincts as the first cop on scene—as a case of Sarah's having been ambushed while asleep or nearly asleep in her own bed. A case of her attacker being a veritable bogeyman who'd been hiding either under the bed, in her closet, or somewhere else in the small studio apartment. A bogeyman now at large and emboldened—walking the streets of Music City and poised to strike again.

One major problem early on in this case was that no one, from experienced detectives to the building landlord, could initially find any sign of forced entry. Whoever had raped and killed Sarah within the sanctity of her own home—and within the larger sanctity of the once seemingly impenetrable and hermetically sealed Vandyland—had done so after making a stealthy entry and leaving no trace of his work. Whether he'd picked the front lock or tripped a window latch after somehow making it to the third floor outside and then slicing the screen with surgical precision, he'd entered under the cover of a winter's night and waited for her to arrive home. He'd been methodical; he'd been patient—he *knew* her routine. He knew that she would have normally been working at her dorm on Saturday nights and would arrive home alone—and late. He'd spent weeks, maybe even months, keeping her under surveillance. He'd stalked his prey.

While Nashville and, more so, the tight-knit university community living within the fairy-tale world of Vandyland were both shocked and perplexed at what had happened to Sarah, Metro homicide cops tried to zero in on some initial and mostly convenient suspects—as was the style at the time. Naturally, her suitor, Tram Hudson, having taken the victim to the movies and then out partying, was initially the prime suspect as the last person to have seen her alive. The cops leaned on him hard.

But Tram was quickly cleared by detectives after a basic serology test—a now bygone pre-DNA method of blood typing suspects through saliva, semen, and other fluids—ruled him out as the assailant. A patent bite mark found on Sarah's upper right arm, however, remained a bit of a mystery. Since innovative and investigative fields such as suspectology and behavioral analysis were still in their nascence at the time—or in many jurisdictions nonexistent—the bite mark, although curious, appeared to have no instrumental purpose in the attack. It was a fact that left the cops of the day stumped. In reality, as we know now with the benefit of hindsight and decades of research, it was in fact an *expressive* form of violence, something done not as part of the modus operandi or MO— which is instrumental to the crime—but instead something that reflected the offender's signature.

Unlike the MO used in a given crime and in which each step has a specific and functional purpose, a signature is something that is sexual in nature or otherwise fueled by fantasy and obsession. Expressive violence is an act that is emotionally cold-blooded—planned, rehearsed, mentally visualized, and later replayed—and which reveals the hollowed-out and darkened center of a killer. While the MO solely reflects the nuts and bolts of a crime, the signature is an addendum to the main crime, much like any signature that appears at the end rather than the beginning of any work. It is something the offender does or feels compelled to do because it fulfills him sexually and satisfies some disordered and destructive fantasy. He *has* to do it before leaving the scene of the crime. It might include the collection of souvenirs, the taking of photographs, the posing of a body, or in this case biting his victim, likely after she was already dead. Indeed, the full implications of the Sarah Des Prez home invasion murder weren't fully apparent to anyone in Nashville at the time—or for a long time afterward, for that matter. No one in February 1975 knew exactly what they were dealing with. They didn't and couldn't in those days know about crime-scene signatures or what are known as paraphilias, the deviant sexual compulsions that prompt these same behaviors. They equally didn't and couldn't know how to prepare for what would inevitably come next. They didn't know and couldn't possibly have known that his killing again soon was an absolute certainty.

Neither had anyone at the time—cops, shrinks, self-proclaimed experts— seemed to have had the knowledge or training to recognize that her killer appeared to have stalked and surveilled her, unseen, with such effectiveness. And no one initially seemed to recognize the significance of the fact that Sarah Des Prez had been raped and killed in her own home by a perfect stranger. Perfect strangers, as Music City would discover in the coming years, are the foremost ingredients in creating the perfect murder. It is as close to a guarantee as the police can get that they—as they were in Sarah's case—are dealing with a moti- vated serial sexual predator, likely a serial killer. The perfect-stranger scenario ended up, however, increasingly becoming a working theory. A background investigation into Sarah's final few weeks alive revealed nothing to suggest she was having problems with anyone, nothing to suggest she was in danger or to suggest that anyone had been giving her the creeps. Combining that with the fact that leads and tips from the public were waning sooner than expected, it was becoming increasingly evident to investigators that Sarah was not only a perfect stranger to her killer but, more chillingly, the victim of what is today known as a targeted-stranger attack—perhaps the most difficult to solve. The term *targeted stranger* describes a homicidal scenario in which a killer identifies, voyeurizes, obsesses over, and then moves in on his prey, often at random. The entire time, the victim has no idea who their stalker is and that they've been effectively marked for death. They have no clue they are living their final days within a dwindling hourglass.

Since there is often no rhyme or reason for why a given person is selected in the first place, the ability to make any immediate or intuitive linkage between a victim and their killer in a targeted-stranger murder is rare. Sometimes selection is simply because the victim happened to fit a specific fantasy mold, one that reflects a killer's equally specific paraphilias and psychosexual disorders, or what is known as a preferred victim. Sometimes selection is entirely random—the apotheosis of bad luck.

Dennis Rader, the self-proclaimed Bind, Torture, Kill (BTK) Strangler, operated for nearly two decades, between 1974 and 1991, in the otherwise benign city of Wichita, Kansas, in this very fashion, killing ten people—including entire families—in what he called "missions" rooted in targeted-stranger stalking. A sadist and garment fetishist who often stole and wore the underwear of his female victims, Rader used the cover of his job as a municipal by-law officer enforcing frivolously Mickey Mouse municipal statutes to drive the suburbs and troll for victims, whose lives he would study in extraordinary detail before killing them. In one case, he was merely driving by a home with an open front door and caught a glimpse of the young family inside. Immediately he knew he had to kill them—and he later did in horrific fashion after considerable planning. Fast-forward to June of 2017 when an inveterate deviant named Brendt Christensen abducted and murdered University of Illinois student Yingying Zhang—whose body was never found—from a bus stop on the same Chicago campus where he washed out as a physics major, simply because she fit his profile of his "ideal" victim. Whether this ideal was constructed through the stalking of similar women or refined over years of indulging in online allurements and viewing erotic images, we may never know. For whatever reason, from the very moment Rader, Christensen, and others see their ideal victims, they are consumed with killing them—all of them they can find. It's often just that random. And terrifying.

But in the winter of '75 this was information that wouldn't be found within the pages of any Metro PD handbook. So as the Sarah Des Prez case started to get colder, opportunities were understandably missed to link her murder with other crimes in the city and region, crimes that we now know fall within the same spectrum of deviance. Today, in an age with standard sex offender registries to track convicts with known paraphilias they can't control, police would now have the means, in theory, to break down the Des Prez slaying to its basic elements. With today's knowledge that most homicidal sexual predators are also experienced burglars capable of precision entry, there would be a basic geographic cross-referencing of the murder to nearby "hot prowl" break-ins, or nighttime burglaries with occupants home and asleep as an intruder skulks around and watches undetected as a matter of arousal rather than theft. The facts of this case would today also have police ideally looking at recent cases of indecent exposure, a well-documented gateway crime to more dangerous acts of sexual predation, including murder. Metro detectives at the time, however, didn't have the luxury of accessing such avant-garde tracking methods. There would be no forays into criminal investigative analysis, or what's commonly mislabeled *profiling*. Even with such tools at their disposal, all that would have taken time. As it turned out, by month's end—just a little over three weeks after Sarah's murder—they'd already run out of time. Before anyone could stop to catch a breath, Vandyland got hit again. This time, it was even worse.

Chapter 3

Thin Mints

The Green Hills neighborhood in Nashville is what might be called the Vandyland annex. Located just off Hillsboro Road south of downtown, it's less than five minutes to West End Avenue and the entrance through the palatial gates to its interlocking-stone driveway into the original Vanderbilt campus. It's an even shorter trek to the newer multipurpose collegiate buildings off 21st Avenue. A number of the more seasoned professors and senior university administrators making the big bucks lived in Green Hills in 1975 and still do today—as do nearly all the doctors at Vanderbilt Medical. As do many of the professional athletes and country stars who call Nashville home. Sarah Des Prez also grew up in Green Hills. It would all turn out to be no coincidence.

Both old and new money have been consistently flocking to Green Hills, one of the wealthiest neighborhoods in America per capita, for over a century. Much of that same money ends up getting spent at the legendary Green Hills Mall that caters to Vandyland's most affluent denizens. It's a place where celebrity sightings, usually of the country-music variety, have always been commonplace. Even in the wake of the Sarah Des Prez slaying, which was still unsolved and had people otherwise double-bolting their doors, Green Hills was perhaps the Vandyland within Vandyland. It was unassailable. It was sacrosanct. Or so the thinking went.

On the afternoon of Tuesday, February 25, Marcia Trimble finished her school day at Julia Green Elementary on Hobbs Road in Green Hills. Weighing just over eighty pounds and with board-straight blond hair, the bright fourth grader with blue eyes and freckles was just a month shy of her tenth birthday when she rushed home that day to her family's residence on Copeland Drive to change into her Girl Scout uniform. After first watching a syndicated broadcast of *Gilligan's Island*, she then donned her uniform for local troop number 802 in order to deliver her final few boxes of Thin Mints, the Scouts' signature brand of cookies, to a woman named Marie Maxwell. Also a resident of Green Hills, Ms. Maxwell was only a short walk away from Marcia's redbrick ranch-style home where she lived with her brother and both parents—her mother, Virginia, the leader of the Scouts' 802 troop.

When Marcia set out that afternoon, the weather was mild enough that she didn't need a jacket for the brief trip. Although Marcia's mother had told her to put on a jacket, she rebuffed her and declared she didn't need one. Spring, she announced, had arrived in the city.

So donning a set of black boots and forsaking the coat her mother suggested, Marcia set out from her family's home that day shortly before 5:30 p.m. proudly wearing—even for a routine delivery—her official Girl Scout uniform consisting, in part, of a short-sleeved blue-checked blouse with a red neckerchief. Marcia figured she'd be gone at most thirty minutes, including the time it took for Ms. Maxwell to pinch her cheeks and talk her ear off, before she was back home again for dinner. Her big brother, Chuck, down the street shooting baskets in a neighbor's driveway, saw his little sister leaving the house carrying a brown box containing the four smaller boxes of cookies, figured she was making a delivery, and left it at that. Within only a few minutes, she'd vanish without a trace. She never even made it to the Maxwell home with the cookies.

When Marcia didn't return home by sundown, her family set out to look for her. By 7:00 p.m., they called for guidance from a family friend who was a Metro cop. Like most decent people who have never needed to use police resources, they were skittish about calling 911. But if anyone should have immediately called 911 that day in Nashville it was the Trimble family. By 9:00 p.m., Metro uniformed and plainclothes officers descended on Green Hills en masse. A full-scale search for young Marcia was soon underway.

An early "Missing" poster created in the wake of young Marcia Trimble's disappearance in Green Hills listed no physical description or other details, but featured three distinct images of the nine-year-old Girl Scout for the news media and volunteer searchers. Courtesy of Nashville Public Library, Special Collections.

When it was clear that something sinister had happened, some searchers began to riff on about how the incident would forever change Green Hills. A few said "God help me" at the very thought of it. Indeed, as impossible as it seemed, some cops conceded that Marcia might have been abducted in broad daylight and in one of America's toniest and safest communities by a stranger who'd seen her coming. In the aftermath of the Des Prez sex strangling, it should have sounded like a familiar refrain. The idea of an innocent child being targeted by a stranger while carrying out a time-honored American tradition was unconscionable and horrific enough. The thought that a child of the tender age of nine could be stalked and targeted by the same predator who had raped and killed an adult woman and Vandy student just weeks earlier was at the time certainly not on anyone's radar. The term *sexual polymorphism*—the willingness by sadistic offenders to toggle between different ages, body types, races, and even genders of victims so long as they have a warm body to defile and murder—was barely known at the time. Even if it had been common knowledge throughout the legal and scientific communities in Tennessee, no one was prepared to accept that a monster of such proportion would ever be found in Nashville, much less Vandyland. Much less Green Hills.

But the truth is that such a monster did exist—more than one, in fact. In time, as hours grew and there was still no sign of young Marcia, the only plausible conclusion the cops of the day could reach, perhaps by virtue of the area's sterling reputation as an enclave of blue bloods, was that the girl must have been snatched off the street. Taken not for some grotesque sexual purpose, but rather, as a hostage to hold for ransom. She *must* have been stolen to be ransomed; no one was prepared to consider an alternative. If nothing else, the theory at least gave hamstrung Metro detectives license to call in the Feds. And so they did.

Johnny Law arrived in full force in Green Hills on the afternoon of February 26, within twenty-four hours of Marcia vanishing. That day, the FBI's Knoxville field office scrambled half a dozen agents, deploying them to the Trimble home, where a reel-to-reel recorder was quick-rigged and hooked up to one of the family's ornate rotary telephones. The agents, working in conjunction with Metro major-crime detectives and investigators with the TBI—the similarly named Tennessee Bureau of Investigation—followed the kidnapping playbook of the day to the letter. It was anticipated that, after holding the girl for a couple of days and proving that he or they meant business, a call to the home would inevitably come with the usual ransom demands. Marcia's distraught parents were counseled on what to say once the call came, how to keep the kidnapper talking and carelessly providing details in order to maximize the ability to trace the call or analyze the voice, and to gather as much background noise as possible in order to reveal a possible location of where the call was made. No one ever thought that Marcia might already be dead. But when the ransom call didn't come after a full week had elapsed, there was a silent minority who began to wonder. Then, on the evening of March 3, the phone at the Trimble home rang. Marcia's father, Charles, picked up the line on his home office desk and said hello.

The voice on the other end of the line was mute, there being only tentative breathing coming through on the receiver. On a hunch, a G-man perched on the edge of the desk threw the switch on the Nagra IV-L recorder linked to the phone line to the setting labeled "No Limiter." Gears clicked, magnetic tape hissed, a single light blinked. Then the voice kicked in: inebriated male, middle-aged, an accent from out of state. It was hoped that it was the call from the kidnapper. Everyone hoped it was *the* call they'd been waiting for and that would confirm that Marcia was still alive. "The man who took her," the caller announced before a dramatic pause. "Yes!" Marcia's father offered back, desperate for something—anything. "Check the mosque," the mystery caller cryptically suggested. "Who is this?" Marcia's father countered. Click—the line went dead. A second call never came.

Although the cops concluded it wasn't the kidnapper, whoever it was had deliberated for some time before making the call and leaving the mysterious tip. While it could have been a kook looking to make trouble, in the preceding week no con men, self-avowed mystics, or cruel pranksters had bothered to call. After the Feds ran a lightning-quick trace on the line, it came back to an AT&T phone booth near the Urbandale Nations apartments, a place miles away from

Vandyland in a literal sense and worlds away in a figurative sense. The mystery deepened. The dread intensified.

It might have been another forty years before the term *Islamophobia* became the popular parlance of social justice warriors, but even in the winter of '75, Metro cops and G-men alike feared that the tip to check out the local mosque might amount to race baiting. It was the only known mosque in Nashville back then, located at 2420 Batavia Street, between Fisk University and Hadley Park. There was some sense that the tip was a convenient pretext to single out a minority community and stoke anger and intolerance. At the very least it reeked of a setup. The triple-crown task force, consisting of Nashville Metro, the TBI, and FBI, which collectively boasted over a dozen full-time investigators, also had no name to work with, nothing to corroborate the tip, and no other details to justify going in and shaking down the Imam or anyone else who might be at the mosque when they arrived. It was all a kettle of fish.

On a whim, however, a pair of curious Metro detectives that included the hard-nosed Captain Sherman Nickens went so far as to make a casual drive-by of the mosque the next day. They did some loose surveillance, as it's known, making a handful of laps around the block in their unmarked Mercury Montego. They did so in the hope that maybe whomever the caller was referring to might stand out as obvious. At one point they parked out front in their unmarked unit—a "plain wrap," as they called it—and considered going in, but their hunches told them that the whole thing had the makings of an ambush. Maybe, after all, the caller *was* the kidnapper. Maybe the whole thing was a ruse, a game of cat and mouse to lure them there and lead them into a trap. In the end, they drove away and never went in. The tip implicating the mosque went unchecked and was deep-sixed out of both political and operational necessity. The caller was never identified. But whoever he was and whatever the reason for his calling that night, he was telling the truth. It would take over thirty years to find that out. To make things right.

Chapter 4

Easter Sunday

It had been thirty-three days since nine-year-old Marcia Trimble had vanished when a man from Memphis named Harry Moffett happened to arrive for a temporary stay at a house on Copeland Drive, a home located just minutes from the missing girl's school. It was Easter Sunday shortly after 11:00 a.m. when the down-and-out Harry ran inside the house to alert the home's owner, a man named John Thorpe, that he thought he'd seen something terrible in the detached garage where he'd gone to grab a spare tire. After Thorpe himself went into the old outbuilding to investigate, he discovered a trail of Thin Mints strewn along the dirt floor of the structure. The trail led to the back of the garage and to the decaying remains of young Marcia Trimble, dead since the day she'd vanished. Marcia had never made it more than about two hundred yards before she met her killer, a man who'd been lurking behind a hedgerow waiting for her, as police later determined. The same cookies she'd had in hand to deliver that afternoon—which brought her into the clutches of her abductor and killer—had been opened and dumped on and around her body, one final indignity by the monster who'd brought her there. Marcia had been raped and strangled, her small and delicate hyoid bone having been fractured by a set of large hands. She was discovered on March 30—two days after what would have been her tenth birthday.

That same garage where Marcia was discovered three weeks after the one and only anonymous call was placed to the Trimble home had actually been checked by citizen volunteers on the afternoon of February 25 during a house-to-house search. It was even searched a second time during a subsequent effort by police and regular Nashvillians wanting to help a few days later. Yet somehow, for whatever reason, no one on either occasion had actually gone into the structure far enough to see her lying there in plain sight. Some citizens and cops alike inevitably chalked it up to being more than an oversight, more than evidence of half measures by well-intentioned but improperly trained and absentminded searchers. What had amounted to a mix-up that managed to place time and distance between the crime and Marcia's killer—and significantly delay the investigation in the process—soon became a major point of controversy. Scattershot theories about what happened to the girl and what *really* happened in that old garage went in all directions and soon divided city, state, and federal investigators.

There were even some investigators who were certain Marcia had been kept alive someplace else before being killed and delivered to the garage only a week or so prior. They believed they had missed their chance to find and save her over the previous month. Although this theory was buoyed by the relatively intact state of the body, it overlooked the fact that the body's presence in the garage during the cool and dry Nashville winter weather had significantly delayed what should have been advanced decomposition and access to the body by scavengers.

The reality of the situation, as others rightfully understood at the time, was that Marcia had actually been lured into the building—there being no drag marks in the dirt floor of the garage—before being sexually assaulted and strangled inside it, out of sight and earshot of passersby. Those who'd discovered Marcia—the property owner along with his temporary boarder from out of town—were naturally investigated as automatic persons of interest. After they were quickly ruled out as suspects, there then followed a snowballing series of additional theories about how a depraved maniac capable of such an unconscionable act could waltz into Vandyland undetected and be so bold as to use a stranger's open garage in the middle of the day to commit such atrocities. How, the cops pondered, could he have known about the garage in the first place? About Marcia? The popular consensus that the interagency investigative team soon arrived at was that Marcia's killer didn't waltz into Vandyland at all. He was a local; he was hiding in plain sight. In the echo chamber of the joint task force, it made complete sense—confirmation bias ruled. It was a cogent theory and an actionable hunch, or so they thought.

It wasn't long before investigators of varying rank soon had a name that seemed to match their theory of the invisible man. They didn't have to look too far to find him either. The initial house-to-house search had already kicked loose the name of a teenage kid investigators found a bit fishy—a boy who had admitted to seeing and speaking with Marcia sometime after she left her home and before she was snatched by her killer minutes, maybe even seconds later. His name was Jeffrey Womack, a spacey fifteen-year-old introvert who lived with his family just up the street at 4102 Copeland Drive, a mere five hundred feet due south of the Trimble home at 4009 Copeland. Womack, likely also the last person to see Marcia alive, had made his way to the Trimble home back in the early hours of the missing-person investigation on February 25 to admit as much. At the time, Metro uniforms, rousting him hard, as they should have, discovered during vigorous questioning that Marcia had, while on her way to deliver the presold boxes to Ms. Maxwell, actually approached him about buying some Girl Scout Thin Mints from her. The story not adding up, or so Metro police believed, Womack was ordered to turn out his pockets on the spot.

The boy, his parents at home and unaware he'd walked to the Trimble house of his own volition to tell the cops what he knew, saw, and heard, complied with the officers' stern demand and turned over the contents on his person: a crumpled five-dollar bill, a half roll of pennies, and a single condom. The cops found this suspicious and made a note of it at the time, particularly since Womack had claimed he shooed away little Marcia because he didn't have any money to give her for the cookies. He of course did. The condom, he said, was reportedly for use with his girlfriend, someone about whose identity he was oddly vague. Because Marcia had turned up murdered so close to Womack's home, police soon shone a light on him as the new prime suspect by default.

The narrative of the Trimble murder soon became one that was reverse engineered to suit Womack as the killer—a weird teenager with "hormones blitzing," as one detective curiously described him to the media—and a kid whom they theorized had become obsessed with and stalked his neighbor Marcia. This, in spite of his never showing pedophilic proclivities or other associated paraphilias in the past. Further, while Marcia had been sexually assaulted, and there was semen discovered on her Girl Scout uniform, there also had been no actual forced penetration. This distinction from most other sexual murders led investigators to believe that the killer either had an abnormally small penis or was too sexually inexperienced to complete the rape. Both scenarios, they figured, might apply to Womack. Their hunches were only compounded when, in the days after the body was found, they made a run at him and challenged him outright on his story.

This time, Womack was no longer talking. Once the boy's mother got wind of the original shakedown during the first day of the search, she phoned a prominent Nashville defense attorney and handed over a handsome retainer. This only intensified the scrutiny of Womack, the collective wisdom in 1975 Nashville being that only guilty men needed lawyers. The whole matter soon became a case study in what we now refer to as "police tunnel vision" where a person, rather than the crime itself, becomes the focus of the investigation and the evidence colored to suit a dominant theory rather than allowed to speak for itself. It's how the majority of murders, either rightly or wrongly, were solved back then in the absence of proper training and forensic expertise. But soon, the cops had a new problem.

The apparent mishandling of the key piece of evidence in the murder—Marcia's checkered blue Girl Scout uniform that contained the suspect's DNA—meant that the analysis of the sample at the TBI crime lab confirmed not one but at least *three* separate suspects. While it was an era before state-of-the-art genetic testing, the use of serology still allowed for the sample to be separated based on blood grouping, a process that had suggested it actually contained three or more separate groups. Investigators floated new scenarios in an attempt to explain the anomaly but still preserve Womack as the killer. They wondered if he might have lured her into the garage where some unidentified friends of his were already lying in wait; they pondered whether he'd initiated the whole thing and then allowed his buddies to do the dirty work. This revised narrative failed, however, to account for the fact that there was no penetration, and that the attack had an amateur, tentative look to it. It was much like the way the Christmas night murder and reported molestation of JonBenét Ramsey in Colorado would be described just over twenty years later, a whodunit that arguably endures as the most contentious cold case involving a child in American history—more so even than the Lindbergh kidnapping. In reality, the more plausible explanation the police had to consider in Marcia Trimble's case was less dramatic. It meant that improper evidence continuity and preservation techniques as the clothing passed through many hands ensured either crime-scene or laboratory cross-contamination. It meant a scenario occurred where people legitimately handling the item as evidence inadvertently left their own DNA on that same item—or transferred evidence from other items. Either way, they knew Womack was good for the murder. They were sure of it. Now they just had to prove it.

What the investigators of the day unfortunately didn't have available was the body of knowledge that the Justice Department's National Center for Analysis of Violent Crime now has, particularly the relevance between where and how a murder victim is discovered and its linkage to some overwhelming common denominators among their killers. For example, the position in which Marcia's body was found corresponds with what is today known as Disposal Pathway #3, that being when a body is left as is by that person's killer at the scene of the murder without having been transported, posed, or concealed in a second location. Killers who use this MO in disposing of their victims tend to have—as over ten years of cases and hundreds of associated victims recently have confirmed—a recurring number of biographical and behavioral commonalities when compared to killers who use other disposal methods.

Murderers who rely on the "as is" pathway tend to split evenly between whites and blacks, most being unmarried or otherwise living alone. Additionally, apart from not owning a vehicle, about half are employed in a part-time capacity at the time of the murder. Nearly one-third of these offenders, it has been found, have also been diagnosed with a major personality disorder or mental illness before the murder. In addition to already being in the psychiatric system, Pathway #3 murderers also have had at least one previous police arrest in nearly 100 percent of the cases. And in almost all cases, the victim is found to have been a targeted stranger, with the killer using trickery to lure him or her to the concealed kill site—in Marcia's case the garage on Copeland Drive. Sexual assault is a common denominator in nearly all circumstances, the victim generally being left partially clothed, just as Marcia was. Most concerning is that sexual murderers who use this method almost inevitably go serial in their killing, with roughly half of them murdering at least three victims before being caught.

Bearing these realities in mind today and using the applied sciences now available, it is clear that from day one, Womack was a square peg in a round hole in terms of his being a fit for the Trimble slaying. This is not offender "profiling" per se or other hocus pocus. Profiling as most people think of it is actually, in most cases, institutionalized guesswork and has, despite unsupported boasting to the contrary and mythologized depictions on film and television in the vein of Netflix's *Mindhunter*, a success rate of only about 4 percent. These same "successes" look suspiciously like luck rather than accurate prediction or deduction. However, examining a disposal pathway to learn more about a killer amounts to basic arithmetic and playing the odds—the metrics of murder used in much the same way that such statistical predictors are used in everything from pro sports to the stock market to make sense of long-term trends. It offers a greater degree of accuracy in prioritizing certain suspects; knowing the numbers allows detectives to triage persons of interest based on recurring commonalities and on the balance of probabilities—knowing that the best indicator of future behavior is past behavior.

The assemblage of detectives working the Trimble case, or Metro Nashville file #75-30512, as it officially became known, the number emblazoned repeatedly on an accumulating pile of banker's boxes, had their own varying theories about Womack's involvement. While they didn't have access to the key data and resources that cops today do, they did have hunches. They also had a dead little girl on the heels of the Des Prez murder, an inconsolable family and surrounding community, and a city on the brink. The media was running stories about Music City's lost innocence while pastors preached about the Devil walking the earth, about wickedness and pure evil invading and sullying the "beautiful South." Meanwhile, nearly nine hundred miles away, events were already in motion to make sure that Metro cops would, in due course, soon have help—that one day they'd have the upper hand, with the Des Prez and Trimble murders solved and the killer behind bars. They'd soon have a pinch hitter who'd arrive in the nick of time. In the interim, the Music City preachers were right—the Devil had come to Nashville, and there would be more blood. The city's Dark Age had begun.

Chapter 5

Beautiful South

North of the Mason–Dixon in the New York borough of Queens, the discovery of Marcia Trimble's body on Easter Sunday never made it to the pages of the *Times* or even the *Post*. The city, after all, had its own problems. These included clocking over 1900 murders that same year—later soaring to nearly 2300 within the next five years, courtesy of the crack epidemic and an unrelated boom in serial murder. Amid this chaos, a native New Yorker returned home at last from the Vietnam War. Transplanted from one battleground to another, he returned to find a city much different from the one he'd left only a few years earlier.

Enter one Patrick Anthony Postiglione. Born in 1951 in Flushing, Queens, to Italian immigrants, he later moved as a young boy to Floral Park on Long Island and then to the historic colonial city of Northport before settling back in the borough of Queens, where his father ran a small and fledgling HVAC business. It was in the Queens of the late sixties where a teenage Patrick ultimately found himself—and found trouble. Like many kids who would one day end up making the best cops, he ran with all sorts of crowds and ran afoul of the law before later championing it. He would hone his street smarts early on and do so under an array of fight-or-flight scenarios that would prepare him for his future career—for the fight of life. From day one he walked the line.

Patrick, or Pat to his friends and family, had by 1971 found an express ticket out of Queens for the short term, as many of his buddies had, by way of the war in Vietnam, ultimately enlisting as a volunteer with Mobile Construction Battalion 1 at age nineteen. By the time of the Vandyland murders, Pat had just finished a two-year tour in Guam clearing jungles with the famed Seabees, the US Navy Construction Battalion. It was the same storied unit whose innovative projects had already stretched from the beaches at Normandy to the tundra of Antarctica, following its creation in the wake of the Pearl Harbor attack during the Second World War. From the streets of Queens to the jungles of Southeast Asia, it was with the Seabees and their motto of Can Do that Pat became whole. He became a man with a plan.

Pat's battalion consisted of similarly skilled tradesmen who, while also maintaining reservist status, could, in keeping with the Seabees's founding principles, spring into action as a combat unit once the heat was on, rather than just duck and cover. It was with the Seabees in Guam and briefly in South Vietnam that a seed was planted in Pat. The unit to which he'd been assigned was a tight-knit group of volunteers that, unlike Pat, hailed largely from the American South. They were men mostly born and raised in places like Mississippi and the Carolinas, Kentucky and Tennessee—especially Tennessee. They were often larger-than-life characters with a certain moxie and worldview that Pat inevitably found ingratiating and purely fascinating as a native New Yorker who thought he'd already encountered every type of character imaginable. They had stories that seized his imagination. Although he'd thought he'd seen it all back home in New York, he clearly had not. Not even by a long shot. His fellow Seabees regaled him with tales about everything from Southern girls and Southern grits to Blue Devils tailgate parties and the blue mountain people of Kentucky. It was sometime in late '72 that Pat realized that if he ever made it out of the war alive, he needed to make it to the "beautiful South." He needed to see what all the hoopla was about—he *had* to see Nashville, as the pièce de résistance. The men in his battalion were channeling Music City. It was calling to him.

A near miss: Minutes after losing control of a defective US Army troop carrier and narrowly evading a pile of explosive acetylene tanks, Pat instead opted to collide with an empty barracks building in the jungle of Guam in the fall of '71 in order to bring the truck to a stop, saving his life and the lives of the entire camp in the process. He is seen here standing in the standard Seabees uniform with what remains of the vehicle, along with a newly broken left hand and obligatory aviator sunglasses. Courtesy of Pat Postiglione.

Pat eventually did manage to make it out of the jungle alive, while many of his buddies new and old never did. Many of those who did never really readjusted, never left the conflict behind them—their own forever war. Many of the same self-avowed hoodlums he'd chummed with in the late sixties were, within a decade, already spiraling out of control—booze, drugs, undiagnosed PTSD, and night terrors—and ended up dead one way or another in peacetime. They were the latter-day casualties of a war that was supposed to be long since over. Pat himself returned home to Queens following an honorable discharge in the summer of '73, doing his best to hit the ground running headlong into a new identity. He resisted being pulled back into the old ways—the old neighborhood and its allurements. He instead buried himself in the sanctuary offered by work, a key strategy for keeping his sanity in future years when he stared into the abyss. Especially when the abyss stared back.

Pat's first job back stateside was as a heating and cooling technician with his father's small HVAC business. And his first gig was doing ductwork in the South Tower of the World Trade Center, opened to commercial tenants just over a year earlier, following nearly six years of continuous construction. After troubleshooting some issues with the tower's fresh-air intake, Pat then went on to do installation work in the other buildings in World Trade Plaza, including WTC 3 and WTC 5, to be unveiled in piecemeal fashion over the next few years. The whole time, aside from the constant itch to head due south, Pat also found himself caught by the cop bug. It was a career aspiration that seemed unlikely at the time, one that was off-kilter at first glance, seeming light-years away from his life before he left for the Vietnam War. Perhaps that's precisely why it made sense. He knew the street; he knew criminals. He also had a cosmic yet common-sense view of justice hardwired into him, a frame of reference that transcended whatever hijinks he'd managed to get into as a hoodlum in Queens and the Bronx. As always, he walked the line.

Pat's time in Southeast Asia had also made him appreciate public service, camaraderie, and the looming sense of danger as a wire in the blood. By the fall of '75, he submitted his first unwieldy paper application to join a league of gunfighters as illustrious as the one he'd only recently left. It was out with the Seabees and in with the NYPD. Following some initial application hurdles, Pat ended up with a tentative offer of employment from New York's finest, short-listed to number 1100 on the roster in a hiring pool of over 12,000 cadets. But in questioning the likelihood of his number ever coming up, his being sent to the academy, and then his being posted to a precinct, Pat was soon starting to second-guess his career choice, looking instead at settling into his HVAC gig long-term and perhaps even one day taking over his old man's business. It was, after all, solid, honest work helping rebuild and modernize Gotham. But that wavering and second-guessing soon ended after Pat caught the ABC rebroadcast of filmmakers Alan and Susan Raymond's gritty 1977 documentary of the NYPD's embattled 44th Precinct in the South Bronx. He watched *The Police Tapes* and was galvanized. He *had* to be a cop—a good cop. It was solid work.

Rebuilding Gotham was one thing, but it was more honest work to *defend* Gotham.

Filmed over the course of 1976 through handheld cameras as the producers rode along with real street cops, *The Police Tapes* was the new hallmark of tragicomic American cinema verité, as well as the precursor to runaway hit shows in years to come such as *COPS*, *Live PD*, and everything in between. An early manifestation of the reality-television boom of the late 1990s, it was part guilty pleasure and part anthropology in action. With real cops barely making a living wage in a crime-and-drug-addled city now becoming television stars, first on PBS and then on a major network, soon, it seemed, everyone was trying—or at least thought about trying—to become an NYPD officer. Although Pat was supposed to have kept his number in line for a spot on the department, the integrity of the whole wait-list system soon came into question after an influx of the brothers and sons of serving senior officers started to apply, seemingly out of the blue. They'd all seen *The Police Tapes*, too.

To speed things up and to expedite his move from slinging dehumidifiers and ventilation ducts to fighting crime as he'd seen on TV, Pat doubled down. He hedged his bets and also applied to the Suffolk County PD, the agency that provides policing services to five New York bedroom communities on nearby Long Island. It was the same agency that had achieved notoriety only three years earlier by leading the investigation into the massacre at 112 Ocean Avenue in Amityville, the reportedly cursed home inspiring the 1977 book *The Amityville Horror*, and later the paranormal film franchise of the same name.

As Pat waited for word from whichever police force might be first to offer him a job, he kept reporting for work at the WTC site and other emerging New York landmarks to install heating and AC ductwork. He would often shoot the breeze there with other Italian Americans hailing from his native Queens and other boroughs—men who had cousins on both sides of the law. It was through them that Pat came to learn the grim truth about what might lie in store, what the real costs of being a New York cop might be. They were the same stories of mayhem and police murders that he'd read about in the *Post* or heard from his coworkers—hardworking men like Nino, Frankie, and Lenny who questioned the logic of police work—about what wasn't shown in *The Police Tapes*. They asked logical questions that defied logical answers. All Pat could offer in the way of rejoinders was that being a cop—in NYC, on Long Island, or anywhere—was his calling. As inexplicable as it was irrational, there was simply no escaping it. It was as if it were in his blood.

By eerie coincidence, that summer of '77 had been the so-called Summer of Sam. It was the precarious and sweltering summer that saw a revolver-toting maniac named David Berkowitz essentially hold all five boroughs hostage, with citizens locked indoors and always looking over their shoulders. Also known as the .44 Caliber Killer, Berkowitz was a dull-witted reprobate who ambushed and killed a total of six people—mostly lovers sitting in their cars—while claiming he was taking orders from his neighbor's dog channeling a rogue demon. Not surprisingly, that same summer heat wave and ensuing crime wave also kick-started a period when it would become open season on NYPD cops. With an average of eight officers slain each year on into the 1980s, Pat realized that he might not be out of the woods yet. He might have escaped the jungles of 'Nam and Guam, but he wasn't necessarily beyond the blast zone. He realized that his career aspirations might amount to pushing his luck; that the luck he'd had back in Vietnam might just run out now that he was back on home turf.

Pat ultimately realized that life as a cop—at least in New York—might very well be a one-way trip. He didn't care so much about the low pay (cops were earning an average of around nine grand, or twenty-eight thousand a year by today's standards); in fact, he didn't even worry about death. He'd seen enough of it, both at home and abroad, to learn how to make some sense of it. His own mortality was always in his peripheral vision—always watching. Waiting. What *did* worry him about checking out of this world early was potentially losing out on his one and only bucket-list item—a chance that he might die in the line of duty before getting to visit the South. He knew that even if he stayed safe long enough to get a paid vacation with the police, the meager salary of the day also wouldn't last long in Nashville. Not by a long shot. It was then, following that infamous summer of '77, that Pat decided it was now or never.

Scrounging the cash—some from the bank, some from the mattress—he'd been saving doing HVAC work for his father, along with some extra military service pay he had on the side, Pat booked himself a flight on American Airlines to what was then still Berry Field Airport in Nashville. Although he didn't know it at the time, he was in for a one-way trip after all. He'd soon discover that it was eminently easier to enter Music City than it was to ever get out. As the

Eagles song "Hotel California," still charting on the Billboard Hot 100 during the Summer of Sam, forewarned: "You can check out, but you can never leave." By the fall of '77, Pat knew that Nashville was the proverbial Hotel California made real and writ large. Queens and his NYC life were now in his rearview mirror—forever. He'd soon be a New York Yankee in Dixie.

As a young Pat Postiglione made his way to Music City to start what he thought might be his last vacation before becoming one of New York's finest—possibly his last vacation ever—things were also still very much in motion behind the scenes of the Marcia Trimble murder. While the Sarah Des Prez slaying from earlier that fateful February of '75 was comparatively cold and saw little in the way of progress, the Trimble slaying had haunted every city, state, and federal cop who'd ever seen the file or even heard the details. Few things stoked that collective fire more than the name Jeffrey Womack—and things were about to get interesting.

By the fall of '77, Womack had been under intense police scrutiny for over eighteen months. TBI and Fed sedans would sweat him wherever he went, and Metro prowl cars would do drive-bys of his family home in Green Hills and even a local diner where he worked as a busboy. Theories varied wildly among investigators as to Womack's role in the murder and the possible involvement of others. Most were convinced that a juvenile delinquent, as they called him, one who lived in the immediate neighborhood, was the architect of the whole tragedy. It was also considered that the lack of more invasive sexual intrusion on the young girl was evidence not only of a premature ejaculation—something we would better recognize today as textbook sadism by someone likely aroused by her screams than any actual sex act—but also of the killer with a "small penis." How the cops of the day figured that Jeffrey Womack fit this profile or how they ever planned on how to introduce this "small" theory into evidence in court, no one knew for certain. And while Womack might not be willing to talk to them without a lawyer, there was nothing that prevented the police from being more innovative and furtive in the approach. The decision was then made to send in an undercover operator to infiltrate the teen's workplace during his table-bussing duties. The fix was in.

But as the finishing touches were put on the undercover project targeting Womack at the now defunct Jolly Ox Restaurant during slow hours when an approach could best be made—ideally to befriend him and eventually solicit some kind of roundabout admission—other deviants had already infiltrated Vandyland to wreak havoc. These malefactors with their dangerously disordered proclivities and violent sexual fantasies should already have been on the short list of suspects for one or both of the Des Prez and Trimble murders once cops got wise to them and their presence in the area. They should have been flagged as persons of interest, at the very least, in even earlier murders in both the city of Nashville proper and the outlying areas of Davidson County. But they weren't. It was a different era of police work. It was siloed and paper-based; it was a crapshoot.

In the late 1970s, these disparate dots of murder were nearly impossible to connect given the limited resources, technology, and accountability of the time. There were no centralized fingerprint databases, ballistics databases, sex offender registries, or even real-time criminal record checks as there are now. DNA databases, taken for granted today, with their ability to genetically profile offenders and link them to crimes, were still the stuff of science fiction of the Philip K. Dick or Arthur C. Clarke variety. Between technological and training handicaps and what was often a pure lack of gumption in some cases, the net result was a phenomenon in murder cases known as linkage blindness, a phenomenon that endures to this day. It was linkage blindness in the late seventies that effectively prevented what should have been interpreted as related murder cases in Music City from being properly consolidated and seen as part of a series—part of a larger constellation that might have allowed a fuller picture and associated narrative to come into view.

In many cities, even on into the twenty-first century, this same trend prevails despite the overwhelming linkage and tracking tools that modern detectives have, compared to their investigative forebears. Interestingly, to this same point, while violent crime has been steadily declining in the United States since roughly the midnineties, the rate of detection—what's known as the clearance rate—has been declining even more steadily. There are far fewer murders per one hundred that are solved today than there were in the 1970s and even the late 1960s, when none of today's investigative technology was available. Although few experts seem to agree on why this is, one theory is that there are simply more stranger-on-stranger murders—including targeted-stranger attacks in the vein of Sarah Des Prez—than ever before. Such crimes are inevitably more difficult to solve because there is no short list of usual suspects and no known connection between victim and killer. By the late 1970s, Nashville was already living this reality. The city was already foreshadowing things yet to come across the whole of America.

Chapter 6

STOMPING GROUND

By the fall of '77, two names had become synonymous with a series of new sex attacks in Vandyland and also Nashville's Midtown, the latter attacks occurring closer to the campus of the almost-as-tony Belmont University rather than Vanderbilt itself. Founded in 1890, Belmont was then and remains today the second-largest private university, and the largest Christian university, in Tennessee. The comparatively dense urban campus has an opulent antebellum look in its architecture and yet a distinctly cosmopolitan vibe to its student body. It's a synthesis of traditional and trendy that, along with a unique program in music business management, has over the years produced a disproportionate number of country stars from its alumni. From Trisha Yearwood to Brad Paisley and Minnie Pearl to half of Florida Georgia Line, the school has churned out charting superstars and industry icons, both old and new. Its uniquely central location in the city—as opposed to the well-insulated and removed Vandyland— also made its co-eds a prime target for the deranged and the dangerous of the city's undergrowth when the city began to change.

The Belmont University campus, as opulent as Vanderbilt's but precariously located in the more urban Midtown district rather than in the secluded arboretum of Vandyland, soon found itself a sought-after destination for sexual deviants, sadists, and other criminals, both old and new, calling Nashville home by the late 1970s. Courtesy of user deldevries.

In the mid-1970s, against the backdrop of the nearly back-to-back Des Prez and Trimble murders farther to the west, there were two specific predators known to haunt the Belmont-Midtown district. One, a dangerous psychopath named Jerome Barrett, a twenty-six-year-old panhandler of no fixed abode, on February 17, 1975, attacked and raped Judy Porter, a female sophomore from Belmont. Barrett was eventually arrested in March of '75 for the crime after being collared for another felony in the nearby community of Berry Hill, a "city" in the official sense with a population of less than five hundred but that managed to maintain, as it still does today, its own skeleton-crew police force.

On the night of March 12—a balmy Wednesday during the last full week of winter—Barrett was busted by a firebrand Berry Hill cop named Tommy Lunn. This was after Barrett had forced open the sliding patio door of a main-floor apartment where a woman he'd been stalking for weeks was fast asleep. Unbeknownst to Barrett, the intended victim was a light sleeper and was awakened by the noise of the door moving along its track. She also happened to be the girlfriend of a Metro cop who'd left her with a loaded .38-caliber Smith & Wesson for protection when she was alone and he was either working the night shift or out of town. The result was that Barrett, having entered the apartment only to find himself staring down the barrel of a gun, quickly opted to flee into the night. He didn't go far. Responding officer Lunn would later find Barrett still on the property of the apartment complex, this time in the building manager's office after he'd forced the door open. He was found rummaging through a lockbox and set of keys hung on wall hooks inside. He was caught red-handed looking frantically for copies of keys for apartments known to be leased by single women—keys he knew likely wouldn't immediately be noted as missing by the manager. Barrett, it seemed, after waking his last intended victim and having his plans thwarted, intended to use the keys the next time he came back to the Bransford House Apartments on Berry Road, to avoid waking his next victim. To ensure his sinister plans weren't interrupted.

But after cuffing and patting down Barrett for weapons, Officer Lunn noted something strange. During the frisk he found that Barrett was wearing two layers of clothing that consisted of completely different colors. It suggested that he had planned to shed and dispose of the outer layer after his attack on his intended victim, both to eliminate any biological evidence and to ensure he didn't fit the description from anyone possibly witnessing him leaving the scene of the crime. It further suggested that Barrett knew what he was doing and had done it before. Particularly disturbing was that Barrett was target shopping for spare keys in the Bransford's manager's office before he was arrested. He *knew* who the single women were and what apartments they lived in. He had been stalking the *whole* apartment complex for months. Maybe years.

Thanks to some solid police work, Barrett never got the chance to strike again, at least not in Vandyland. He was soon linked to the rape of Belmont student Judy Porter as well as another home-invasion rape with a bizarrely sadistic verve to it since both husband and wife were targeted. That case, occurring in March of '75 in the Acklen Park neighborhood of Nashville—also within the boundary of Vandyland—involved Barrett breaking into a home, tying up the woman, and then waiting for her husband working the late shift to return home just after midnight. After beating and robbing the husband, he then made the husband watch him rape and nearly kill his wife. By all accounts, he had a similar plan for the Nashville cop and his girlfriend in Berry Hill before things quickly went awry and he got intercepted by Berry Hill PD. Linked to other crimes as well, Barrett ended up being sentenced to a combined total of twenty-six years hard time for several counts of aggravated rape and sent to the infamously dangerous and decrepit Tennessee State Prison.

In the meantime, back near Midtown, another predator named George Mitchell remained on the prowl. In his earlier years, the neighborhood kids had another more apropos name for him. They simply called him Kill.

George Mitchell, also known as Kill, was by the late 1970s a fixture around the area of Nashville's Belmont University and became infamous for a particularly peculiar—and dangerous—fetish. Courtesy of the Maury County Archives.

Raised by his grandmother in 1950s Section 8 housing, North Nashville's subsidized public lodgings, Mitchell could be routinely found during his formative years wandering the debris-strewn common area of the John Henry Hale projects, named after a benevolent African American physician from Nashville's Meharry Medical College. While on his walkabouts, the odd and solitary Mitchell would frequently brandish a stolen BB pistol, aiming and occasionally shooting it at anyone or anything that he stumbled across. Mitchell's cold affect and apparent disregard for life and property—in particular his fixation on his purloined pistol—had even the hardened lifers at the John Henry Hale apartments figuring him for a future killer. Hence his telltale nickname: Kill. In the end, Mitchell's BB gun obsession would prefigure a different kind of fetish. While today's cutting-edge long-term analysis and consolidated research by the Center for Homicide Research in Minneapolis suggests a correlation between specific handgun styles and finishes, specifically chrome finishes, that often denote a sexual attraction to guns and predisposition to rape, in Mitchell's case no one—police, school officials, neighborhood guardians, and Section 8 drug pushers alike—knew what to make of him or what he would do next.

As it turned out, George Mitchell was and remains an anomaly in not only Nashville history but the annals of American crime more generally. While usually dismissed outright as a freak and sex offender of the most bizarre variety, he still stands out as an important and yet lesser-known case study of how paraphilias remain in flux—always evolving and devolving—over an offender's adult life. One example is the way in which what begins as part of an MO for some other apparently nonsexual crime can ultimately become an end in itself—devolving into more of an expressive signature than as a means to an end. It's a phenomenon that was first noted in a rash of interstate robberies. In that example, a stickup man was found to be targeting only female clerks and groping them before stealing money while hitting a series of banks out in the boondocks. Investigators came to realize the robberies had never really been about the money—the money was only the justification, the rationalization, the cover story. The robberies were, rather, primarily sexually motivated and were surrogate rapes where the objective was to punish women who had a certain look to them. The clerks were both targeted strangers and preferred victims, and the stickup man was later found to have also been wearing women's lingerie under his disguise in each case to intensify the arousal he got from terrorizing them. But George "Kill" Mitchell's future crimes—while similar to this notable and contemporaneous 1970s case—proved even stranger still.

Sometime in 1968, nobody's exactly sure when, Mitchell's customary roaming ground moved from the Hale projects to the Belmont U campus and its surrounding Midtown neighborhood. Eventually he was to move toward Hillsboro Village, the Gulch, and even Downtown Nashville, where there was always a stocked pond of suitable victims. At one point he even began turning up in other cities as far away as Atlanta, with the same MO. Having evolved from a young wastrel in North Nashville into an adept pickpocket, purse snatcher, and shoplifter—the latter a petty crime but, some hold, often a distant early warning of possible future sex crimes—by the early 1970s Mitchell was given a new nickname. This ominously cold, withdrawn, and mute boy once known as Kill soon became known by a moniker that more accurately described his new adult fetish. They called him the Nashville Footstomper.

Mitchell's first crimes targeting women's feet involved his wandering around areas where young females, predictably wearing high heels year-round and sandals in the Tennessee summertime, could be easily spotted and followed. While sometimes Mitchell would simply wander around looking for a suitable target, other times he would purposely loiter in front of stores or in public places known to be frequented by these young women, usually walking alone. In either case he would approach his target and, without saying so much as a word, stomp on one of the woman's feet with steel-toed work boots, crushing the victim's arch and toes in the process. The assaults were the perfect distraction that allowed Mitchell, once his target fell to the ground or otherwise recoiled in pain, to snatch her handbag and make a run for it. If for whatever reason the stomp missed the mark and his victim maintained her composure, the MO was also subtle enough that Mitchell would simply chalk it up to an accident—or his being drunk and stumbling—and then offer a phony apology before disappearing around a street corner. Most of the time, however, things worked out as planned, in many cases leaving the women seriously injured and immobilized. Official Metro PD communiqués and the Nashville rumor mill alike soon began circulating word of the brash daytime mugger who, rather than brandishing a knife or pistol, stomped on his victims' feet to both immobilize and distract them, while onlookers were oblivious to what they were seeing. What no one realized at the time was that Mitchell didn't do it for the money but because the foot-stomp assaults were in actuality sexual assaults. He was just getting warmed up.

Ten years later, following intermittent stints in and out of the county jail for similar strong-arm robberies and other felonies being plea-bargained by public defenders on account of Mitchell having a compulsion with which he was grappling, the so-called Footstomper had by then abandoned any pretense of his attacks being used to facilitate purse thefts. From the summer of '77 onward—the same time Pat Postiglione set foot in Nashville—Mitchell had escalated to the point of no return. By then, he was simply stomping on women's feet and running off with great erotic delight. The bizarre act had metamorphosed into an end in itself; what had once been thought to have been his MO was now shown to be his paraphilic signature. It had likely been all along. After over a dozen convictions for similar conduct, Mitchell himself was well aware of the fact. There was no longer any purpose in dressing the conduct up as being a robbery.

Mitchell was that rare and often undetected breed of fetishist known as a partialist, or someone sexually fixated on a single and typically unusual body part, sometimes to a dangerous level. Many partialists now satisfy their secret libidinous needs in private by going online, where they can find an endless variety of visual stimuli. Alternatively they may sometimes rely on consenting, sometimes paid, adult partners to indulge these fetishes, including the more common varieties of foot fetishes. But when this erotic fixation is paired with violence, and when arousal is enhanced when it involves *non*consenting and frightened partners, the sky seems to be the limit in terms of the depravity and cruelty that some partialists are prepared to resort to.

Take for instance the so-called "Milwaukee Cannibal," Jeffrey Dahmer, who first became obsessed, while still a teenager, with his male neighbor's bare chest after Dahmer witnessed him jogging shirtless. After unsuccessfully trying to ambush and kill the young man to carve out his chest as a plaything, Dahmer later turned to the acquisition of street kids whom he dismembered before keeping—or in some cases eating—single body parts he found arousing. Charles Albright, "the Dallas Eyeball Killer," while similarly a young man, became sexually obsessed with women's eyes as stand-alone surrogate sex toys, after, like Mitchell, first beginning his criminal career as a petty thief. Following failed attempts to become a medical doctor—an ophthalmologist, no less—Albright instead chose to murder women and surgically remove their eyes as trophies for his collection. Consider also Oregon's Jerry Brudos, "the Shoe Fetish Slayer," who murdered at least four women in the late 1960s, in one case amputating and then keeping in his freezer the foot of the victim, using it from time to time to model the high heels he would place on the severed appendage. Brudos placed some of his victims in high heels after he murdered them, to then be posed and photographed. His obsession was so great that, following his arrest, conviction, and incarceration, Brudos was found with a stash of shoe-store mail-order catalogues hidden in his prison cell. Just as was the case with George Mitchell in Tennessee, authorities in Oregon had no idea what to make of Brudos—they had no clue what they were really dealing with. They equally had no inkling of what he might do next.

Things could have gone either way for George Mitchell given the intensity of his deranged foot fetish, predisposition to violence, and what remains known about his childhood—he could have very well been Music City's Jerry Brudos or even worse. One thing that is for certain is that he should have been looked at closely for other violent sex crimes—including the Des Prez and Trimble murders—that occurred in Nashville when he wasn't in custody on other charges. But he wasn't looked at. Nor was Jerome Barrett, the Belmont and Berry Hill nighttime prowler and sadistic rapist—the intruder caught looking for spare keys and prepared to play the long game while meticulously stalking his young female victims. As it turned out, Barrett even wanted to boast about that same psychopathic patience, his cunning methods, and how he always got away with it, the first chance he got.

Just over three years into his twenty-six-year stint in the state penitentiary, Barrett was overheard making a strangely cryptic overture to a fellow inmate after a dustup in the prison cafeteria. Angrily yelling as some kind of apparent intimidation tactic meant to have his opponent back down, Barrett made a self-incriminating admission, claiming to have "killed four blue-eyed bitches" back in Nashville before getting locked up on the Berry Hill beef. Upon hearing the bravado, a blue-ribbon jailhouse snitch, doing a five-year bit on a grand theft auto plea, quickly brought the information forward to Metro detectives through back channels. Yet, in spite of the specificity of the claim, the informer was just as quickly dismissed as an opportunist telling the authorities what they wanted to hear. As such, the information was never properly vetted and the statement by Barrett never looked into further. The informer, by that time already a frequent flyer in the business of diming out fellow inmates, had previously burned bridges with cops all over Tennessee. Since he had become the correctional-system equivalent of the boy who cried wolf, the tip was ultimately dismissed outright. It was viewed as a selfish attempt by what some might call a stoolie to reduce his own sentence by giving false information and even perjured evidence. It was also a time when all eyes were still on Jeffrey Womack, the presumably homicidal busboy and shifty neighbor of Marcia Trimble. On that front, the cops were finally about to make their move.

Chapter 7

Session 7

About the same time Barrett was boasting about what he may or may not have done to four of Nashville's women and girls before getting locked up at the state pen, the city's resident foot fetishist, George Mitchell, was serving his last Tennessee prison term for his bizarre stomping attacks on Nashville's sandal and heel-clad women. It would be one of the last stints of a total of eighteen years of his life spent in custody for his brazen sexual assaults first veiled as muggings. It was also about the same time when Pat Postiglione, for the first time, touched down in Nashville on February 15, 1978, to start his vacation.

Pat would spend his first three months in and around the city working odd jobs while his dad still held a seat for him with the family HVAC business in Queens. But while Pat's father may have been hopeful that his then twenty-six-year-old son was coming home, Pat had no intention of ever going back, something he realized after only a few days in town. It took him little time to decide to drop anchor in Music City, even though it was a place where no one seemed able or willing to pronounce his last name (*post-a-glee-own-ee*) correctly. He nonetheless considered Nashville his new home, just as so many others before him had. Although he didn't know it yet, Pat's decision to stay in town and settle there was one that would set sliding doors in motion. In time he'd rewrite history and also write the book on how to solve murder cases, especially cold-case murders. He'd write the book on how to hunt monsters without equal and live to tell the tale. Of the countless possible future paths he might follow after finally arriving in Nashville, the one that seemed to make the most sense was old hat. It was the one he had always felt was fate: police work.

Pat dropped off an application in May of '78 and waited. The lack of a follow-up response made him wonder if the paperwork had been properly filed or even looked at by anyone. He later called to check. He then called again—and again. While he waited, he spent his time working odd HVAC gigs around Tennessee—Knoxville, Chattanooga, Memphis, Murfreesboro—and then as far south as the "Ole Miss" campus, the University of Mississippi in Oxford, Mississippi. By August of '80, persistence had paid off and he was at last on the books as a confirmed Metro hire, a little over two years after first landing in town. He'd be going to the police academy on Nashville's Tucker Road in the final class for 1980, one that began later that same month—an intake they referred to as Session 7. The Metro PD recruiting captain who called the rent-by-the-week apartment where Pat was staying at the time to give him the good news, in the same breath proclaimed him as the "most persistent son of a bitch" to ever try to make his way south to Tennessee—or at least who wanted to stay and be a cop there. He was right.

By that time, Pat's future colleagues had already arrested busboy Jeffrey Womack on the Marcia Trimble murder and quickly released him due to a lack of evidence. The original investigators were bitter, and the girl's family was left irreparably heartbroken again. Pat's instructors at the Metro academy's Session 7 even talked about it. They riffed in lectures on criminal evidence and procedure about what went right and wrong with the arrest and release of Womack. They also talked at length of the Trimble case itself. They discussed its having occurred so close to the Des Prez murder and how, while markedly different in MO, both murders brought winds of change to Music City. They talked about innocence lost. But the timing was uncanny. As both tragic 1975 cases became academy parables, and the actual investigations into the murders went into deep freeze, the one man who would ultimately solve them both, along with a record number of other cold-case murders, was just getting started. Change was on the horizon.

After he breezed through the Session 7 academy class, the plaster was starting to set by the winter of '81. The plan that Pat had put into motion—the turning points that fate had consistently handed him since discharging out of the Seabees—was finally coming to fruition after twenty-two grueling weeks of training that had begun the previous August. Graduating at the top of his class in phys ed and firearms, middle of the pack and deceivingly mediocre in all other areas, Pat had a first assignment as a Metro patrolman not unlike the detail inherited by most rookies straight out of the academy. He worked a lonely one-officer radio car in the south end patrolling Section 8s, what was known as 12South.

By the time Pat hit the beat in South Nashville for the first time, even iconic streets uptown were in complete disarray. Famed routes like Printers Alley, once a quintessential tourist haven hawking grotesquely garish and sequined jackets and boots, along with all things George Strait and Dolly Parton—had devolved into a perilous gauntlet lined with muggers, pickpockets, pimps, and pushers. South Nashville was more like the New York that Pat had left than the Nashville his Seabees buddies had extolled with such passion. As would become commonplace for him, Pat soon found himself catching radio calls that led him to people and places his background as a self-described hoodlum in Queens—or even his time in Vietnam and Guam—could never have prepared him for.

After graduating Session 7 at the Metro police academy in December 1980, Pat Postiglione was soon set to embark on a career that most cops of the day would say was reserved for Hollywood. Within a matter of years, he was on his way from being a member of the uniformed patrol to catching what is thought to be more serial killers and solving more cold cases than any other detective, living or dead, on the record books in America. Courtesy of Pat Postiglione.

It was a sultry summer night in 1981 when Pat would catch his first murder case, as a twenty-nine-year-old street cop dispatched to JC Napier Housing projects—Section 8 apartments—for a report of a possible homicide. When he arrived—far older at the time than most other street cops catching their first murder—Pat determined the tenant in question was lying dead on the timeworn kitchen linoleum. The victim was a nineteen-year-old single mother, the killer her live-in, down-and-out, garden-variety loser boyfriend. The dispute that ended in murder, as Pat soon figured out, began over who would get the second half of a ham sandwich.

As Pat—gun drawn—searched the tiny ramshackle unit for any sign of the killer, he noted a crimson trail that led to a quivering infant less than a year old. The victim's child had crawled across her dead and bloodied mother and then all over the house, leaving a trail of blood behind her—tiny indiscernible finger and palm prints embossed in gore. It was senseless. It was all for nothing. It was Pat's calling within a calling. Murder would soon be his bailiwick. It already was. The more senseless the kill, the stronger his resolve to catch the killer. It was a basic corollary.

By the fall of '87—now at age thirty-six—Pat had made detective, quickly being transferred to the homicide division by virtue of his no-nonsense ability to put down tough cases. Once there, Pat worked under Detective Sergeant Robert Moore. Like most senior Metro detectives, Moore knew Pat's name long before he was brought into the fold, as Pat had handed Moore's team an impressive number of murder suspects while he was still working as a street cop—the ham sandwich slaying being just one of them. Moore and the other brass clearly recognized Pat's formidable work ethic and refined intuition.

From September '87 until September '88, the transfer meant that Pat would unofficially head a run-ragged graveyard unit within general homicide, a citywide flying squad of murder cops affectionately known within the department as the Midnight Watch. It was a necessary rite of passage. Many saw the hours required as tantamount to a bottom-of-the-barrel detail, an initiation ritual for newcomers to the squad or a purgatory for veteran murder detectives who had demons that foiled daytime productivity—guys who had screwed up big-time in the field and needed to ride the pine for a while to get their mojo, sobriety, or manners back . . . or sometimes all three.

Not surprisingly, Pat saw things differently—he always had. From the Seabees to crawling through the ductwork of the WTC, he had always been a bit too smart for his own good. By the fall of '87 he learned to forgive himself for it and to own it. The midnight watch as a plainclothesman, in his mind, was where true detectives cut their teeth during the witching hours. He reasoned it was a lonely but also an introspective and very necessary solo gig—police work's version of life in a monastery—that imparted a certain sense of humility and wisdom. It also enabled a certain appetite for ingenuity. Pat knew that great disruptive innovators and industry pioneers seldom if ever slept through the night. Pat was by then also acutely aware that the "Early to bed and early to rise" mantra of Ben Franklin was pure bunk. In reality, it was the inverse; the world came alive at night. It was also more likely to die at night. When it did, Pat wanted to be there. He knew that *real* police work occurred during that same twilight zone—the nether region between the Tennessee dusk and dawn—when the brass-buttoned pencil pushers and other police politicos were fast asleep in their beds, banking on the few remaining true cops to keep them safe.

By the time Pat was on straight midnights in general homicide, footstomper George Mitchell had officially become another state's problem. Two years earlier, Mitchell had taken the advice of his parole officer and hit the road south to Florida to try his hand at a new, less risky compulsion—hustling pool. The new vice didn't last long.

After pulverizing the feet of some women in a smoky and seedy arcade and pool hall near Jacksonville, he found that people there weren't afraid of him like they were back in Nashville's Midtown. What they did was hit back—and hard. After nearly being throttled to death by a group of angry locals, Mitchell decided to begin managing his violent fetish by getting a couple of chump-change jobs and using the extra cash to pay strippers to allow him to massage and lick their feet—among other things. He still had never been so much as questioned about the Vandyland murders, not even after Womack was, at least officially speaking, off the hook. Besides, the War on Drugs and War on Crime soon had cops all over America fighting offensives on two fronts—tilting at all kinds of windmills. The Vandyland murders of 1975 were, quite simply, yesterday's news.

While many Metro detectives thought Womack was good for the Marcia Trimble murder and were still reeling over the charges being dropped, Pat wasn't buying any of it. Even as the new kid on the block he was already thinking differently and was liberated from the echo chambers that most detective bureaus tend to become. In reality, the math was simple; based on everything he knew about the case—which by 1987, over a decade after the fact, was a lot—Womack was no serial killer. However, labeling the still-unknown killer with the "serial" designation in this case made sense to Pat because he knew, deep down, that Marcia Trimble's killer had done it before. The scene, although disorganized and impulsive, also reflected a certain criminal confidence and experience—a certain homicidal acumen. He even started to think that the Trimble and Des Prez cases, in spite of conventional thinking at the time, must be connected; he just wasn't sure how. There *not* being a connection between them bordered on the impossible, he thought. There had to be some missing link yet to reveal itself. Suffice it to say, other Metro detectives didn't share, or like, his unconventional thinking. Police hunches at the time were, after all, supposed to epitomize the principles of Occam's razor, that the simplest conclusion is always the right one—that logic should always flow downhill and follow the path of least resistance. Luckily for Pat, his colleagues *did* like his results. Before long, Pat would become known as the Closer, with a diamond-plated clearance rate, or solved average, to prove it.

One of those solved cases occurred on Christmas Day 1987, when Pat was called to the infamous Tennessee State Prison, a foreboding and ominous structure he'd driven by countless times but whose doors he'd never actually stepped through until the early morning twilight of that cool December 25. While most maximum-security penitentiaries across America were, at least by 1987, built out in the boondocks to deter escape and provide advance warning on any approaching threats, Tennessee's flagship prison, having admitted its first inmates back in 1898, ended up near Nashville's hopping downtown a century later as the city built up around it during the intervening time. In theory, its imposing Gothic facade—one that epitomized the term *stony lonesome*—served as a center-stage deterrent, one readily visible to anyone who might have thought twice about crossing the law and who might need a reminder of where they'd end up. In reality, the spooky fortress-like structure and its archaic electric chair also made for a coveted location to film prison movies—particularly once the facility officially closed in 1992—with everything from the Oscar-nominated film *The Green Mile* to infantile tripe like *Ernest Goes to Jail* and a handful of country-music videos being filmed on location there.

As though Pat making his first visit to a quiet state prison before first light on Christmas morning wasn't strange enough, stranger still was that it was to death row. There, Tony Lorenzo Bobo, a convicted murderer waiting to ride the lightning, had beaten to death another inmate awaiting his own capital punishment. As a con-on-con murder in death row of a maximum-security institution, the case should have been open and shut. Yet there was something about it that didn't smell right to Pat. True, Bobo was a heartless fiend and sociopath who'd been convicted of robbing and shooting a woman in cold blood at a Memphis bus stop in the winter of '83 and gleefully admitted to as much, once busted by local cops. True also that as of the previous March, Bobo had the appeal of his death sentence quashed by the Tennessee Supreme Court, and at first blush, he seemed like a man with nothing left to lose. However, the beating death for which he was now accused was reportedly over a drug debt incurred over the refusal to mule in new product. To Pat, notwithstanding its being Christmas, the circumstances of the murder seemed a little ill-timed.

It struck Pat as odd that a career criminal like Bobo, who knew the system and who had additional appeal options as well as clemency requests up his sleeve, would murder another doomed inmate on a small death row wing over a comparatively petty drug beef. It seemed even stranger that a low-witted low-roller like Bobo could, in the few months he'd been at the prison, be the "heavy" on the wing running his own drug ring from the inside. To Pat, it had all the markings of a new kid looking for juice, for profile, and respect among other inmates. Moreover, it read like a new kid following orders. Someone being coerced to do another, more senior, inmate's dirty work.

Once again, Bobo admitted to what he'd done. He admitted to the murder without conscience or much of a second thought. He said he acted alone, and that was that. He was prepared to take ownership of his death sentence, and for the time being, bask in the glory of being the guy not to be messed with at one of the most infamous prisons in the South. The guards reminded Pat that it was Christmas and that he should take the confession and evidence at face value and head home to his family and be done with it. But on his way out just a few hours after he arrived, and still looking at an afternoon's worth of paperwork as a two-finger typist back at the office, Pat stopped by and spoke with the prison's priest, who was on-site offering Christmas morning communion for inmates—especially the death row inmates whose souls it was thought were in greatest need of salvation.

The meek and diminutive old man with a rich accent and a pallor as chalk white as his clerical collar told Pat that he'd seen the "troubled" Bobo recently communicating with another inmate named Jerome something or other through an elaborate note-passing scheme known in the prison as "flying kites." He described Bobo as looking deferential, even frightened upon opening one particular "kite" recently passed to his cell—a lengthy missive with double-encryption, one no doubt passed from the general prison population to death row with the assistance of guards playing favorites for one reason or another. The priest described Bobo as looking genuinely scared while reading the note. On his way out of the towering medieval doors of Nashville's dark castle, Pat checked the laminated clip-on badge that read "Visitor" and collected his revolver and cuffs from a rusted tilt-drawer gun locker. He ran the name Jerome past the prison desk man on day shift. He confirmed that Jerome was in all likelihood Jerome Barrett, a hulk of a man with abnormally large hands who got popped for the rape of a Belmont student and an attempted rape of a Metro cop's girlfriend a few years before Pat arrived in town and got on the job. The same Jerome Barrett who boasted of killing "four blue-eyed bitches" and getting away with it during a cafeteria dustup shortly after arriving to serve what was supposed to be over four decades in hard time. Pat wrote the name in his book and then made a long walk through a brisk wind to his unmarked and aged Dodge Diplomat in the lot outside. The name Jerome Barrett meant nothing to him at the time, but if the priest knew it, he figured so should he. He figured the name might be important one day.

Chapter 8

M SQUAD

As the calendar flipped over from 1987 to 1988 Pat threaded his way through the heavy caseload and inevitable politics of general homicide. In so doing, he would also almost single-handedly inherit a deluge of horrific violence that had made its way to Nashville from what seemed like out of nowhere. These were still the days before he would go on to create and lead one of the first dedicated cold-case units in America, ultimately exploiting the newfound ability to test old crime-scene samples against the DNA of known offenders—convicted rapists and killers often turned loose from crowded prisons and back on the streets. For the time being, however, conventional sleuthing would have to suffice. As serial murder was about to leave its mark on Music City, the Trimble–Des Prez cases, Pat's binary pet project since graduating from the police academy, would have to go on the back burner until at least the fall. That was, after all, when things always seemed to get interesting.

TVPD: The reality and fiction of eighties' law enforcement converge as Pat (left) rubs shoulders with actor Bruce Weitz (center), who played Sergeant Mick Belker, and former NFL running back turned actor Ed Marinaro (right), who played Officer Joe Coffey in the acclaimed police drama Hill Street Blues, which aired on NBC from 1981 to 1987. Members of Metro general homicide, on a rare slow night, were tasked to serve as a plainclothed protection detail for the show's cast while in Nashville on publicity in early 1987. Courtesy of Pat Postiglione.

Metro's internal transfers and promotions used to always take effect on September 1. While entirely arbitrary to outsiders in terms of timing, every police department has a similarly annual "draft" day based in fiscal budgeting. So it was on Thursday, September 1, 1988, when Pat was moved from general homicide to the so-called Murder Squad. Insiders called it the M Squad for short, an elite mystery-murder and special-circumstance homicide unit with citywide discretion and authority. It was Nashville's equivalent to legendary detective units like the LAPD's Homicide Special Section that had fielded the Manson cult murders and other high-profile cases going back to the late sixties. It was the crème de la crème.

Like all homicide units, despite the reward of the work and thrill of the chase, it would inevitably also take more than it gave back. True to form, even as the senior guy in charge and soon to be promoted to detective sergeant, Pat never shied away from getting his hands dirty. Without pause he volunteered for the thankless, on-call position of catching any major case that came in during the wee hours. He had developed a special fondness for the graveyard shift following his twelve months on the Midnight Watch over the previous year—the exhilaration of being the first on the scene and the first one hot on the trail. During his transitional period from the Midnight Watch in general homicide to the M Squad, Pat, often on his own time, began to make connections between historical cases beyond the Trimble and Des Prez sex slayings that so consumed him. These were other, lesser-known cases that also predated his arrival in Nashville, back when he was still installing rooftop AC units in NYC. This macabre time travel work all began almost by chance.

In perusing some archived dossiers, including open-but-unsolved robbery-homicides, sexual homicides, and murder-for-hire schemes—and every outlier in between—it was on a random weeknight in the summer of '89 when Pat realized that the M Squad was a Rosetta stone that linked old with new. It translated once opaque information into a common language. It brought different vernaculars and documentation systems together in one place—it consolidated and collated information that otherwise floated around and lacked context. Information that was otherwise dormant going nowhere. It dawned on Pat, while scouring historical cases under the light of a desk lamp at his Spartan office on James Robertson Parkway, that with its own private file collection, in addition to its citywide mandate and veto power, the M Squad—combined with a person's own street smarts—could become a limitless treasure trove for those who knew what to look for. Pat had always known what to look for—and where.

As a kid in Queens, Pat knew that right and wrong were not necessarily synonymous with legal and illegal, much like he was now realizing that *unsolved* and *unsolvable* were not synonymous descriptors. They were poles apart. As a hand-picked M Squad investigator, he knew how to sort the good cases from the bad cases. He also would learn how to sort the bad people from the *really* bad. Sure enough, within a year, Pat would catch the case of Kevin Hughes. The Hughes case would be the whodunit that kicked off what would become one of the most tireless and effective homicide units in the country for the next decade—a case that epitomized the ambitious mystery-murder mandate of the M Squad. It would also be the litmus test that would prove the newly minted detective sergeant's spirit.

In March of '89, twenty-three-year-old Kevin Hughes was a self-proclaimed reformer of the country-music scene who sought to expose the bribery, chart fixing, and general seediness of Nashville's new country underbelly—the dark side of the industry that people didn't see on CMT or at the Opry. Hughes, arriving in Nashville in an attempt to make a name for himself in the behind-the-scenes world of market research and chart-trends analysis, quickly drew the ire of some dangerous power brokers and made enemies instead. He found big trouble in what seemed like the most unlikely of places, the city's famed Music Row.

By the mid-1980s, Nashville's Lower Broadway, often mislabeled as "Music Row," was the epicenter of the new-country tourist trap that had subsumed much of the downtown. The real Music Row was less obvious, an off-the-beaten-track type of place where there would be few witnesses after dark. Courtesy of Metro Nashville Archives.

In 1989 Music Row was, and still is, the epicenter of the country, gospel, Christian, and bluegrass music scenes in Nashville and the whole of America. Contrary to what many people think when they hear the name, there is no actual public music performed there; in fact, there is really nothing to see there at all. Located southwest of the main downtown and more obvious attractions along Broadway, Music Row is a largely contiguous set of recording studios, management companies, and marketing agencies—some being obvious storefront operations, most being nondescript converted homes with no signage at all—that serve as the lifeblood of the country scene in particular. Headquartered mostly along 16th and 17th Avenues, this densely packed and key commercial area also includes the handful of corporations entrusted with keeping track of sales and listener metrics, collectively serving as the proverbial nerve center for some of the industry's biggest record labels and their marquee stars. In early 1989, this included country music's leading competitor to the long-standing *Billboard* magazine, a publication known as *Cash Box* magazine.

The now defunct trade journal, an index of top-charting country-music albums and singles, along with artist interviews and profile pieces, had since its inception in 1942 been a key source of publicity for Nashville's up-and-comers. Kevin Hughes, hailing from a small town in Illinois, decided to accept a job there as a researcher and indexer, bringing with him a certain good-natured naïveté. He apparently arrived there believing the country industry at the time was clean and—at least compared to the well-known exploitation that pervaded Motown acts and boy bands—operated largely by the book. He was devastated to ultimately learn that it was likely even worse. He discovered that fellow *Cash Box* executive and sleazy promoter Chuck Dixon was allowing record labels and talent agents to make secret cash payments in exchange for preferred chart positions in the magazine. It was chart fixing; a pay-for-play scandal that needed to be revealed. It was why Kevin Hughes felt morally compelled to make things right and why he had to act and shine the light on country music's dark side. It's also why he ended up dead.

Although this Nashville payola scheme wasn't invented by Dixon or *Cash Box* magazine, Dixon certainly took it to a new level. His MO was to lure emerging talented (and talentless) dream chasers, all enamored with the look and sound of new country as it exploded in the nineties, with big but empty promises. Promises of musical stardom and fancy cars, of mansions in Green Hills or nearby Belle Meade, and of the legions of groupies and sycophants that would no doubt follow. Dixon would, as many had before, often take the meager life savings of aspiring hopefuls as a "start-up" fee or other retainer before contractually then making them his slaves—exploited serfs with no way out. Although it was the oldest show-biz grift known to man, Dixon and his entourage managed to introduce a new twist.

By virtue of his senior position at *Cash Box*, Dixon could artificially inflate what were supposed to be genuine and vetted numbers on album sales and radio airplay, moving select newcomers up in the magazine's rankings to present the illusion that they were breakout stars and making waves in the industry and selling out record stores. So long as the money kept rolling in from either the artists themselves, their agents, or their usually independent record labels, they could maintain a preferred chart position rooted in bribery. This manipulation of the charts in turn led to word-of-mouth publicity and a domino effect—and in theory to a deferred return on investment not unlike a pyramid scheme. DJs who weren't already playing the listed tracks dominating the *Cash Box* charts, upon seeing how well they were ostensibly performing, would of course decide they should start playing the tracks—even if they'd never heard of the artist in question. It was all one big propaganda machine underscoring the impressionable nature of people and their insecurities. Chuck Dixon, like all polished fraudsters, knew human nature and human greed like the back of his hand, and he knew how to leverage them.

Cash Box magazine became something of a bad pun, with cash payments in exchange for chart rigging in the journal's pages becoming more and more flagrant and Dixon's methods becoming increasingly cavalier. Kevin Hughes, having stumbled across the scam through his various conversations with Dixon and watching chart metrics get printed that defied his own research, increasingly felt morally and professionally compelled to act—to become the country-music industry's first real whistleblower. The tipping point for him was when Dixon's scam eventually started creeping into the magazine's annual award-selection criteria, placing the entire industry in jeopardy. A young, hopeful new country act named Mickey Jones was named *Cash Box*'s male vocalist of the year in 1988 even though he hadn't sold a single album. What he had done was borrow and pool money with some other stakeholders in order to pay Dixon for the mirage of success and ensuing surge in profile. That was when Hughes threatened to pull the curtain down on the whole charade; it's when he threatened to go public.

It was a few months later, on the night of March 9, 1989—a Thursday—when Kevin Hughes spoke by telephone from a recording studio on 16th Avenue in Music Row for the last time with his brother back in Illinois. His brother could tell, even over the line, that something was amiss, that Kevin didn't sound quite himself. He sounded distracted, ominously preoccupied. For Kevin to be evasive about what was eating at him wasn't his nature. Whatever it was, there was a distinct element of fear in his voice. Although no one knows exactly what Kevin knew or thought he might know about what was going to happen next, his brother on the other end of the line was right when he sensed that Kevin, at the very least, wasn't alone. That night, Kevin had been meeting at the recording studio with a legitimate breakout artist, a twenty-one-year-old country star in the making named Sammy Sadler.

The two men had stopped at Evergreen Records' 16th Avenue studio so the new country prodigy, Sadler, could call his family back home in Texas. Kevin Hughes, who was chauffeuring the rising star at the time, followed suit and called his own family in Illinois, perhaps sensing that this might be his last chance to do so. Minutes later, as the two men emerged from the Evergreen studio and walked to Hughes's car parked on the street outside, a lone figure emerged from the shadows, veiled entirely in black. The figure's face was concealed with a ski mask, also black. It was textbook "hit" attire. As Hughes and Sadler took note of the shape rapidly approaching them and the implications of what they were seeing, the mysterious figure then produced a pistol from his black jacket, took aim, and opened fire. A single shot hit Sadler in the shoulder, and he dropped to the pavement in a matter of seconds. At that point, Hughes, likely realizing that he was the primary target, decided to make a run for it.

Fleeing and screaming southbound into darkness, running for his life down 16th through the heart of the after-hours Music Row—all other studios and offices long since closed—Hughes was struck in the back twice when the phantom attacker unloaded with volleys of fire from a .38-caliber revolver. With Hughes lying wounded and writhing on a dark street devoid of witnesses, and Sadler bleeding profusely behind the parked car, the assassin had made it clear he had purposely stalked the men to the studio that night. It was to silence Kevin Hughes. Walking up to the kid from Illinois with a brazen coldness, the shooter, almost casually, stood over him and fired two more shots into Hughes's brain at point-blank range before disappearing back into the night. The ordeal ended just as suddenly as it had started. By the time it hit the morning news, it was already known as the Murder on Music Row. It had a certain morbid ring to it.

Pat arrived on the scene around the same time as staff reporters and the *Tennessean* stringers. The predawn twilight soon also brought out the joggers, dog walkers, and keener Music Row interns arriving early. They would all inevitably become the audience for the inauguration of a new M Squad partnership. Pat Postiglione and a veteran homicide detective named Billy Pridemore, an out-of-stater and Yankee himself, would be working their first murder case together. Born and raised in the Midwest north of the Mason–Dixon, Pridemore was an army brat who'd spent his formative years all over the country before his father finally moved the family to Tennessee. Joining the Metro PD a few years before Pat, Pridemore had pushed a black-and-white prowl car in nearly every district as a patrol officer and then worked as a K9 officer before becoming an unlikely recruit into general homicide. Pat and Pridemore were soon partners on the dreary Midnight Watch, and inevitably drove each other nuts. But in between their bickering, they worked cases hard. They also *solved* cases like no other duo.

Investigating the Hughes case in tandem, Pat and Pridemore soon found themselves listening to all kinds of crazy theories about what *really* happened to the kid from Illinois that fateful night on 16th Avenue. Some said it was industry related while others said not, that it instead had something to do with the Satanism scare sweeping the South. The conspiracy nuts had a heyday with it all. Some said it was the work of a disgruntled new country washout whose songs Sadler had stolen. Others suggested it was the work of an emerging or existing country star—names ranging quite incredibly from Clint Black to Alan Jackson—set on either settling a score or burying an ancient Nashville secret. Within the first forty-eight hours, there were no fewer than a hundred named suspects, half of them charting country acts. But amid the fog of innuendo, there was a common denominator to all the tips and folktales: Chuck Dixon and the dubious charts at *Cash Box*.

As the murder on 16th Avenue went from hot to cold, *Cash Box* itself quickly went broke. With the murder of Hughes and the maiming of an emerging star throwing a long shadow over the glitz of Music Row—the whole of Music City, for that matter—the magazine seemed to lose its already rusty luster. It went from being a fake chart index and repository of fake news to being a glossy-paged obituary. And while other entertainment industries had had their own problems in terms of cutthroat tactics, the case, at least to Pat, presented a new nationwide low.

On a Friday evening in early April, just two weeks after Kevin Hughes was gunned down in the heart of Music Row, Pat and Bill Pridemore had something of an M Squad mind meld. They first argued for an hour about where to meet for a drink, a prelude to what would be an almost daily debate about everything to do with food or drink, which would go on to define their often mercurial working relationship for the better part of the next decade. Once they finally agreed on a charming hole-in-the-wall known as the Villager on 21st Avenue, they ran scenarios. Slouching on barstools, they soon agreed that Hughes was likely murdered in cold blood in order to assure his silence. The enduring question was, Silenced over what? Better yet, Silenced by whom?

The prime suspect and most motivated person to keep him quiet, Chuck Dixon, had an airtight alibi for the night of the murder—an almost too perfect story backed by a dozen witnesses. It was a story that had an air of rehearsal to it, as though Dixon had been prepared to be asked and had been practicing for weeks.

It was then and there—at the Villager of all places—that Pat had an epiphany. It was a realization that confirmed once and for all that he needed to follow his gut—his New York intuition. Pridemore as a fellow Yank inevitably concurred. The Hughes murder, they both agreed, had marked the start of a new generation. They were at the tail end of the eighties and already the next decade was looking ominous. The two plainclothes cops agreed that the worst was still yet to come—a storm was gathering. It was right about then that the bartender cut them off and handed them each a cab voucher and put an abrupt end to their commiserating. Pat took a Nashville Yellow Cab. The radio played Waylon Jennings. It was the start of a commercial-free classic-country all-hits weekend. It was a requiem. It was an elegy for the Nashville of old.

Part II

THE MOTEL MURDERS

"One wants to wander away from the world's somewheres, into our own *nowhere*."

—D. H. Lawrence, *Women in Love*

Chapter 9

Whistling Dixie

It was just before 7:00 p.m. Central Time when the rain came. A low-pressure system out of Arkansas moved into West Tennessee by midmorning, and after first deluging parishioners leaving Sunday church services in Memphis, ominous gray skies soon pushed eastward with a vengeance. They soon opened up over Music City in the early evening of June 18, 1989—Father's Day—with Centennial Park on West End Avenue seeming to get it the worst. The Nashville Parthenon, the park's signature landmark and a scale replica of the ancient Greek Parthenon, served as an impromptu shelter for the dozens caught in the torrential downpour unleashed just before dusk. Those dozens included a group of Civil War buffs—men hailing from across the state of Tennessee and who still called it the War of Northern Aggression—who were reenacting the Battle of Hatchie's Bridge in period regalia, just as they did in the park every other Sunday. Huddled between the columns of the majestic structure, one reenactor donning sergeant's chevrons wiped his brow with a kepi cap. Another guy used his bayonet to shotgun a can of Keystone.

The Nashville Parthenon, a scale replica of the Greek Parthenon, was built in 1897 to commemorate the Tennessee Centennial Exposition and today serves as a popular gathering point in Centennial Park. Courtesy of Mayur Phadtare.

A few miles away on Linbar Drive in South Nashville, the same driving rain would help wash away the potential evidence left by a teenage miscreant and deranged sadist named Jerald Gregory. The boy was in Nashville for the Father's Day weekend, staying with his aunt as he often did whenever his mother could offload him for a few days or, ideally, months at a time. Normally a resident of Clarksdale, Mississippi—an iconic town in the history of Delta blues and Southern rock—fourteen-year-old Gregory was no musician. In fact, he wasn't much of anything other than proof positive that, just as the day's weather promised, a storm was coming to Nashville. The boy was precisely what the Music City preachers had warned about in the wake of the Des Prez and Trimble sex slayings, the wicked force that would make the South dirty once more. A harbinger of further evil yet to come.

In addition to Jerald Gregory over the decade to follow, Nashville would serve as an early forerunner to what's now called the "murder mitten" phenomenon: how—like contiguous fingers in a mitten—one thing heats, sustains, and enables those things of similar constitution beside it. It describes how homicidal violence, like kinetic energy, can affect nearby objects through its own type of convection—through direct or indirect contact. In terms of serial killers lying in wait, the Vandyland murders would similarly heat up and awaken psychopaths previously in stasis not only in Nashville, but all over America. Hunting season was on.

During that same fateful Father's Day weekend in Nashville, Gregory, staying with his apparently clueless Music City aunt, became a temporary neighbor to young Candy Moulton, a twenty-two-year-old young wife full of life and residing in an adjacent building within the same apartment complex. It was the pure misfortune of having leased an apartment so close to Gregory's blood relative that would seal Candy's fate for reasons she could never have predicted.

Due to circumstances beyond her control and beyond any semblance of fairness, from the day Candy Moulton moved into her modest apartment with dreams of a family and things to come, she was doomed. Her unwanted legacy would be that she would also go on to become—at least among those who know of the case—the subject of a key study on how to predict the same type of targeted-stranger attack that had also claimed the life of young Sarah Des Prez in Vandyland in the winter of '75. More recently we have also come to see the Candy Moulton murder for what it really was: a sexual home-invasion murder, a scenario that unfolds more commonly than people are prepared to acknowledge. It was the nightmare of all nightmares, an act committed by a killer in pursuit of a very specific fantasy. It was a fantasy for which previous warning signs had been missed.

The real tragedy is that neither Candy nor the uniformed Metro cops who responded to earlier break-ins at the apartment complex—beginning the first summer Jerald Gregory stayed with his aunt on Linbar Drive—recognized that someone had been in area homes for reasons other than theft. Even today, many police departments have yet to realize that roughly one-third of all break-ins are not just about money or the property. It has taken nearly a hundred years for law enforcement to get wise and begin to understand that the motives for residential burglary, perhaps more diverse and complex than any other crime, often go—much like armed robbery—far beyond any financial gain. It's likely for this reason that, as confirmed in a 2017 study, residential break-ins are the second-most common gateway crime for violent sex offenders, far more than other offenses that one might typically consider to be warning signs, such as incidents of exposure and even fire starting and kidnapping. More tragically, only a handful of police departments acknowledge this reality in their policies and training even today.

This is also why when nothing is noted as being stolen in a B&E, it is often assumed—wrongly—that the burglar got interrupted or scared off, and why many times a formal report isn't even filed. In reality these are the cases that may be the most essential and important to investigate. Even when conventional items deemed worthy of stealing—electronics, liquor, money, guns—are found missing, that is not necessarily a reliable indicator as to the real underlying motive for entry. Any incidental theft is often little more than subterfuge and, sadly, a prelude of what will come next.

By contrast, sexual burglars *want* their presence to be known. Not only bold and indifferent to being detected, they, in many cases, even instigate being found or otherwise lure a homeowner into discovering or seeing them. Sometimes, however, unless matters escalate to an actual attack, it can be tough to tell the two apart.

No one is sure which of these motives brought Jerald Gregory to Candy Moulton's apartment on Father's Day '89, or whether he was responsible for the voyeuristic burglaries committed in the area before that, or even whether he knew Candy was home that afternoon. It was after 6:00 p.m., just before the rain came, when Candy's husband, Kenneth, returned home from work as a small-wing pilot to their one-bedroom walk-up apartment to find his new wife dead in their bedroom. After first being bound to the bedposts with electrical extension cords, Candy had been stripped naked, partially strangled, and blindfolded with one of her husband's neckties—all implements of opportunity found at the scene by Gregory, who had managed to stealthily enter the home earlier in the afternoon and ambush Candy, who was home alone. After the psychopathic teen raped Candy, he stabbed her a total of eight times. Having severed an artery in her chest, he then watched her bleed to death over the course of a few minutes.

Strangest of all, before leaving the scene and coolly making his way back to his aunt's unit to watch *Life Goes On*, the killer teen also took the time to insert four wooden cooking spoons in Candy's vagina. It's unclear whether this process—a signature indicative of extreme sadism and visual fetishism, and a strong indicator toward serial murder at such a young age—occurred while she was still alive or after she had bled to death in the bed. It did, however, ensure that Gregory left something of himself at the horrific scene. It ensured—as the rest of Nashville could soon be thankful—that he was apprehended in record time. As usual, Pat and the M Squad caught the case.

While DNA testing was still in its infancy in June of '89, the genetic material left at the scene along with a partial fingerprint on one of the spoons would allow Pat Postiglione's M Squad to collar Gregory before he could go serial and claim other victims. But even with the physical evidence, the case wouldn't break easily.

Candy Moulton's murder received a one-page play below the fold in the *Tennessean* when Jerald Gregory, by then eighteen years old, was finally arrested in June 1990 after he returned to the same apartment complex, from his native Clarksdale, Mississippi. He had begun stalking a new summertime target while, once again, staying with his aunt. Gregory's arrest no doubt saved that next woman's life.

As the case moved its way through the Nashville criminal justice system, the murdered housewife's story receded farther and farther from the public eye. By October of that year the case had been relegated to page 16 of the *Tennessean*; by November, to page 19. And so it went, until, by the time Gregory was finally convicted and sentenced to Tennessee State Prison for a term of twenty-five to life, the case was all but forgotten in Nashville. The Candy Moulton case had been a tragic and horrific matter involving a youthful and, as it seemed, first-time murderer. But by the time of Jerald Gregory's conviction, other murders were piling up. By then it was also clear that the city was under siege by a new type of predator who, in the literary tradition of the Southern Gothic, epitomized the surreal and the grotesque—the unexplained. The Jerald Gregory case was a disturbing and inexplicable one for Pat and his new partner Pridemore to try to make sense of, both of whom also soon became household names and the fodder of dinner-table conversation, at least among their fellow Metro cop buddies. The real test of their nerves, however, was yet to come. As would be, within the next decade, the most dangerous game they would ever play.

Chapter 10

No Vacancy

On Thursday, October 3, 1991, a ghoulish out-of-towner going by the name Terry Duncan checked himself into room 23 at the Esquire Inn on Dickerson Pike in Nashville.

The Esquire (which would later be shut down by Metro PD in 1998) was rough trade, home to the lion's share of the prostitution and drug activity from across the city and region. Rooms at the Esquire rented for anywhere from twenty-five to forty dollars nightly, with a surcharge of ten dollars for "sex rooms" to ensure the desk clerk's discretion and willingness to allow guests to check in off the books. In time, the dodgy joint would also earn the additional dubious distinction of having Nashville cops dispatched to a record 230 radio calls in 1997 alone, mostly for drugs, prostitution, and disorderly conduct. But six years earlier the Esquire, while inevitably on the downward slide, did manage to attract occasional law-abiding clientele in search of short-term lodging on the cheap. Many of the customers were interstate truckers drawn to the nearby fuel and food options on Dickerson Pike. Looking to avoid the hordes at the TravelCenters of America on 1st Street, they would opt instead to crash at the Esquire as the closest—and cheapest—place to bed down in Music City for a night.

Although the neon sign in front of the Esquire Inn that night read "Vacancy," the desk clerk told the lone man who arrived in Nashville on nondescript "business" to check in that the sign was a mistake. The clerk swore to him that it was no ruse, no bait and switch. He assured the man calling himself Terry Duncan that, with the rooms unexpectedly now booked solid, he'd merely forgotten to turn on the "No" portion of the weathered neon sign. The clerk was telling the truth.

Less than a week after a Country Music Association award ceremony at the Grand Ole Opry House, a gala event hosted by Reba McEntire, which had coincided with the enormity of the Garth Brooks album *No Fences* that had taken country music mainstream, the city was still packed to the rafters. All sorts of dream chasers and industry hangers-on were still flooding into Nashville, still tying up the city's hotels and motels. While accredited media, record-company parasites, and genuine stars had booked up all the top hotels downtown and along West End Avenue, places like the Esquire absorbed the overflow drawn to the city to capitalize on the week-long CMA party.

Amid these hijinks and despite the "No" now displayed on the Esquire's street-facing sign, the man checking in that night was able to work out a deal with the clerk on duty. In leasing room 23, one of the off-the-books sex rooms, for the standard room rate of twenty-five dollars and signing the name Terry Duncan on the motel's requisite three-by-five registry card, the phantom tenant, claiming to live on 53rd Street East in Dallas, said he would require two room keys for his one-night stay. One would be for him, and one for an unseen female friend waiting outside. Only one of the two guests would ever check out.

The clerk that night knew not to ask questions, and that, as for most men checking into the joint without ID, the moniker—Terry Duncan—was an alias. It was an alias that, on this particular night, was designed to conceal what he had planned next—what he knew would go down in the room soon after check-in. It was a morbid reprise of what he'd done before—as recently as one week before—and what he would endeavor to do again soon. What he would hope to do in other cities after leaving his mark on Nashville. While, within a matter of hours, the man calling himself Terry Duncan had vanished from the Esquire, he had been sure to leave behind something for others to discover. A discovery of water leaking from room 23 would soon reveal what would be Nashville's first in a series of serial killer sagas that would reshape Music City forever. The first in a series of horrific cases without precedent that would also contour the path of Pat's career—and his life.

The Esquire chambermaid passing by the motel's "suite" 23 just after 11:00 a.m. the following day quickly noticed water seeping out from beneath the door of the room. After a series of imperious knocks and declarative "housekeeping" announcements failed to elicit any response, the maid jostled the rusty round copper knob to find the door unlocked. Swinging the door open wide to a room in darkness, save a flickering fluorescent light above the vanity in the bathroom, she soon heard an ominous gushing noise. The faucet for the stained and skeezy-looking bathtub had apparently been left on full throttle—the right metal knob labeled "Hot" cranked all the way on and the drain plug left in. It was pure mischief, or so the chambermaid thought, another reason why the sex rooms normally warranted an extra surcharge.

With water billowing over the sides of the tub's chipped porcelain, the room had likely been flooding for the better part of a few hours, she figured. It was then that she caught a glimpse in the near darkness of something on the dilapidated queen-sized bed to her left. As it turned out, the bathtub stunt was no random or petty act of mischief. Terry Duncan had become consumed with washing away the blood of his crimes. It was one of those "out, damned spot" obsessions in the vein of Lady Macbeth, what is known in murder cases as an act of *undoing*. It's something compulsive and repetitive that simultaneously destroys evidence but also psychologically relieves the killer of what they've done. Undoing of this nature is also thought to be the reason why a great many victims of murder are burned postmortem, even when there is no advantage to the offender in doing so. Fire, like water, is thought to be a powerful erasing force that allows the killer to carry on pretending it didn't happen. The man calling himself Terry Duncan engaged in this same cleansing ritual. The open bathtub faucet in room 23 at the Esquire was, despite eventually drawing the attention of witnesses, one sure means, at least in his deranged mind, of erasing the horror of what happened overnight on October 3. He was almost right.

After turning off the faucet and pulling the drain plug from the bathtub, the chambermaid dried her hands on what appeared to be the lone remaining towel—a yellowed, threadbare rag hanging askew on a wall rack—before making her way over to the queen bed in the suite, where, amid the pile of pillows and a balled-up, spore-ridden comforter, she saw what appeared to be the silhouette of a human form. Seemingly oblivious to the risk of electrocution while standing in an inch of water atop a saturated shag carpet, the maid threw the switch for the ceiling fixture. As a yellow bulb housed in a sconce over the top of the bed threw light on the seedy room, it spotlighted the body of a woman later identified as twenty-four-year-old Donna Bacot, lying faceup and eyes wide open. She'd been dead just over an hour or two, the body still warm to the touch.

Donna Bacot, like both Sarah Des Prez and Marcia Trimble over fifteen years earlier, had been left as is and partially naked at the scene—what FBI profilers refer to as Disposal Pathway #3—but with a twist in this latest case. Beyond the time-delay evidence-destruction tactic—the Macbeth MO—the acid-washed jeans Donna Bacot was wearing, partially pulled down, had been curiously sliced to ribbons. Horrified by her discovery, the maid ran back to the main desk and had the day clerk dial 911. Within an hour, Nashville Metro cops and the M Squad's plainclothesmen, led by Pat, had boots on the ground at the Esquire and were canvassing room to room. The canvass for witnesses turned loose some cogent items of information; some seemed to be viable investigative action items and some obvious distractions. All the while, the real leads were still back waiting to be discovered in room 23. The water from the bathtub, as it turned out, had washed away nothing but the roaches.

Chapter 11

Tourniquet

Young Donna Bacot, a newish housewife married to a Nashville trucker who was on the road when she was killed, to this day remains one of the Esquire's more puzzling visitors. Overnight on October 3, 1991, she had been raped and beaten about the face and head in room 23—but she didn't die from the beating. In an already bizarre case with a peculiar reliance on an equally unusual weapon of opportunity, the killer who had checked in under the name Terry Duncan had used one of the two hand towels normally on the rack in the bathroom as the murder weapon. After subduing and controlling Donna, her killer had used the towel to fasten what could be described as a Boy Scout knot—a basic figure-eight pattern—around her throat. The woman's autopsy at the medical examiner's office the following day revealed that her assailant, over the course of nearly an hour, had engaged in a progressively more sadistic torture session with Donna as he slowly twisted the towel in a clockwise fashion. The towel, functioning like a jerry-rigged tourniquet, was made to slowly and incrementally close and eventually crush Donna's windpipe. The MO spoke to a certain madness; it reflected the darkest and most wicked of fantasies—a killer undoubtedly with a history of increasingly cruel sexual experimentation. It nearly guaranteed he'd killed before and would again soon.

Bringing his victim to the point of unconsciousness before raping her, bringing her back to consciousness, and then starting over, the killer carried on this process time after time. By the point that Donna finally succumbed to the trauma, slowly and horrifically, the towel, cutting nearly two inches into the flesh of her neck, had almost severed her trachea in two. The killer, it appeared, had finished by raping Donna's dead body in a grisly act of necrophilia, either unaware of the fact or uncaring that she was no longer unconscious but actually dead. In the case of homicidal necrophiles, murderers who are aroused by death, there exists an even rarer subset of the already rare and grotesque disorder. Known as pseudonecrophilia, it's when a psychopathic sadist is so aroused by the process of killing and the aesthetics of his murder that he needs to carry on sexually with the corpse as a type of spontaneous indulgence—almost as a reward for his work. Key case studies in this behavior include the infamous "Campus Killer," Ted Bundy, who, in traveling the United States and killing over thirty women during the mid-1970s, and likely even earlier, exhibited this same behavior in order to exert control over his victims even after death. Now a little over a decade later, another psychopath going by the name Terry Duncan seemed to be channeling Bundy's nightmarish methods. Like Bundy, it seemed as though he was also a killer on the open road.

Pseudonecrophiles are further distinguished from other death fetishists by the fact that a first experience may change them in their future choice of victims. Sometimes finding that the act of murder in itself is no longer sufficiently arousing, they may begin changing their MO to kill their victims more quickly or efficiently in order to acquire a corpse to relive their definitive and transformative first experience. As the pseudonecrophile evolves to exhibit behavior classified as "true" necrophilia, the dead in turn become a preferred "type" for the offender. The result is the inevitable development of even darker and more violent fantasies that can significantly escalate the frequency and brutality of future attacks. In the summer of '91, Pat and his M Squad team of high flyers didn't of course have the body of forensic knowledge or training available today to know this. They nonetheless still knew they were dealing with a new breed of killer entirely, at least by Nashville standards. Modern advances aside, what Pat and his Metro cronies did know for certain was that whoever had killed Donna Bacot had unquestionably killed before. Since her killer was likely also a dive-motel habitué, his confidence and MO were both evolving based on what happened at the Esquire. Terry Duncan was escalating, and he'd no doubt resurface soon, and with a new name and victim, while applying even more cruel and heinous methods. Pat also knew that the anonymous, soulless drifter claiming to hail from Dallas would not stop killing until he was caught.

Before the autopsy results on Donna even made their way to the M Squad office at 200 James Robertson Parkway, Pat managed to pry loose another key piece of evidence from room 23 at the Esquire. Of particular interest was a man's white T-shirt recovered by Metro evidence techs. Pat noted that the shirt, while soaked by water, still had what looked to be a medium-velocity blood-spatter stain intact. Better yet, the blood didn't belong to Donna Bacot. The working theory Pat developed was that, once it was evident that things were about to go bad for her, a terrified Donna had lashed out and punched her killer in the nose at close range as a last-ditch effort to fend him off—or at least to leave her mark. While the medical examiner didn't find skin or any other evidence beneath Donna's fingernails, the T-shirt bloodstain seemed to suggest that, although unable to scratch or claw at her attacker, Donna had managed a quick jab to her attacker's face before being subdued, restrained, and tortured to death with the ratty bathroom hand towel.

Beyond the bloodstain of unknown origin, within the first forty-eight hours of the investigation, three other key leads worth pursuing were considered and afforded equal weight. These included the periodic trucker connection to the motel, the pseudonecrophilic behavior—without calling it that at the time—as a crime-scene signature, and the name Terry Duncan with the Dallas address on the motel registry card. Separately, each item of interest meant little; but together, they filled in the four corners of a case that was starting to come to fruition. The evidence, in aggregate, started to draw a picture of who had killed Donna and why he'd chosen the Esquire as the place to do it.

Pat knew that all experienced liars, criminal psychopaths, sadists, and even necrophiles have some kernel of truth in each of their lies—they leave some trace. It's why, after all, they are able to lie so effectively. There is something inherently truthful in their tall tales that allows them to easily memorize their lies and take ownership of them. Even psychopathic and pathological liars—the most experienced and dangerous of fibbers—tend to stick to a script. As such, Pat knew that the alias used by whoever killed Donna Bacot when he checked into the Esquire that night was bunk. But it was familiar bunk; it was rehearsed bunk—bunk with a pinch of verisimilitude. He figured a check of both local and National Crime Information Center (NCIC) databases would soon confirm it. It was the Texas connection, Pat was now certain, that was the elusive kernel of truth. He rolled up his sleeves and dug deeper into his Lone Star State theory.

Within only a couple of days, Pat was able to verify that the address used by the killer when renting the room actually existed in Dallas—and that the associated zip code matched, no less. While no one named Terry Duncan was living there or had apparently ever lived there, the killer's apparent familiarity with the city and area went beyond the trivial in those pre–Google Maps days. The killer, previously living or still living in Texas, had either lived or worked in the vicinity of the address in question—he had some connection to the neighborhood to be able to pull the address and associated zip out of a hat as he did. Pat banked on it.

After a set of partial fingerprints recovered from a crushed can of Busch found in the room's garbage was ruled out as belonging to Donna Bacot after elimination prints were taken from her lifeless body—the can, like the T-shirt, apparently having been overlooked or forgotten about by her killer—Pat sent copies of the partials to both the Texas Rangers and Dallas PD to check against known felons in their Automated Fingerprint Identification System (AFIS) data-bases. The first time around, nothing matched. It seemed to be a dead end. But then came a new lead.

Once Donna Bacot was positively identified as the victim at the Esquire, the final known few hours of her life soon began to help fill in the blanks. Earlier on October 3, she and a friend had been out for happy-hour drinks at a dive bar near the Esquire and even closer to the Pilot truck stop just down the street. A man using the name Terry, whom the friend described as a white male about thirty, slim build, neat brown hair, and cowboy boots—generally the same description offered up by the clerk at the Esquire—soon cozied up to the two women. Like so many sexual psychopaths, he had a certain shallow charm and rehearsed manner of speech that, when combined with the half-price booze, allowed him to lure Donna for an overnight tryst—not initially at the Esquire, but at her own home.

With the mysterious man from the bar and her friend both back at Donna's modest house on Picture Ridge Terrace—the one she shared with her husband who was at work on the road at the time—Terry, as he had called himself, had quite incredibly, almost inexplicably, managed to then lure Donna from her own home back to the motel as a more discreet alternative to staying at her place. It struck Pat as a most unusual MO since Donna's own residence—given that the killer had no previous connection to it—would serve as an equally neutral and available place to rape and kill his victim as any motel. If anything, given that moving locations to the motel inevitably *introduced* other potential witnesses and other forms of evidence—the night clerk, other guests, the registry card, and a room whose continuity and cleaning records could be used to establish the origin of any physical evidence recovered—the tactic actually seemed counter-intuitive. There had to be something, Pat figured, that the Esquire Inn offered the killer that Donna's own home could not. It simply wasn't his fear of being interrupted or his need to control the environment, seen in the cases of murderers who use recurring kill sites—their car, a tool shed, a remote location or confinement space to which they have exclusive access—as much as it seemed to be like the Texas connection. It seemed to be something personal and familiar to the killer. He'd done it before, and it had worked. He was sticking to what he knew, and he knew low-rent motels. It was familiar terrain. Donna unwittingly went along with the death trap.

Within a week, Pat, even during the fledgling days of offender DNA testing in the early 1990s, had managed, through the expertise of the TBI Forensic Services Division, to retrieve a usable genetic male profile from the blood found on the T-shirt. The lab had beaten the odds by managing to isolate a sufficient number of loci, or genetic markers, in the blood despite the partial obliteration of the stain following the flood in room 23. It also turned out to be a suitably sized sample to allow for testing against known suspects or other crime scenes where DNA might also have been left. The problem was that, unlike the AFIS database that compares fingerprints using automated software, in 1991, DNA testing was still so new that there existed no such national or even regional network. It would have to be done manually, tediously, and in piecemeal fashion.

Prior to 1994 when an act of Congress allowed the FBI to establish and administer the country's Combined DNA Index System (CODIS) as an inte-grated database for all offender and crime-scene samples nationwide, DNA test-ing required that exhibits like the one recovered by Pat from the Esquire Inn be tested case by case. It was a time-consuming process similar to the way firearms were for many years submitted for ballistic comparison but without the technical specs to help narrow the search. The haystack in the case of DNA samples at the time was, however, even bigger—in theory, the entire male population of the United States—as investigators searched for the elusive needle. Worse yet, if a detective were to guess wrong too many times, the original crime-scene sample would eventually diminish to the point of being useless since a quantity of DNA is permanently eliminated with each new comparative test. It was a frustrating Catch-22 situation: burn weeks of work playing the DNA lottery and hope to get lucky testing against potential matches, or strike out in the process and lose the case forever. In most cases, police departments chose to do nothing but sit and wait.

A preferred alternative would be to somehow apprehend what Metro cops and city press were calling the Motel Killer before he struck again, something he'd no doubt do again soon. It was an unlikely prospect given what the police had to work with. In fact, it seemed so unlikely that one of the M Squad's more cynical detectives, an old-timer named Joe Thornhill, told Pat it was impossible. He told Pat the Motel Killer was a ghost—that he was as good as gone and never coming back to Nashville, and the case would liquidate too many Metro resources with little to no chance of success. He warned Pat about the hot-hand fallacy—that Pat's recent winning streak, including the bust of Jerald Gregory in the Candy Moulton murder, wasn't a predictor of future success in the Bacot case. He also warned him about the sunk-costs fallacy—that the more you irrationally invest in something to recover your time or money, the more you are destined to *never* recover it. He told him to give it up. He chalked it up to advice from a thirty-year guy that Pat should take at face value.

But what Pat really considered was that the clock was ticking and that sometime, somewhere, the killer of Donna Bacot—a man who drank Busch by the can, a man who could lure a married woman from her own home, a man who knew a thing or two about Dallas—would be back on the road to kill again under the name Terry Duncan or some other pseudonym soon. But he also knew that the more DNA tests he ran against names he thought might be a good match—high-risk parolees, sex offenders new to the state, suspects never properly cleared in earlier open or unsolved strangle jobs across the South—the more he used up his key piece of evidence. Pat would need to play it smart.

Pat's fire-rated, street-tested Queens-to-Nashville hunch told him that the Esquire Inn necro-creep from Texas he was chasing wouldn't just kill again. He knew from being at the scene at room 23 at the Esquire that he'd killed in a similarly sadistic and methodical fashion. Donna Bacot wasn't his first kill. It was too high-hatted by the standards of necrophiles to be his first foray into sexual homicide. Pat knew that if he could find the cocky and deadly lothario's first murder, it would reveal rookie mistakes that might uncover what the scene at the Esquire had managed to conceal about who Terry Duncan really was.

But after the cops with both the Dallas PD and the state's Department of Public Safety—the iconic Texas Rangers—were both unable to get a positive match on the prints recovered from the beer can using the AFIS database, Pat turned his attention back to the bloodstained T-shirt in earnest—the DNA smoking gun unwittingly left behind in room 23. In a committed and methodical campaign of hunt-and-peck on a scale that even in the digital world of today would be nothing short of extraordinary, Pat proceeded to manually cold-call the homicide divisions of each and every police department—hundreds of them—within a three-state radius of Tennessee in search of a name to run the limited DNA sample against. Pat already knew that time was running out before the killer's next victim would be discovered in a seedy motel somewhere. He also knew that between the roach motel, the specific ligature, and the grotesque necrophilia, the list of similar cases in other cities—even in the most crime-ridden of cities—should stand out as inherently unusual.

Calling and speaking with either the detective sergeant or lieutenant helming the homicide unit of every police department on file with the FBI or with an otherwise publicly listed telephone number within a day's drive, Pat made a brief introduction before walking whomever he talked to through the basic facts of the Bacot murder. Imploring them to check their open/unsolved files for anything that looked remotely similar, he told them he had a solid male DNA profile and that they might be able to help each other out—how two birds might be felled by one stone following a single test at the TBI crime lab. He stressed the motel factor in particular, the elaborate and sadistic strangulation, the precision of the improvised tourniquet, and the appearance of a rehearsed scene—all seemingly second nature for the killer.

As it turned out, he didn't need to look too far from home before he stumbled on a case that stuck out, an open but inactive homicide file, growing colder by the day, which bore startling similarities. The case was a dead ringer for the Esquire job start to finish and had occurred only a week before Donna Bacot was murdered. Within a few weeks, Pat finally had traction. It turned out that the killer was moving more quickly across the country than previously thought, his MO evolving and his violence escalating more expeditiously than Pat had feared. The lingering question was whether "Terry" was still in Nashville on the prowl or had already moved on.

Chapter 12

CONVERGENCE

As Pat soon discovered via detectives in Cincinnati, Ohio, a week earlier to the day of the Bacot slaying, a little over 250 miles northeast of the Esquire Inn, a man using the name Scott Campbell checked into the seedy Dennison Hotel at 716 Main Street in Cincinnati's East End, paying a mere ten dollars cash for a standard room. That was the morning of September 26, 1991. The signed registration card—as in Nashville—bore a Dallas, Texas, home address, this time on 15th Street. The similarities would not end there.

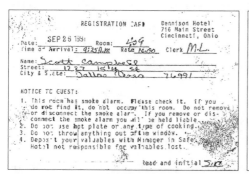
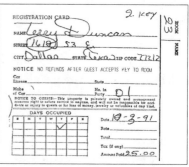

Left: The original registry card submitted on the morning of September 26, 1991, at the Dennison Hotel in Cincinnati by a man calling himself Scott Campbell. Right: The registry card, completed and signed by the same hand, for room 23 at the Esquire Inn in Nashville on the night of October 3, 1991, this time in the name of Terry Duncan. With murder victims found in both rooms, Pat would soon zero in on a subtle clue that would ultimately point to the Motel Killer's place of origin. Hotel registration card for the Dennison, courtesy of Pat Postiglione. Hotel registration card for the Esquire, courtesy of Pat Postiglione.

Pat grabbed his now increasingly occasional partner Billy Pridemore—the latter now in his third decade on the job and ever more consumed with his new-found golf game—and the pair hopped in an unmarked '87 Impala to make the four-hour trek to Cincinnati. The two made the trip, under Pat's signing author-ity as the M Squad's detective sergeant, to the so-called Queen City to meet with Detective Ed Zivernick of the Cincinnati Criminal Investigation Section.

After nearly four hours of fighting congested traffic on account of a caravan of gravel trucks headed north, traffic thinned alongside the Ohio River as Pat and Pridemore made their way to the Cincinnati PD's Major Offenders bureau. It struck Pat as being an even better detective brand than M Squad. It was badass. But, as usual in the police world, it was also false advertising. Most of the cops who clocked in there and handled cases of a lifetime were charlatans who didn't appreciate the importance of the role they had. Instead they watched Reds games on duty and marked time. The status quo ruled.

Pat and Pridemore soon resigned themselves to this banal reality of cop work in Cincinnati as they waited in the CID foyer for a few minutes while cops in uniform, off-the-rack suits, and civvies all walked by with exaggerated gaits and sized them up as trespassing outsiders no doubt looking to make trouble. Finally Pat caught a glimpse of a frumpy but friendly-looking bespectacled man walking toward them who looked more inviting. He was carrying an envelope that read "Do Not Bend" and a paper bag labeled "Evidence," and Pat realized it was the man they had come to see. It was Detective Zivernick. Pat got ready to compare notes as Zivernick took the Nashville cops into a breakaway interview room with no windows and muted lighting. Together they stood ready to try to break the stalemate with the Motel Killer.

The reality was that while the slaying at the Dennison in Cincinnati was only a little over a month old by that time, and no one, including Ed Zivernick, was prepared to call it cold, it was certainly stagnating in abeyance and not being actively investigated—at least by M Squad standards. The list of suspects also still stood at zero in what was a stranger-on-stranger strangle job. It was a seemingly random motel murder where, unlike back in Music City, the victim was a known local sex-trade worker and drug user named Ida Mae Bladen.

The Bladen murder at the Dennison was one of a handful of stubborn outliers in Cincinnati that year. It was a year in which, of the fifty-four mur-ders committed within the limits of the city proper, the cops had managed to maintain a stellar clearance rate of about 90 percent. It was a number far better than the national average, which still stands at closer to 66 percent, with roughly four of every ten killers never being identified much less arrested, indicted, and convicted. In the absence of other leads—and in order to preserve other ongoing investigations—Ed Zivernick's strategy in the Dennison case that September was to therefore future-proof the one piece of forensic evidence they had on file and then play the game of wait and see. They'd wait patiently for DNA-testing technology to improve; wait for it to catch up with Ida's killer and, in the meanwhile, bide their time. But another DNA sample that might link to the Motel Killer was a veritable game changer for Pat and Pridemore, validating their investment in a road trip to Ohio. The disclosure spontaneously made by Zivernick of the mothballed offender DNA from the scene at the Dennison naturally caught Pat by surprise. The revelation made within the confines of the drab cinder-block room that afternoon also led to an obvious if not excited response from Pat of "*What* DNA?" It was a perfectly rational question. It was, after all, something he was hearing about for the first time. In no time flat, the breaking news offered by Zivernick would change everything.

A prewar firetrap with 105 one-star rooms, the Dennison in East Cincinnati was a no-tell hotel if there ever was one. In September of 1991, a man calling himself Scott Campbell developed his MO there, one that would later resurface in Nashville, where he officially became known as the Motel Killer. Courtesy of 5chw4r7z https://www.flickr.com/photos/5chw4r7z/25618932134/in/photolist-FXidM2-F2RHYs-RVnyJs-5eXRBN-eXDYJr-9txBrf-tELQcF.

While Pat had made the drive to examine the murder site of Ida Mae Bladen in person and maybe look at some photos from the brown "Do Not Bend" envelope based solely on the apparent link in MO and low-rent lodgings, this latest piece of information had been entirely unexpected. It soon turned out to be the missing link Pat never saw coming. Replying that the forensic recovery team had "recovered semen from the bedding in the room, you know, room four-oh-nine," Zivernick went on to clarify that whomever Pat had spoken with by telephone previously likely didn't know about the DNA since it was hold-back evidence that police were playing close to their chest. It was evidence that was being withheld even internally to prevent department leaks and not spook the killer into fleeing town if he turned out to be a local. As with all large-scale systems replete with problems of communication and efficiency—medicine, transportation, education—getting information was all a matter of timing and who you knew. Zivernick reminded Pat and Pridemore of as much.

It was then that Pat had one of those light-bulb moments. Communication breakdowns aside, while the DNA Identification Act that would allow the FBI to establish CODIS (and the equivalent of a genetic dragnet across the nation) was still a few years away, the technology existed, even in the fall of '91, to confirm a common offender between two or more crimes—what's known as a scene-to-scene hit. In order, however, to justify the comparative test, one that would use up a significant portion of the sample held by each police department and limit their future options if they were wrong, Pat would first need to satisfy himself that the Motel Killer, Terry Duncan, and Scott Campbell were indeed one and the same person.

In reviewing the crime-scene images from room 409 at the century-old Dennison Hotel (eventually razed in 2017 to great acclaim), Pat decided that it was possibly the most decrepit and rancid-looking hole-in-the-wall he'd ever seen, worse even than some of the Section 8s back on his Southside beat in the early eighties. Despite the hotel's imposing historic facade, room 409 looked unfit for human habitation and made the Esquire Inn look like the Ritz by comparison. It was then that Pat had a serious case of déjà vu. The crime-scene snaps of the room confirmed that Ida Mae Bladen's naked body had been sprawled on the bed just like Donna Bacot's body was a week later in Nashville. Those mid-range photos taken by the Cincinnati PD crime-scene tech confirmed a look of abject horror on the victim's face that was hauntingly identical to Donna Bacot, as though a death mask of Ida Mae had been created by her killer and then overlaid with precision onto Donna's face at the Esquire. It was, however, the close-up images of the victim's body that told the full story—one even more horrific.

Still fastened around Ida Mae's throat when she was found by the Dennison's cleaning lady on September 27 was the electrical cord for a lamp on the room's bedside table. Like the towel at the Esquire, the cord had been fashioned into an improvised tourniquet—the same Boy Scout figure-eight knot seen on the tortuous ligature used in the Donna Bacot murder back in Nashville. While both crimes were equally seedy and already had a common MO—the sordid motel room, the forgery in the registry, the forced sexual intrusion—more importantly, they also now had a common criminal signature. They had, like all such signatures, something individuating and subtly consistent between a series of slayings that reflected a killer's personality, paraphilias, and view of himself and the world. Between the towel at the Esquire and the lamp cord at the Dennison, it was the nature of the fatal knot that carried the most weight. Pat knew that two men in different cities having the same MO *and* the same signature bordered on a mathematical impossibility.

By day's end, Pat shook Detective Zivernick's hand and headed back southbound with a shot. While making his way through the tranquility of northern Kentucky with Pridemore by his side, he took in the big picture of the apparent connection between the Esquire and the Dennison. He and Pridemore ran scenarios once again. Pat knew that the use of the lamp cord as the improvised ligature, the necrobondage, in the murder of the earlier Cincinnati victim; registering at the hotel; and killing Ida Mae Bladen under the pseudonym Scott Campbell reflected a specific set of fetishes and paraphilias with a much earlier beginning. Today we recognize these offenders as what are called process-focused killers—cruel sexual sadists whose priority is relishing the actual process of murder as an end in itself, looking to prolong their amusement rather than using murder as a means to an end. Pat knew that, whether as Scott Campbell, Terry Duncan, or whatever names he'd used before, the Motel Killer who'd come to Nashville simply enjoyed killing.

Murder was a leisure pursuit for him, a pastime not unlike boccie ball, Ultimate Frisbee, or knitting. He was a murder tourist who'd made his way to Music City, as had so many other serial killers Pat had seen and would see over his career. The Motel Killer had used Nashville as a different kind of holiday destination entirely. Perhaps it was the city's unique geographic position and equally symbolic place in the American landscape, the largest urban center in a state bordering eight other states and accessed by numerous interstate routes and lonely county roads. Or perhaps it was Nashville being a place where dreams are both made and broken, a place that captivated the imagination and conjured old-world Dixie charm but also a place that seduced the soul with celebrity and grandiosity. Perhaps he saw it as a place where everyone was too busy and caught up in their dreams to notice the monsters arriving in their midst. Either way, Pat now had a tentative handle on who he was dealing with.

While some of these abstract philosophical questions as to motive and method intruded on Pat's thoughts as he tried to anticipate the Motel Killer's next move, a more pressing question would soon offer a definitive answer. It was an answer to a question he'd had since he and Pridemore had left Ohio: Were Scott Campbell and Terry Duncan the same person—the same killer? With the window of opportunity forever narrowing, Pat knew that if he was dealing with the killer of Ida Mae Bladen in the case of Donna Bacot—a highly mobile necrophile and process-focused serial killer fixated on prolonging the act of murder and the suffering of his victims—the killer would be growing restless. He'd soon be back on the move, checking in to another skid-row motel with a new victim in tow. It was all but inevitable.

Chapter 13

Burger College

It was early June of '92 when the ever-consistent TBI came back to Pat with a common offender profile. The blood found at the Esquire Inn the previous October 3 and the semen found at the Dennison Hotel the week prior were an exact match, at least as close as DNA matches could be "exact" by 1992 standards. The first person Pat told of the match was Bill Pridemore, one desk over in the M Squad office, followed in short order by Ed Zivernick over an AT&T office line back in Cincinnati. Joe Thornhill, Pat's consummate doubter, conveniently had the day off when the news came in. He didn't get to see that the goalposts were now in sight and, against all odds, that his naysaying and nihilistic predictions had been off the mark.

While not yet having a name or a location for the newly confirmed serial murderer, Pat knew that he could now be unequivocally certain that the same person was responsible for both murders, spaced exactly a week apart. Had Pat not reached out to the cops in Cincinnati and made the trek to Ohio in person, not only would the link have never been made, but the gruesome torture, rape, and lamp-cord-ligature murder of Ida Mae Bladen at the Dennison Hotel would likely have never seen the light of day. As a marginalized sex-trade worker, young Ida had even fewer advocates in life than she had in death; while Detective Zivernick with the Cincinnati PD Major Offenders Unit had worked the case as best he could under the circumstances, the linkages made by Pat gave the M Squad eminent domain over the case and the ability to take the lead in both files—two crime scenes nearly three hundred miles apart now confirmed as connected—from that point forward.

Nearly eight months after the fact, Pat returned to Esquire Inn's infamous room 23 and its even more infamous bathtub flood with a renewed perspective and with fresh eyes. He paced the parking lot and looked at the types of people checking in there, the cars they drove, the license plates. He noted a lot of trucks, mostly big rigs riding bobtail—tractors without trailers—with the drivers laying over in town and waiting for a new load rather than deadheading it back home. Noting the many plates from Texas affixed to those rigs, he thought back to the motel registry, back to the check-in ledger bearing the dubious name of Terry Duncan with an address of 53rd Street in Dallas.

Pat rightfully considered the commonalities between the Nashville and Cincinnati scenes beyond just the DNA evidence linking them to a common killer. He thought beyond the low-rent lodgings, the inner-city settings, the quick access to the interstate, the transient and trucker traffic coming and going, and, of course, the Texas connection to both aliases on the three-by-five cards at the front desk upon check-in. Knowing he had to take one more shot at the fingerprints lifted from the beer can at the Esquire, Pat later faxed the paperwork to the Dallas PD, which, as he'd recently discovered, had one of the more sophisticated AFIS terminals in the nation. It was an agency that could circumvent the Texas Rangers and run both state and regional fingerprint checks on its own, in effect cutting out the middleman. Within a few hours Pat hit pay dirt. Persistence, as he had learned long ago, always paid off. What a difference two weeks—the time elapsed since he'd last had the prints from Esquire checked—had made. In those two weeks, the Motel Killer had popped out of the reeds, albeit in an unlikely manner.

The Dallas cop who called Pat with the results of the latest AFIS check knew nothing about the motel murders. Knowing nonetheless that the specificity of the request meant that he'd helped hook a big fish, the officer who rang Pat's desk that day was almost giddy about the circumstances of the match. "You wanna know who this guy is? . . . You *really* wanna know who this guy is?" the unnamed detective asked rhetorically again and again, sportily and somewhat smugly keeping Pat in suspense. "Well, I'll tell you who your guy is!" he continued before Pat could even answer. The Dallas detective then told him who "your guy" was: Michael Scott Magliolo, forty-one years old and, of all things, the general manager of a McDonald's restaurant in Jasper, Texas, who had recently matriculated at the so-called Burger College, the unofficial name for Hamburger University in Illinois, where McDonald's lifers are sent for managerial training and social engineering. The Texas hunch had been right all along. The prints from the beer can yielded an AFIS hit this time because, as it turned out, the aspiring Burger College grad had gotten himself pinched by Jasper PD officers for an open-and-shut DUI—a bust that only a week prior had landed him in the state's fingerprint database. Until then, he'd been entirely off the grid. Now he was in play. Now, at long last, he was in the M Squad's crosshairs.

The timing was nothing short of remarkable. Within a matter of days, first through a DNA match and then a fingerprint match—both definitive by the standards of the era—Pat had boxed in a serial killer that no one but he ever went looking for. A killer no one ever knew existed. A series of unforeseen events had put Michael Magliolo on police radar for the first time in part due to good detective work and in part due to the sheer luck of his being arrested while driving pie-eyed on his way to a bar with a car full of teenage girls and being reported by a passerby. When printed and booked on the driving rap, Magliolo of course had no idea that, nearly seven hundred miles away, Pat Postiglione had made the scene-to-scene match linking him both to Donna Bacot in Nashville and his earlier victim, Ida Mae Bladen in Cincinnati. He had no idea that Pat had recovered partial prints from a discarded beer can at the Esquire that, by dint of the unforeseen DUI bust, would soon prove to be the proverbial nail in the coffin. It would be what Pat had been waiting for, what the Metro cops and Davidson County DA would need to stop Magliolo—the *real* name now assigned to the Motel Killer—from killing again.

Chapter 14

LUMPER

While Billy Pridemore hit the links off Elmington Avenue to play eighteen holes and work on his handicap, Pat took an economy-class Northwest Airlines flight to Dallas and met there with Detective Zivernick, who, on the flimsy Cincinnati PD budget, had to take three trains instead. Together they interviewed Michael Magliolo in a room at Dallas PD headquarters that looked not unlike the one back in Cincinnati where Pat and Zivernick first met just weeks earlier. As it turned out, Magliolo was no master-class criminal. He certainly wasn't the supervillain who'd never allow himself to be caught—the phantom killer that the skeptical and cynical Detective Thornhill thought he was. In the end, in the bowels of the building on South Lamar Street in Dallas, Magliolo broke easily; he confessed to everything. Without pause, he admitted to both the Nashville and Cincinnati murders and even added a third murder—his first kill—a year earlier in Hammond, Louisiana, that had previously gone undetected. Had it not been for Pat's sleuthing, Magliolo would have kept at it for years; he admitted as much. He simply loved killing. It was just good sport.

The next day, Pat's return flight on Northwest became a de facto *Con Air* as he returned Magliolo in cuffs and leg irons—still in economy class, no less—back to Nashville. It all went down textbook smooth. Yet, before booking him for murder one at the Criminal Justice Center on 2nd Avenue, Pat had to make one slight detour. As one last order of business, he rerouted Magliolo from the CJC to the M Squad office at 200 James Robertson Parkway not too far away, equidistant between 2nd and 3rd Avenues. It was a slight detour, but it was an important one.

Before Magliolo was booked and printed at the CJC and had his mug shot taken by some anonymous uniform like every other crook in Music City, Pat first snapped a pre–mug shot Polaroid of the elusive Motel Killer. It was a candid portrait of a now humbled Michael Magliolo in cuffs, sitting at, of all places, Detective Joe Thornhill's desk in the M Squad office. Pat left that revelatory snapshot in a place he knew Thornhill would find it, leaning against his sullied coffee mug emblazoned with the words "World's Best Detective." It was officially over, complete with photographic evidence. It was proof positive that the hot-hand fallacy might not be a fallacy after all.

Told Ya So: The elusive Motel Killer, Michael Scott Magliolo, newly arrested and extradited from Texas, sits smugly at the desk of the skeptical Metro detective Joe Thornhill, the M Squad investigator who had vocally decried Pat's attempts to locate the mysterious interstate serial killer. This Polaroid photograph taken by Pat was left on Thornhill's desk to be found at the start of his next scheduled shift, along with a colorful personalized inscription, also from Pat. Courtesy of Pat Postiglione.

Furthermore, while Pat and Ed Zivernick's interrogation in Dallas had been fruitful, it was once Pat was back in Nashville that Magliolo really started to sing. In fact, it seemed as if he couldn't *stop* talking, not just to Pat and Pridemore, but also to a reporter with the local CBS affiliate about his other victims. Plural. Between Jasper and Nashville, it seemed as though Magliolo's earlier victims had gone from one in Louisiana to eight in various other cities across the US. While Magliolo eventually boasted of at least ten other victims scattered across five states—Tennessee, Ohio, Pennsylvania, Louisiana, and Arkansas—only one other victim could ever be verified beyond Donna Bacot and Ida Mae Bladen. That is not to say that he hadn't killed nearly a dozen victims in dive motels across the South and Midwest, as he claimed. It's only that, due to many of the police agencies in these states failing to keep diligent records of these murders—much less exercising the same due diligence that Pat did—these crimes seemed to have fallen between the cracks in the period from the mid-1980s to the early 1990s. As unfathomable as it may seem that cases of murder can be lost, mislaid, forgotten about, or even, for any number of reasons, made to disappear, the tragic reality is that it's far more common than anyone could ever imagine—even today.

The state of Illinois, for example, managed to get away with not reporting and otherwise suppressing all its homicides required for annual reporting to the FBI for more than twenty years, from 1994 to 2015 inclusive. Even when compelled to release these figures following a lawsuit filed by the nonprofit homicide think tank the Murder Accountability Project, in early 2016, only what is believed to be 80 percent of the estimated 2100 murders to have occurred over this period were ever accounted for. The remaining 20 percent—roughly 420 murders—remain lost to history and are likely unrecoverable, victims and their killers alike swept into the dustbin of American crime history.

In Magliolo's case, of the additional ten plus murders that he claimed to have committed, Pat did manage to find that the Hammond, Louisiana, killing was verifiable. As likely the first murder he ever committed, it would serve as Magliolo's origin story—a partial explanation for how the horror that came to end in Music City at the Esquire Inn first took shape. It also seemed to explain the connection that both the Dennison and the Esquire had with neighboring truck stops and interstates.

It turned out that before becoming a McDonald's manager in East Texas, Magliolo had held a variety of odd jobs. One of these jobs would become part of his MO whenever he had an extended stretch off from booking children's birthday parties and fielding complaints about cold french fries. Serving as the perfect cover, it allowed him access to the open road along with the anonymity he needed to acquire his victims across multiple states. This side job was precisely how Magliolo ended up in Nashville in October of '91. It was also how he had ended up in Cincinnati—at the Dennison Hotel—a week prior. It was the same reason he was in Hammond, Louisiana, in 1988, when he first got a taste for murder.

Working as a freelance lackey exchanging hard labor for free passage, loading and offloading cargo in exchange for a lift down the interstate on long-haul rigs—what's known in trucker lingo as a "lumper"—there is no telling how many truck stops and seedy motels and hotels in various states Magliolo managed to visit over the years by way of this pretext. Even when gainfully employed back in his native Texas in a management position with McDonald's, Magliolo felt compelled to revert to this line of work on his days off, hit the open road, and troll the nation's highways and drifter lodgings in search of victims to rape, torture, and murder with increasing specificity.

Lumper work, however degrading, was to some extent the perfect cover story for Magliolo, any payments always being made under the table in cash, no questions asked. In most cases, a ride to the next spot on the map was payment enough. At the same time, any personal identifiers offered or accepted—as the custom went—consisted of first names only or, more often, some type of alias or anagram. Neither a lumper nor the trucker offering them passage wanted any backlinks to their real identities beyond the open road and its allurements. Names like Scott Campbell and Terry Duncan were, as such, taken at face value. The passengers on board long-haul trucks and using these names while working off the books—no license number, no DOT number, no other personal identifiers—ensured they could never be traced back to anyone or any place in particular. It was the prelude to the perfect murder: a stranger killing a stranger, with no known motive and in a town where he knows no one and no one knows him. It had certainly worked for Magliolo more than enough times before.

As strange, foolhardy, and fraught with predation as it might seem by today's standards, lumping was a socially acceptable and even widely sanctioned form of hitchhiking in the early nineties. It enabled Magliolo to slip almost invisibly in and out of cities entirely undetected. To some extent, Detective Joe Thornhill was right—Magliolo was as close to a ghost as one could get in Big City USA. There was never a shortage of rides to and from any place on the map Magliolo wanted to travel, not to mention truckers prepared to give him a lift in exchange for whatever. It would always, in his mind, be worth the fare. The lumper MO proved especially easy during Magliolo's first confirmed murder, when he had also been traveling with his wife. She was the perfect decoy.

As far back as 1988 and likely even earlier, Magliolo had used a combination of lumper work and conventional hitchhiking to make his way around the South with his one-time spouse—usually with murderous intent. Often for weeks at a time, the hapless couple lived as wandering vagabonds, sleeping beneath bridges or in unlocked cars, foraging for food in dumpsters, subsisting through petty larcenies, and even turning to the sex trade if need be. On occasion Magliolo would take to *geeking*—a term for male prostitutes who secretly turn tricks for other men in the trucking, traveling carnival, and other nomadic scenes—in one case meeting a man in his midseventies named Jimmy Pemberton in Louisiana. It was during the experience that followed that Magliolo learned that motels provided the perfect environment for a murder. The staff didn't ask too many questions, and the other patrons made it their business to mind their own business, most of them being there for nefarious reasons themselves. For this reason, low-rent motels of the ilk of the Esquire fall squarely within what the FBI now classifies as *known vice areas*, one of the leading locales where all breeds of serial killers either acquire or kill their victims.

Not unlike Nashville's infamous serial footstomper, the diverse sexual deviant George Mitchell from a generation prior, what began as part of Magliolo's MO soon became his signature after finding he had a penchant for sexual murder as an end in itself. Just as Mitchell's foot stomping was ostensibly for the purpose of distracting and robbing his female victims, Magliolo's first murder ostensibly was also to facilitate a robbery of the man who took him to the hotel for paid sex. Like Mitchell, he too would find that the MO awakened some otherwise dormant and unexplored latent deviant sexual urge within him. Soon there would no longer need to be a second felony. Magliolo's previously preferred method of carrying out his crimes would soon define his identity as a predator. It would become his signature.

As Magliolo's first victim, Jimmy Pemberton had made the mistake—like Donna Bacot and Ida Mae Bladen after him—of bringing the sadistic Texan back to a motel room. In that case the room was a squalid set of quarters located near a Tangipahoa Parish truck stop, about an hour from Baton Rouge. Magliolo had reportedly offered the aged Pemberton some kind of sexual favor in exchange for a little cash—what in Nashville they call "walkin' around money." Magliolo's intent the entire time, as he later admitted, was to get the sad old man into the room alone and then kill him for his jalopy station wagon parked outside the door to the suite. It was robbery-homicide that would provide Magliolo an item that could serve as both transportation and shelter for him and his equally destitute wife, who all the while was left waiting back at the truck stop, seemingly none the wiser about what her husband was really up to. Or so she claimed.

By the time Magliolo had killed anywhere between three and ten people in various roach motels across the southern and midwestern United States, his wife, apparently finally aware of his lumping and geeking routine—or perhaps just tired of it—had packed her bags and left. The two had been divorced by the time Magliolo was working at the Jasper McDonald's and was arrested for the DUI with a carload of jailbait high school girls. By the time Pat had her ex-husband back in Nashville and on ice, the timeworn woman was prepared to cooperate fully with the investigation into the three slayings. While acknowledging their nomadic existence together as they traveled all over the country for months on end sleeping wherever they could, she made it clear that she had no idea what her husband did when he was away from her—which was most of the time. She agreed that her one-time hubby was probably good for the up to ten murders he boasted of—that he'd likely killed even more. She also suspected him of killing her own brother years earlier, a case that was still unsolved at the time of Magliolo's arrest. She considered that the fifty-one-year sentence he eventually received for the Bacot murder was far too lenient. She wondered why Tennessee didn't execute men like Magliolo more often. The reality is that they would never know whether Magliolo's wife was genuinely—and blissfully—ignorant of his murderous sojourns at motels and hotels across the country or rightfully terrified of being his next victim and didn't want to poke the bear.

However, Magliolo's pursuit of lumper work wasn't ever really "work" to him. It was leisure. Just like his murders. All adults, from the most slothful and unproductive of people to inveterate workaholics, divide their waking hours, knowingly or not, into four categories: work, obligatory nonwork, free time, and leisure time. Most people, depending on how much free time they have, choose to occupy that time pursuing hobbies and pastimes that offer them what work cannot—the activities that define them. That's what separates leisure from free time; leisure is supposed to challenge, excite, empower, or distract. More importantly, you're supposed to be good—and get better—at it the more you do it. If the challenge is too high with no personal value added, people tend to get frustrated and quit. If the challenge is too low, people get bored and want to increase the challenge to justify the investment in time and money. That's why our leisure pursuits reflect who we really are—they are windows into our core identities. Murder is no different.

As emerging research has come to suggest, and as Michael Magliolo demonstrated between 1990 and 1991 (and maybe even earlier), serial homicide appears to be, above all else, less a compulsion than a hobby—a sadistic pastime. Like in Magliolo's case, where his extended days off from McDonald's were used to hit the road and kill for fun before having to drag himself back to work, new evidence is mounting to suggest that serial killers are more likely to murder when they simply have the free time and corresponding physical and mental investment to allow for it. They're also more likely to increase the frequency of the murders as they get better at it while simultaneously increasing the difficulty level to stay challenged, much like all pastimes pursued to test one's mettle and find purpose—from playing golf to building model airplanes, gaming, and long-distance running. This could mean being more daring in where and when they strike, experimenting with a new MO, or in targeting more demanding and challenging victims. It could also mean—as has been seen in countless cases—baiting authorities with phone calls or letters, returning to the crime scene, or generally taking unnecessary risks to keep the thrill alive. In Magliolo's case, the challenge meant coaxing Donna Bacot to leave the comforts of her home to go to the Esquire—a gambit that ultimately got him caught.

No one knows how far Magliolo would have pursued his skills if he hadn't made the additional mistake of killing in Nashville on Pat's watch. One thing for certain, however, is that serial killers like Magliolo all have a dream job in mind. It's the same dream job everyone else has: to do what you love for a living—to get paid to pursue your pastime. Much like Pat's soon-to-be ex-partner, Billy Pridemore, had a dream retirement job in mind—as many men do—of working at a golf course, where his leisure time and work time might seamlessly dovetail together as one, so, too, do serial killers seek out occupations that align nicely with their preferred pastime. As Pat and his team would soon learn the hard way, some killers are better than others at figuring out how to pull this off. They figure out early on how to love their work and get paid for it.

Part III

THE DIVE BAR MURDERS

"That is the remarkable thing about drinking, it brings people together so quickly."

—Erich Remarque, *Three Comrades*

Chapter 15

Force Majeure

It was October 15, 1993—a Friday—when the Universal Pictures thriller *Judgment Night* went into nationwide release. Boasting a cast that included nineties mainstays such as Emilio Estevez, Cuba Gooding Jr., and Denis Leary, together with a soundtrack replete with top-40 acts like House of Pain and De La Soul, the film, though a critical flop, was, like *The Police Tapes* nearly two decades prior, an autopsy of the American psyche. The film's plot depicted a group of middle-aged, middle-class men in an RV who, after taking the wrong exit en route to a sports event in Chicago, end up being targets in a deadly game of cat and mouse with the ruthless gangsters who control the area.

At its essence, the film was a hackneyed voyage-and-return story that's been told and retold since antiquity, one reframed to capture the mass hysteria surrounding urban gangs like the Crips and Bloods at the twilight of the twentieth century. By that fall of '93, America had both an obsession with and visceral fear of these and other gangs that were, until then, thought to have been limited largely to the LA area. That city's widely televised riots, killing nearly sixty people in the summer of '92, only served to intensify that fear. It was a paranoia that was galvanized when news footage of mob rule and the reach of these gangs hit the evening news across the country, even more so once Crip and Blood franchises began to show up across the Midwest and the South within the next year.

Most of these knock-off gangs weren't *real* Crips and Bloods. For the most part they were no more than cabals of small-time punks—loosely joined pop-up shops and poseurs—arbitrarily choosing to wear red or blue in order to claim affiliation with one of the two West Coast gangs. They were at best imitators who co-opted those same gangs' brands and names to frighten both their underworld rivals and law-abiding locals alike. They were phony-baloney and then some, but the ruse worked. Appearance was then, as it is now, reality. Especially in Music City.

By October of '93 a number of Section 8 neighborhoods had teens jealously guarding their turf as either satellite Crips or Bloods—sometimes both—skulking around in either red or blue bandanas and T-shirts just as they'd seen on TV. In both East and North Nashville in particular, some kids on bikes could be seen flashing hand signals to older men sitting on porches or in parked cars; some buildings in the Gulch were tagged with gang graffiti pledging allegiance to either blue or red. It didn't matter that no gangs were actually headquartered or operating in that neighborhood; the tags created the perception that they were. Studies into graffiti have consistently shown its mere presence creates the illusion of increased danger; it reinforces the fear of crime and the fear of losing control—of a person's space being invaded and conquered. The Nashville Bloods and Crips might have all been playing pretend and mimicking their LA role models, but they were also playing for keeps. They were winning a psychological war of attrition where there would be mounting casualties. Like other cities across America where LA gang brands were being counterfeited, there were very real deadly consequences to come.

Nashville had by that fall of '93 set a new record for murders committed inside the city limits; for the remainder of that decade the city would see an annual average upwards of eighty-five slayings a year. While the faux Crips and Bloods setting up shop all over Music City weren't single-handedly responsible for all the inflated bloodshed, they had certainly helped inspire a new reign of what criminologists call social disorganization. The theory suggests that the order of society, as the LA riots of '92 showed in such sobering detail, is tenuous at best, only ever one power outage, Stanley Cup win—or loss—or unruly public demonstration away from complete implosion.

At any given time, there are dozens of forces pushing on a given city's character for control. Most people go along with the status quo, play by the rules, and pay their taxes because the disincentive to not doing so—jail, financial ruin, loss of reputation, or embarrassment—is stronger than the enticement to participate. But compliance with the rules laid down by society ceases when those disincentives no longer matter—when the repercussions become malleable and negotiable. When people see other people getting away with things they shouldn't be, it has a cascading effect on societal conformity and any appetite to play nice—the willingness to defer gratification rather than summarily claim what you think is yours.

The opposite of social disorganization is what's known as the social contract. It is the view that a person's moral and political obligations, rights, and freedoms are dependent on an implied contract or agreement made by all those in the society in which they live. It's why people close ranks to help and protect their neighbors with no expectation of a material return; it's why people build communities, raise barns, donate clothes and money, and help ensure the welfare of citizens they've never met. It's why all civilized societies are bound by the rule of law. But it's also a house of cards. A day late or dollar short, the social contract buckles under its own weight. Like any other contract, it just takes one departure from the agreement for the whole thing to fall apart. For years the social contract was strong in Nashville. That was before 1993. Before a massive chasm opened up beneath the city and pulled the whole thing in.

The murder of Leanna Shoulders on April 2, 1993, had arguably been the tipping point, the force majeure that dissolved the Music City social contract for much of the next few years. Like all force majeures it was unforeseen and catastrophic. It revealed the now inarguable epidemic of violent crime subsuming the city—the dawn of a dark age when people would be truly afraid. Whether it was pulling up stakes or battening down the hatches, there was a citywide sense of foreboding going into the nineties. The twenty-five-year-old Leanna had been working as the night clerk at the Dickerson Road Days Inn when two teens looking to make a name for themselves—looking for juice with the fake Crips and Bloods and the soon-to-be very real Gangster Disciples out of Chicago—gunned down the part-timer for thrills. It was the senseless and bloody punctuation mark on an already senseless and sophomoric robbery. One shooter was Emmanuel Edwards, a well-known down-and-outer looking to hitch his wagon to any gang he could. The second assailant was named Jason Clark, a kid who by June of that year the district attorney would successfully try as an adult for murder one. It was a get-tough-on-crime good-faith gesture, even if a little too late.

Pat and Pridemore worked the Shoulders murder and caught the two shooters within the first forty-eight hours of the crime. Others also worked the case from behind the scenes, though not in the conventional sense. The Metro chief, the Nashville mayor, the Chamber of Commerce, the puppet masters controlling Music Row, management at the Opry, they all tried to put out the fire. They tried to provide some assurance as fast as Pat had made the two arrests that Music City was still safe. They claimed the killing wasn't a gang initiation as many were saying and that it was just a blip on the radar. Unfortunately, what had started as a cabaret act in Music City by those looking to emulate the West Coast gangs became a stinging indictment against the rule of law and the leadership of city officials. But it would also inspire one citizen to go on to seize what he saw as his destiny as a killer most strange. He was the last person in Nashville anyone would expect to do such things. That's precisely how he nearly got away with it.

Chapter 16

Last Call

The same Friday that *Judgment Night* premiered at the Regal Cinema in Opry Mills, Pat paused to look at the whiteboard in the M Squad office—to assess the state of things in the city and marshal his thoughts. It was the same board used by all his detectives in the office to record the year's murders in vertical columns with each detective's name at the top. When a murder first got logged, the name of the victim and the file number were written in red. Once the case was solved and a suspect was arrested—if it got solved—the red entry was erased and rewritten in black marker. It was a visual indexing system that allowed the team to see with a glance how their efforts were stacking up, a system accurately replicated in any number of cop shows, most notably the long-running NBC drama *Homicide: Life on the Street*. But leaving the open/unsolved cases in red also ensured they were a constant distraction. It was a stats sheet that held both bragging rights and shame, depending on the amount of red versus black appearing under a given officer's name. With the weekend just starting, Pat knew that, based on events of late, there would likely be more red names going up on the board in the next forty-eight hours. He was right but couldn't possibly have anticipated the circumstances.

Just over a day later, in the early morning hours of Sunday, October 17, Pat and the rest of the M Squad all received wake-up calls at home, pulled from their beds with a rude awakening. When Pat picked up the corded General Electric telephone on his nightstand at just after 3:00 a.m.—four rings in— the Metro watch commander on the other end explained that the Nashville

Fire Department had responded to a three-alarm blaze at a hole-in-the-wall bar known as the Corral Club, or simply the Corral, on Lebanon Road that turned out to be more than first met the eye. After fire crews had extinguished a massive blaze that had risen like a midnight sun in the dark of the Tennessee night—one with all the telltale signs of arson—the fire captain conducted a quick search for the point of origin for the fire. Once it was safe to enter what remained of the structure, he began to survey the still-smoldering debris of the tavern. He soon determined that the fire had been started near the main bar with the use of an accelerant, thought to be gasoline, based both on pour patterns and the fact that a partially melted plastic jerry can had been found inside. The fuel for the fire—or the material upon which the accelerant had been poured—wasn't, however, the wooden bar top, the floor, or any of the dozen or so tables inside. It had been a human body.

Located inside the husk of the Corral was the charred corpse of an adult male—burned beyond recognition—sitting on what remained of a chair beside the discarded fuel canister. Despite the horrific charring that ensued once the body, whether alive or dead, had been doused with gasoline and set ablaze, Metro cops were soon able to figure out who their victim was. A patrolman with the South Precinct, one of the first to arrive on scene along with firefighters, had located a wallet, picked clean, in a mud puddle behind the receiving doors for the bar. While the cash was gone, a Tennessee driver's license gave Pat his first clue. The victim—apparently the lone victim—of the arson murder was a forty-six-year-old man named Ronnie Bingham, the owner of the Corral.

Given the intentionally set fire and the discovery of Bingham's wallet outside, the scene had all the markings of a robbery-homicide, albeit a rather unusual and grisly one. But Pat knew that the whole concept of "a robbery gone bad" was a misnomer—one of the most misattributed of all criminal motives. With less than 0.02 percent of armed robberies ending in homicide in the United States over the last fifty years, the more common scenario when murder is involved is that the theft was an impulsive afterthought, as Pat was confident had been the case at the Corral. This was especially obvious when he found amid the charred ruins that the cash register and fireproof safe hadn't been touched. As well, real robbers as a rule don't carry around jerry cans of unleaded gas to their crimes. It seemed to Pat, as he followed the crime-scene techs through the charred remains of the building, that Bingham was likely killed for some other reason and had been left in the bar after closing by a killer who had obtained the accelerant from his car nearby. The killer must have then doused the body to destroy evidence, taking the whole bar to the ground in the process. The wallet was likely pulled from Bingham's back pocket before he had been set alight. It suggested the whole affair came together suddenly and was perhaps unplanned. It was as impulsive as it was maniacal. Bingham's killer had likely already been in the bar for another purpose before closing time, his car parked in the rear lot outside. For some reason he'd decided to kill Bingham once he had him alone.

Pat's hypothesis was confirmed the next day, the afternoon of October 18, when an autopsy performed by a forensic pathologist with the Davidson County medical examiner's office found lodged in Bingham's skull a single .38-caliber bullet, a round of the semiwadcutter variety commonly used in revolvers. He'd been shot in the head, execution style, relieved of his wallet, and then set on fire. While the sequence of events was now clear, the circumstances surrounding the murder were only growing more puzzling. Digging into Bingham's personal and financial life for clues as to who might have had it out for him failed to provide much clarity, or at least not as much as the cops were hoping for. For someone running a dive bar in the big-city South, Bingham was actually about as squeaky clean as they came. He had some enemies, naturally, but no one who seemed capable of such mayhem. No bad debts, no business beefs, no love triangles, no disgruntled ex-employees, no booze or drug problems, and no rivals in organized crime or enmity among his competitors. With that, and not wanting another *Cash Box*/Kevin Hughes whodunit in the red column to juggle into 1994, Pat realized that he'd need to look beyond the usual suspects and motives. After getting a list of regulars at the bar from Bingham's bereaved and shocked staff members, he expanded his canvass of potential witnesses by narrowing down who was in the bar on the night of the murder—who might have seen who *else* was there. It was a wise move. Before long, Pat had statements from two women, both regulars at the bar who knew Bingham and were able to describe a man they'd never seen there, alone after the last call for drinks at about 1:30 a.m. He also was the last customer in the bar at closing time when the women left.

The man was generally nondescript—five foot eight, medium build, medium brown hair, glasses, and a little on the chubby side—a standard-issue nobody. And yet, they did manage to note something peculiar about him. What stood out was that the mystery customer wasn't drinking; rather, he was compulsively putting quarters in the video poker machine. With a seemingly endless supply of change in his pockets, the man was obsessively and passionately working the machine as if he were playing for his life.

Through a contiguous set of underworld informers with an array of motivations to dime out fellow crooks, Pat also soon learned that an unnamed old-timer from somewhere near the city of Gallatin, about thirty miles north of Nashville, had sold a .38-caliber revolver off the books to a man named Tom Steeples, a local computer-store owner, only a few months before the murder. While by 1993 in Nashville, it had become de rigueur for a successful store owner to have a gun for "protection," it turned out that Steeples, unlike most upper-middle-class gun owners, was a little too giddy about owning a gun, enough that it struck the black market seller as weird. This was especially the case when, before buying the gun, Steeples test-fired it with glee by firing round after round into the earth beneath his feet. Steeples liked it so much, Pat learned, that he would routinely shoot it while in his backyard before and after work. Sometimes it was to test his aim, other times just to see what it felt like to shoot it. Most often, Steeples would shoot the rounds into an old fifty-five-gallon oil drum resting at the back of his expansive upper-middle-class property in the upscale suburb of Mount Juliet.

Nearly a full decade before a similar method was used to catch the better-known Beltway Snipers in Metropolitan Washington DC—the older of the two serial shooters, John Allen Muhammad, having regularly shot into a large tree stump in his backyard as target practice—Pat managed to obtain a search warrant for Steeples's home on South Mount Juliet Road, again focusing on an item used for target practice. Included in the items to be searched for was an empty plastic barrel situated in plain view on the property—a barrel full of bullet holes and which, it was hoped, would contain projectiles that would match those found in the soil at the gun seller's own home. That they were the same .38 caliber rounds already found to match the bullet lodged in Ronnie Bingham's skull.

Pat, Pridemore, and the Metro PD forensics team's best of the best, normally delegated to assist the M Squad with its key tasks, arrived on October 21 at the sprawling Steeples home, where they hauled away the old oil drum from the backyard. They were later able to pluck a handful of spent rounds from the item, most of which were still intact enough to allow for a ballistics comparison. That subsequent comparison revealed that the spent projectiles pulled from the barrel were a match to the .38-caliber bullet taken out of Bingham's head on October 18 by the medical examiner, as well as the rounds test-fired by Steeples back when he first bought the weapon. Beyond the overwhelming forensic evidence linking Steeples to the murder, it also turned out that he lived in the area of Bingham's bar and, it was learned, had occasionally been there before. As cold and bizarre as it seemed, it was as if on that particular night, Steeples had merely grown tired of firing into the empty oil drum and had selected Bingham at random for his next round of close target shooting. Although Pat never found the gun used in the murder itself, the bullets were the next best thing.

The arrest went down on Lebanon Pike, just down the street from the Corral Club where Ronnie Bingham was murdered, on the afternoon of Saturday, October 23. The setting, however, seemed light-years away from the scene where Bingham had been shot and immolated with such cruelty—killed for reasons Pat was still trying to figure out. It was "family day" at the Hermitage Lanes, today the Hermitage Strike and Spare on Lebanon Pike, when Pat discovered Tom Steeples with his wife and two kids beginning their seventh frame at the sprawling facility jammed with birthday parties, league players, and weekend-access parents. By day Steeples, playing the family man, worked his own business as a successful Nashville computer wholesaler, back in the dial-up internet days when piecemeal PC hucksters in strip plazas controlled the hardware and software markets. But by night he lived a second secret life, scoring and smoking rock by the G-note and dabbling in rough sex with Music City escorts. Before long, nearly everything Steeples earned running his business on Elm Hill Pike, going under the rather banal name of Computer Forms and Supplies, had been squandered on drugs.

Yet when Pat and Bill Pridemore, along with a small retinue of Metro uniforms, crashed family bowling day that Saturday, they didn't get the chilly reception they were expecting. It almost seemed as though Steeples was expecting to be caught, as though it was no big deal and just all part of his endgame; one with an unhappy ending he couldn't avoid. He'd been waiting for the other shoe to drop since killing Ronnie Bingham for something some were suggesting was trivial as revenge for losing at his bar's video poker game. The reality is that Steeples likely didn't have a motive at all. When Pat approached and asked, "Are you Tom Steeples?" Steeples didn't even have to inquire who was asking. Instead he simply asked for a lawyer. Within an hour he had retained Jack Lowery, one of the highest-priced lawyers in the Nashville area. Although most of his disposable income had been going to drugs, Steeples still had assets he could leverage to pay for the best. Awaiting his bail while in custody at the Metro lockup, the Criminal Justice Center (CJC) then located on 2nd Avenue, Steeples was not only an alleged murderer but what we recognize today as an activated psychopath.

One of the hallmarks of serial killers, what in part separates them from mass murderers such as school shooters—who tend to be psychotic or suffering from a schizoid disorder—is a diagnosis of psychopathy. By definition, a clinical or criminal psychopath is an individual who scores thirty or higher on a standardized test known as the Psychopathy Checklist Revised (PCL-R), a test designed and later revised by Dr. Robert Hare, a Canadian experimental psychologist and pioneer in the field. The PCL-R, sometimes cited as the Hare Checklist, measures four types of distinct behaviors, known as facets, which relate to personality traits ranging from impulse control and malignant narcissism to parasitic, manipulative character traits and a general lack of empathy. Hare's work in this area built on an earlier version developed in the 1940s known as the Cleckley Checklist, similarly named for its creator, Hervey Cleckley, whose research suggested that the psychopath could in part be summed up by what he called an "innate fearlessness." They are brazen predators who love the thrill of the chase and the satisfaction of controlling people in all elements of their lives.

While not all psychopaths go on to become murderers—and they can find comparatively less lethal outlets for this innate fearlessness, bizarre grandiosity, and need to dominate others by seeking out specific occupations (business executive, lawyer, chef, doctor, and journalist being among the most common careers)—the activated psychopath, like Steeples, is a rare breed who effectively has had a switch thrown in his head to awaken him from sleep mode. There then occurs a sudden shift in perspective and a new inability to exercise restraint when that psychopath pushes the limits once and is able to get away with it. It's an awakening that occurs when a psychopath who's been playing by the rules decides to take off the mask of normalcy and start taking bigger risks to appease a twisted ego and various sexual urges. This period of self-actualization is typically irreversible. Ronnie Bingham was that awakening. Steeples, now activated, would feel the need to keep on killing.

Chapter 17

Amateur Night

After retaining marquee Nashville defense attorney Jack Lowery, a legal guru known as a Mid-South Super Lawyer, who rolled between cities across the US in a private jet, Steeples quite incredibly managed to make bail after being charged with murder one, arson, and indignity to a body in the death of Ronnie Bingham. Leveraging his store and its assets as collateral, he played the upstanding citizen and pillar of the Nashville business community in court, and the judge bought it. He'd also played coy with Pat during his in-custody interview and hadn't said a word, no doubt using the time alone in the interrogation room to stare at the pegboard walls and contemplate his next moves—whom to kill first once he got out, and how. It was with bond set at $150,000 and a strict list of conditions to abide by that Steeples soon managed to secure his liberty while awaiting trial. Lowery had convinced the bail court judge that Steeples, a man with no criminal record, who had a young family and was the sole breadwinner of that family, needed to be free to run his computer shop until the trial to settle the matter of his guilt or innocence. In reality, Steeples needed to get out of the pokey because of some other business to attend to. The people of Music City had no idea the danger that they—all—were already in.

As is the rule with most awakened psychopaths, Steeples didn't immediately get sloppy. While eager to take ownership of his new murderous persona and indulge his dark fantasies, he also knew from years of blending in that he couldn't immediately go all out. He knew, at least for the first little while, that people would be watching him and scrutinizing his every move. He knew that the tiny Mount Juliet Police Department, at the request of the M Squad, might even drop by to make random bail checks to ensure compliance. From the time he bailed out on October 24 through the holiday season, Steeples played the role of an innocent man who'd received a bum rap. He kept his head down, went to work, and talked with friends and neighbors about what he was calling a big mix-up—about how he'd have his day in court and be vindicated as he claimed Jack Lowery had told him. He also filed and soon retracted a divorce petition and made at least one attempt at suicide by carbon-monoxide poisoning before deciding he wanted to plod on into 1994 and try his hand at a new type of murder. In the meantime, while celebrating Thanksgiving and Christmas and doting on his kids the way that was expected of him, and as the fateful year 1993 became 1994, Steeples's closet drug habit soon began to reveal itself. Money started to get tight, and the pressure mounted. He was entering a period of what's known as decompensation—when the stress of playing nice and the rigamarole of daily life begin to wear on the psychopath, and the urge to kill returns with a vengeance.

It was the night of Monday, March 7, 1994—almost five months since he made bail—when Steeples decided it was time at last to indulge that urge. For one reason or another, he ended up at yet another Music City dive bar, now long since closed, this one known as the Stagecoach Lounge on Murfreesboro Road in South Nashville. Back in his element, he sat down by himself as he had at the Corral and started cranking happy-hour cocktails. Even among drug addicts like Steeples, it's actually hard alcohol that serves as the most consistent and preferred disinhibitor, one thing that the vast majority of serial killers, especially organized psychopathic killers, have in common before their crimes. On this particular night, while Steeples didn't have a specific plan on whom to kill or how, he was keeping his options open. Although the evening had started slowly, Steeples realized that he'd hit the jackpot. He'd arrived at the bar on an open-mic amateur talent night.

It was at the start of the amateur showcase, around 7:00 p.m., when a newly married couple, twenty-four-year-old Robb and twenty-eight-year-old Kelli Jean Phillips, showed up at the Stagecoach. They had driven a battered old GMC pickup over two thousand miles east from San Diego to come to Nashville with big dreams. Robb originally hailed from Charleston, South Carolina, and was a US Navy veteran who'd served aboard the aircraft carrier the USS *Constellation* for two years before moving with his new bride to San Diego to start a band. By 1994 he'd decided to make a go at a solo career in country music as a singer-guitarist. That left him only one option in terms of where to head next: Music City.

Like the thousands of people arriving by the month in Nashville to this day, Robb and Kelli Phillips came chasing the country-music scene and all its derivative industries. Hoping to take odd service-sector jobs and gigs wherever he could, Robb was determined to ride the wave of "new" country's mainstream success and get discovered. His wife was unwavering in her support, either believing in her husband's talent or just being too sweet to tell him he was lost in space, and served as both his publicist and manager. She was also his rock, even agreeing to uproot their lives to head to Nashville after having already been burned once during Robb's first attempt at a solo career. The young couple had, by then, already been lured to Mexico and fleeced of their modest savings by a slimy industry "insider" with "connections" in the vein of Chuck Dixon at *Cash Box* magazine. By the time they arrived in Music City on the afternoon of March 7, they should have been once bitten and twice shy. Tragically, they were not. They still managed to trust people to a fault and believe in their dreams. Family nest-egg money now gone, and down to their last few dollars—their hopes and their battered old pickup truck both running on fumes—Robb and Kelli had checked into a declining Econo Lodge earlier that same day, one located just down the street from the Stagecoach Lounge. The sign out front read: "Where the Stars Stay." To Robb, it was a good omen. Kelli agreed. It was also a decision that sealed their fates.

In the only known surviving image of Robb and Kelli Jean Phillips, the young couple are seen posing during happier times in an undated photograph—before the road took them to Music City and into the clutches of their killer. Source unknown.

As Robb took the stage with his Yamaha acoustic guitar, stepping up to the microphone to perform some Toby Keith covers for the motley-looking crowd, Kelli sat at a table in the front row and beamed. It was then and there that Steeples took note of her and hatched his plan. Having correctly concluded that she and the man on stage were married, a newly reactivated Steeples honed in on her with a sinister confidence and an innate fearlessness that allowed him to manipulate and exploit the young couple's desperation. Chalking Steeples's charm up to genuine Southern hospitality, not knowing he hailed principally from Illinois and all sorts of other places, Kelli didn't mind when he pulled up a seat beside her. Hearing the words "I'm in the record business," Kelli's ears perked up; he seemed believable. They were, after all, in Music City. "I think your man has real talent. I could introduce him to some of my people. I could introduce *both* of you." Kelli smiled; he talked the talk; he looked like he had money, and they needed money. "Let me buy you a drink," he told her. The lure was cast.

By the end of Robb's set, Robb joined his wife and the stranger beside her for a drink, quickly won over by Steeples's ruse. They figured him for the real deal. They'd been in town less than twelve hours, and it already seemed that Robb was about to get his big break. Their booking into a room at the Econo Lodge, where they were told the stars stayed, now seemed to be a self-fulfilling prophecy. It seemed too good to be true. Of course, it was.

After about two hours of buttering up Robb and Kelli and buying them round after round of drinks, Steeples, having played out the charade of the spendthrift and well-connected music producer, managed to elicit all the details he needed to proceed to the next stage of his plan. Bidding them farewell, he promised to call the couple in their room once he had more details on when Robb might get to meet the real players in Music City, when he might even get some studio time. It might be in the morning; it might even be later that same night. Robb and Kelli Jean were elated; they were also half drunk and not thinking straight. They were numb to the danger they were in. Shortly after Steeples walked out of the bar, they left and made their way back to room 112 at the Econo Lodge, Kelli hopping right in the shower while Robb tried on bedazzled country-star outfits. At the same time, Steeples was at home getting his tools.

It was a little past 9:00 the next morning, Tuesday, March 8, when two short knocks followed by a third and an announcement of "housekeeping" prefaced the door to room 112 being swung open by the motel chambermaid. It was eerily reminiscent of three years earlier and the actions that came immediately before the discovery of Michael Magliolo's homicidal handiwork at the Esquire Inn. With history, it seemed, on autoplay, the maid entered the suite on that morning to find a scene of abject horror—a sight she'd never be able to unsee, and one that would forever change her. As the shag carpet beneath her feet squished—every fiber sopping wet with blood—she found Kelli naked on the bed, lying on her back. Her head and shoulders hung over the side of the bed, where her long blond hair dripped blood and brain matter like a saturated paintbrush onto Robb's body on the floor below. Still dressed in the stage outfit he'd planned on wearing for the record execs, he was beaten beyond recognition, his face and skull pulverized.

Meanwhile, back at the M Squad headquarters, Pat was consolidating some discovery materials for the forthcoming trial in the Ronnie Bingham case as the loose-leaf versions of the unsolved Trimble, Des Prez, and Hughes murders all lay open amid the other clutter on his desk. They were the files that were always close at hand, never far from his sight or his mind. The Trimble and Des Prez files, the murders that predated his arrival in Nashville by two years but which he learned during his time at the academy were the slayings that definitively reshaped the city—the cold cases that had become the bête noire of every Metro officer to have served since 1975—troubled him the most. They nagged at him. They might just also be, Pat thought, the justification for the creation of a dedicated open/unsolved unit one day. Pat couldn't help but think that not only were the murders somehow related, in spite of popular opinion around the department to the contrary, but that the killer of both girls was already in the system, possibly already in prison for an unrelated crime. It would explain why the murders suddenly stopped as quickly as they started and why there weren't more with a matching sexual MO as the seventies and eighties rolled on into the nineties. He couldn't help but think that he might have even crossed paths with the killer before and that he might very well again.

It was as Pat was stickhandling these intrusive thoughts that the phone on his desk rang. It was Pridemore. He asked if Pat was listening to the uniformed radio band. He said that a call just went over the air announcing that three units were at the Econo Lodge on Murfreesboro for a double homicide—a bad one. While he wasn't sure how he knew it at the time, Pat at once had a worrying inkling—maybe because of the location and the bars nearby, maybe because of the grotesqueness of the scene Pridemore had hinted at—that it somehow might be Ronnie Bingham redux. His gut told him that it was connected to Tom Steeples. It was one of those times that he hated being proven right—that Steeples should have never been allowed bail in the first place and should have been kept under twenty-four/seven surveillance despite the cost. That he should have never been turned back loose on the city with no one watching.

Arriving at the grim scene in room 112 a little over an hour later, Pat realized he was growing weary of brutal murders in motels. Even considering the Magliolo slayings and the brutal shooting of Leanna Shoulders just shy of a year earlier at a Days Inn, Pat found himself at a loss to understand the scale of what he was looking at. As he took in the totality of the scene—the sheer brutality of the crime and the overall narrative of the murder—the precise sequence of events could be gleaned from the gore pervading the room. The blood itself told most of the story.

With no sign of forced entry, it seemed as though Robb, having let someone into the room that he knew, had then turned his back to walk toward the television when he was surprised from behind. The blood on the soles of his shoes suggested that he'd been bludgeoned and was bleeding profusely even before falling to the floor, that he'd walked in his own blood before losing consciousness and then being bludgeoned further. Based on the lack of a struggle in the room and the wet towel at the threshold of the bathroom door, it also seemed as if Kelli had been in the shower at the time and had heard nothing. When she walked out of the bathroom, she, too, was surprised by the killer, who then overpowered her and, based on the ligature marks on her wrists, handcuffed her on the bed before raping her and beating her to death. High-velocity blood spatter on the ceiling, TV screen, and as far away as the bathroom mirror all but confirmed, along with the devastation of the head wounds, that both Robb and Kelli were beaten with some type of metal object, likely a lead pipe or tire iron. It was overkill; it was pure rage—it was what we now recognize as a lust murder. The rape of Kelli hadn't been enough to satiate the sadist responsible for this latest Nashville massacre. The postmortem violence and the severity of that violence spelled surrogate sex through mutilation.

Today we understand more about gratuitous mutilations, constituting lust murders by definition, where maximum violence, gore, torture, and eviscerations by stabbing or bludgeoning can satisfy a sadistic killer in a sexual manner, with or without an accompanying act of rape. While stabbing has historically been understood as the preferred method of violence, given that it so overtly simulates sexual penetration and bodily intrusion, it is now recognized that any repetitive thrusting, swinging, or probing action that causes extreme blood loss and makes interior organs visible serves the same twisted psychopathological function. We also understand that the precise number of blows is equally important. With emerging cutting-edge research suggesting a magic number of twelve or more stabbing, sharp-force, or blunt-force wounds after death indicating a sexual motive, the over-the-top beatings of Robb and Kelli clearly fit the mold—they were both victims of lust murder. It was Pat's belief, assuming this was once again the handiwork of the activated psychopath Tom Steeples, that what happened in the Bingham murder at the Corral—the act of lighting the body on fire—might not have been about destroying evidence after all. As in the Econo Lodge murders, the desecration and mutilation of the victim's body after death may have been more sexual and emotionally expressive in nature than it was logically instrumental in helping him get away with the crime. By then Pat had already dealt with enough firebugs aroused by flames—a disorder known as pyrophilia—to know that a great many sex offenders also have at the very least *some* accompanying interest in fire. It seemed as though Steeples was now expanding his repertoire.

Chapter 18

Person of Interest

While Pat's horrible feeling continued to be that the murder of the young couple was somehow related to Tom Steeples, other scenarios were also being batted around the M Squad. Some of the Metro brass, fretting about the case in the wake of the Motel Killer panic, suggested that the couple was perhaps on the run and their past had caught up with them their first day in town. As usual, Pat had a different theory entirely.

Later that same night, Pat found himself driving the latest car in the M Squad motor pool at the time, a '93 Chevy Lumina with a massive aerial that gave it away as a cop car from a mile out. He found himself driving the area of the Econo Lodge, back and forth along Murfreesboro Road. He pondered why the young couple from California had been staying there, of all places; he wondered whether there might be a connection to one of the nearby dive bars out near the airport. He decided to check out the Stagecoach Lounge as the most logical starting place. It was, after all, a half-mile straight shot door to door between room 112 at the Phillipses' motel and the bar. It turned out to be a good hunch.

Using the couple's driver's license photos to canvass the staff, Pat learned that Robb had been at the Stagecoach for the open mic night less than twenty-four hours earlier and was later seen sitting with a woman thought to be his wife or girlfriend. The bartender described them as both being with a second, older man for the better part of two hours and said that the older man was buying drinks and tipping generously. He said the old guy was making a show of it, that it all seemed meticulously choreographed. The other staff witnesses who recalled seeing the same thing all offered essentially the same description of the man. It was also the same description offered by the patrons at the Corral of the last man left in the bar the night it had burned down the previous October—the night Ronnie Bingham ended up murdered. They painted him as a stocky but otherwise generally nondescript middle-aged white male with brown hair, maybe five foot eight or five foot nine, sporting a cheesy-looking mustache. They were in effect telling Pat what he already knew. They were describing Tom Steeples.

After three witnesses from the Stagecoach Lounge successfully picked Steeples's mug shot out of a photo array in preference to a dozen other similar-looking men—a process known as a photographic lineup—Pat had the probable cause he needed to get records of phone calls placed to and from the Steeples home in Mount Juliet on the night Robb and Kelli were killed. Some of the other M Squad detectives thought it was an unusual first move, but those records ended up providing a most useful link. Pat knew that if Steeples was indeed involved in the double murder of Robb and Kelli, Steeples would have likely made a call to the house to offer some excuse for his being out late while out on bail and subject to strict rules regarding his movements. Alternatively, he might have been calling to set up an alibi with his wife. The location of the call placed to the house would help confirm Steeples's proximity to the Stagecoach Lounge or the motel. In reality, the call log, or pen trace as it was sometimes known, confirmed that the call in question was made *from* and not to the Steeples home.

As it turned out, just before midnight on what was still March 7, about thirty minutes after the couple had been seen leaving the bar, Steeples had called the front desk at the Murfreesboro Econo Lodge from his home's landline and been patched through to room 112 by the desk man. It was the call he'd prom-ised Robb back at the bar that he'd make—*the* call to confirm his rendezvous with Music City's record honchos. Steeples's true purpose in calling was of course to make sure both Robb and Kelli were in the room and were alone—that Robb would be expecting him and would answer the door so he could kill him first. The fact that Kelli was in the shower when he arrived was just an added bonus Steeples hadn't counted on. He would not have to kill him in front of her and risk losing control. As always, it was meticulously choreographed.

Despite the seemingly incriminating phone records, it wasn't quite enough to make a move on Steeples a second time. While Pat knew the case against

Steeples for Bingham's murder at the Corral was solid, he wanted to ensure that all the *i*'s were dotted and *t*'s crossed on this one as well. If not, anything less than an airtight case would ensure that superlawyer Jack Lowery would be all over it and have Steeples out on bond again. Pat also knew that if the Econo Lodge case wasn't rock solid, it might even jeopardize the earlier case—that Lowery might just argue that Pat had an ax to grind, that all the evidence collected dating back to the previous October was ill-gotten. It was then that Pat had another idea. As unorthodox as it was bold, it would at least save the life of Steeples's next intended victim.

In complex and dynamic investigations, especially involving serial killers still at large, police have a wide variety of options available for what's known as stimulating a known suspect. Depending on the jurisdiction, the techniques range from the sneaky to the theatrical. In some cases it means releasing disinformation to the media to prompt the suspect either to let down his guard or to panic, effectively leading police to a hidden body or other missing piece of evidence they otherwise wouldn't find on their own. In Canada, an even more intrepid technique exists, known as a Mr. Big sting, or simply the Canadian Technique in other Western nations where the practice is outlawed, in which an undercover officer infiltrates the suspect's circle, usually his workplace or an existing social group. Once rapport and trust are built, the infiltrator, playing on the suspect's psychopathic need for grandiosity and exclusivity, gives him the opportunity to join an elite criminal organization subject to a series of tests of loyalty.

That organization is always headed by a shadowy figure who, as a parody of the 1973 James Bond film *Live and Let Die*, goes by the metonym Mr. Big. He's a sinister kingpin who must give final approval for all new prospects. The suspect being targeted in these highly theatrical investigations is warned ahead of time, as part of the ruse orchestrated by the undercover investigator, that Mr. Big will be looking for absolute honesty, fidelity, and an ability to follow orders before giving approval. When the suspect and Mr. Big—also an undercover officer—finally meet, a tense truth-or-dare challenge ensues with the suspect, unknowingly on camera, confessing to a previous murder as evidence of his criminal acumen, inevitably providing details only the killer would know.

It's a complex and high-risk social experiment rooted in the predictable greed and braggadocio of most killers; it's premised on the notion that they will confess to the right person if they think it will get them something in return—money, power, respect, or membership in an exclusive criminal club. In one notable case from 2014 involving a killer who worked at a furniture store, the undercover officer, using a fake name and social security number, obtained a job on the same shift at the same store for over a year, deeply embedded under an assumed identity as a mattress salesman. Managing to break the company's annual sales record, he also managed to get the suspect to confess to the murder of his wife years earlier. As widely known as the technique has become, it remains a ruse that many people keep falling for.

But in April of '94, Pat's idea for stimulating Tom Steeples was far more direct: Pat publicly named Steeples as the leading person of interest in the gruesome slaying of the Phillips couple. In naming him and releasing his earlier mug shot to the public through the media, it reminded everyone in Nashville that the person of interest was also the same man currently indicted and heading to trial for shooting and torching bar owner Ronnie Bingham just a few months earlier. Stopping short of calling him the prime suspect, Pat opted instead for the less committed—and completely defensible, in terms of any accusations of slander—title of person of interest. The difference is a subtle but important one.

A suspect is someone whose involvement in a crime is near certain or who cannot be eliminated from the investigation. *Person of interest*, on the other hand, is a term often used in the early stages of an investigation when the cast of characters is still being sorted out; it's someone who *may* be involved and who is either eliminated from the investigation or later elevated to the status of suspect. While Pat knew that Steeples was indeed more than just a person of interest, he played down that fact in the papers and on the evening news. One of the advantages of being the detective sergeant in charge of the M Squad was that he had both the resourcefulness and ranking authority to make these judgment calls. It also helped that he had gumption in spades. In this case he pursued the strategy to see what Steeples would do next, anticipating that he'd slip up. He also wanted Steeples to know that he knew what Steeples had done and then done again, that he'd soon be back behind bars. More importantly Pat wanted the public to know. He wanted them to be vigilant and to know who the latest monster in their midst was. Pat's timing couldn't have been better.

The night of April 8, 1994, when Steeples's face hit the evening news on all three Nashville network affiliates, one of the people watching was a twenty-year-old girl from a good neighborhood and loving family off West End Avenue. In recent months, however, she'd fallen in with a bad crowd that had led to drugs, more bad crowds, and even worse decisions. Through a series of unfortunate events, she ended up resorting to doing outcall escort work through carefully worded classified ads placed in the *Tennessean* and pinned to the walls of various dive bars—the same bars Tom Steeples had trolled for his victims. That's how and why, in a strange twist of fate, that same girl had ended up naked on a bed in a rented room at a seedy Ramada Inn on Spence Lane, not far from where Steeples lived with his wife and kids.

Steeples had seen the girl's ad and called her to the motel that night. She was to be part of an elaborate and twisted game where it seems he wanted to replicate the murder of Robb and Kelli by renting the same style of room at another Nashville motel and re-creating the murder from the victim's perspective. Dennis Rader, the BTK Strangler operating in Wichita, Kansas, and mentioned earlier, had done much the same thing, taking photographs of himself imitating his victims and pantomiming what happened to them, fantasizing between his crimes about the terror he must have inflicted upon them. On this particular night, Steeples was in the shower originally, playing the role of Kelli, his young date left in the room on the bed waiting for him. Then getting out of the shower, as Kelli had, he would change roles, metamorphosing back into the killer. His plan was presumably to walk out of the shower and see the room from Kelli's perspective before he had killed her. He would then go on to murder the eighteen-year-old escort on the bed, as he had Kelli. This was apparently the plan he had concocted for what was to be his fourth victim. But on this particular night, fate would intervene.

While Steeples was obliviously planning his attack in the motel shower, the story of his being a person of interest in the recent Phillips murders was the top story on the news at eleven. Watching the story while she waited on the bed, the girl Steeples called to the Ramada immediately recognized the picture on the screen as the john who'd hired her for the night, the same john who'd brought her to the room. The same john who, in spite of having money and a nice car, insisted they had to get together in a low-rent dive—that it *had* to be a seedy motel. With all the pieces now starting to fit together, the girl clued in to what was likely in store for her. Her mind racing, she then remembered that the man had also curiously come to the room with a small gym bag—too small to be an overnight bag. Quickly scanning the room, she eyeballed the bag sitting on the floor by the slightly open bathroom door, where steam was beginning to seep out.

On instinct, the girl grabbed the blue nylon bag and unzipped it. Inside, a cursory inventory of the bag's contents foretold the horror story that awaited her once Steeples was done in the shower: a roll of duct tape, a lead pipe, and a fresh box of surgical finger cots. It was a rape kit and a kill kit. It was also the same kit Steeples had brought to the Econo Lodge on Murfreesboro—to the fateful room 112 a month earlier. While Steeples's intended victim that night didn't know it, it was the finger cots that were the dead giveaway about his intentions more than anything else.

The need for direct skin-to-skin contact between killer and victim is why these killers would ultimately be compelled to remove their gloves to touch and molest the corpses of the people they'd murdered without an intervening surface, even at greater risk of leaving evidence behind and being caught. It's the same reason why a sexual psychopath like Steeples opted for cots instead of gloves. It's the same reason why sexual murderers don't use condoms even during crimes indicative of significant organization and preplanning. It seemed that for Steeples, wearing foolproof gloves versus laboriously applying—and later collecting—individual latex coverings for each finger ultimately failed to offer the heightened sensation he needed with respect to the actual act of killing. In other words, the risk of identification and arrest posed by not wearing full gloves was negotiable; the risk of not maximizing the sensational stimuli of the murder through the use of cots and *some* direct skin contact was *not* negotiable. It was at precisely that moment that the girl also realized that the door to the room had been triple locked, that the night chain had been drawn, and that she'd been locked in. It was then that she heard the shower turn off and the sound of metal gliding on metal as the shower curtain was being pulled open.

Frantically sprinting the short distance to the door, the girl tried to quickly summon her fine motor skills to undo all the locks before Steeples walked out of the bathroom. After finally spinning the third lock, she flung the door back only to have it catch on the night chain and swing back. *The night chain.* She'd forgotten about the night chain. Now out of time, the girl caught the door before it relatched, managing to squeeze her petite frame between the door and the frame with the chain still on, taking off some skin in the process but escaping with her life and running and screaming stark naked through the deserted parking lot.

She ran for the first light she saw, to the motel manager's office, where an old-timer who was pulling the night shift saw her coming and stood from his chair. Sadly, it wasn't the first time a woman had been found running naked through the parking lot at this particular location. But this time, especially given the girl's age, the clerk knew something was different. "It's the guy on the news!" the girl kept screaming in between panicked pants of "He's going to kill me!" The clerk instinctively ushered the girl into a rear adjoining office and hit the lights before returning to the main desk and calling 911. The terrified girl, later identified by local papers as Denise Sloan, called her mother and a friend, who also called police. By the time Metro cops arrived, the client who had checked in under the name Tom Steeples but with a bogus Memphis address and phone number was long since gone. The girl had escaped as a consequence of the media stimulation strategy publicly putting Steeples's face and name front and center on the evening news. The girl soon became Pat's best living witness. She'd met Steeples and had actually lived to tell about it.

Chapter 19

General Hospital

After the near miss at the Spence Lane Ramada following the impromptu—and lifesaving—discovery of Steeples's bag of tricks by his next intended victim, Pat knew he finally had the upper hand. While the uniformed officers responding hot to the call of the hysterical girl, holed up naked in the manager's office at the motel, had missed Steeples and the kill-kit evidence linking him to the Phillips couple's murder by a matter of minutes, Pat would make sure Steeples didn't slip through Metro fingers again. Circumstantial or not, Pat knew the case against Steeples was buttoned up as tightly as it could be before he inevitably went on to kill someone else. He knew he needed to tighten the noose on Steeples and officially upgrade him to prime suspect and arrest him before time—and luck—ran out. It was time to hit his house in Mount Juliet with a second search warrant. It was also time, on the heels of the success of his media stimulation tactic, for further brinkmanship—to push the limits with a newly permitted area of criminal investigative methodology. It was time enough at last to swear out a court order requesting a sample of Steeples's DNA. A new investigative era had dawned.

In the spring of '94, DNA technology was still in its infancy in terms of being able to link a crime to a specific offender. Only a few months since Congress had passed the DNA Identification Act, it was also still four years before the national DNA databank known as the Combined DNA Identification System, dubbed CODIS for short, was to go online. Pat had seen the writing on the wall, knowing that DNA technology was the future for solving many cases.

It would serve as the ideal complement to time-honored hunches and old-school street smarts, still the epicenter of real detective work. He also saw a future where Steeples would be locked back up—this time for good.

After the recent havoc with the call girl, it had become obvious that Steeples felt compelled to keep killing, even when out on bail and on thin ice. Pat knew he couldn't afford to lose track of him again. By the end of April he decided to have him placed under loose surveillance for two straight weeks, an unmarked tail car following Steeples to and from work and wherever else he went. Steeples knew of the tail since the cops working that detail were told to make it obvious, to make Steeples feel squeezed. On the afternoon of May 13, the cops then made their next move. Perhaps more accurately, Steeples made the move for them. The ploy to sweat him and make their presence known ended up working better than expected. Just after 3:00 p.m., after blowing off work early, Steeples finally cracked.

While driving down West Trinity Lane—by eerie coincidence past another Nashville Days Inn that recalled the Leanna Shoulders murder as but one of a spree of motel slayings in the city—Steeples spotted the latest Metro unmarked tail car in his rearview mirror and floored it. He might have been paranoid or looking to bait the cops. He might have even had more sinister plans and some kind of grand finale planned out. Either way, Steeples having so conspicuously caught the attention of police, the plainclothes detective on his tail called in Steeples as driving recklessly, trying to evade police, and possibly being DUI. Most of the cop's hunches were right.

Once some marked Metro cruisers caught up with Steeples, the uniformed cops weren't sure of what they were getting themselves into but knew, upon seeing the caravan of unmarked units already on his tail—Pat and Pridemore in a Lumina at the end of the line—that it had to be big. They checked their "hot sheets," the list of outstanding stolen cars from the last forty-eight hours, but found no matches. A radio check of Steeples's plate number by those inclined to call it in then revealed the outstanding murder charges from the Corral and the associated bail conditions. The first cop in line—the black-and-white Ford that had become the pace car for the fledgling chase—quickly hit a switch on the console to activate the roof lights; a quick chirp of the siren followed to let Steeples know the jig was up.

After Steeples was pulled over and taken into custody on suspicion of DUI and reckless driving, the arrest then permitted cops to search the immediate area of Steeples's driver's seat for any evidence of those same offenses. A search of the cabin of Steeples's Chevy Impala—ironically the same make and model as half of the unmarked units that had been following him—turned up all that was needed to lickety-split revoke his bail: a vial coated in crack cocaine residue. It was a vial that looked recently purchased—a vial recently opened and used as well.

The crack bust, totally unforeseen, struck Pat as being too easy in the end. Tom Steeples, who had murdered three people in cold blood with remarkable cruelty, had still been walking around a free man. For him to end up getting collared for possession of a controlled substance and, by extension, violating the terms of his bail recognizance, seemed almost like an anticlimactic way to get Steeples back in custody. As unexpected as it was, Pat would still take the back-door victory; it bought him time to solidify the case against him for the slaying of the Phillips couple. It also provided him the probable cause he needed to get the second warrant for Steeples's home, as well as a third warrant. A warrant for his DNA.

Later that same day, warrant in hand for Steeples's DNA, Pat took the man he knew was good for the Phillips double murder to the old Nashville General Hospital on Albion Street to have the blood drawn. At the same time, Pridemore, canceling a late-afternoon tee off with some retired TBI officers, obtained a second warrant for Steeples's palatial house in Mount Juliet. This time around, a toss of the house turned up nothing new with the exception of one item that some uniformed officers searching the garage the first time seemed to miss: a plastic jerry can of gas almost identical to the molten can found at the scene of the Ronnie Bingham slaying. Although purely circumstantial, it spoke to Steeples's carelessness—or perhaps mere laziness. It's what's known as the least effort principle, a condition to which all killers are susceptible, though some more than others. The principle is rooted in the idea that offenders will exert only the minimal effort required to cover their tracks and no more. It also explains why a serial killer's first murder is such a telltale affair—how if it can be discovered amid an ongoing series, it will usually reveal the greatest number of oversights and help expedite their identification and arrest. This cornerstone of the emerging specialty known as suspectology holds that as the reason police will always have time on their side. It has been and always will be their chief advantage in both serial and cold-case murders.

In the unsolved slaying of Robb and Kelli Phillips, another advantage was of course that the Metro cops now also had the killer's DNA. Following the judicially authorized blood draw, Steeples was a match to the DNA left by the killer at the Econo Lodge gore fest. After the precision match cleared the way for Pat to officially charge Steeples with the rape and murder of Kelli and the murder of her husband, Robb, the aspiring country star who would never be, Nashville went berserk. The press could not get enough of the story about the duplicitous millionaire who'd made his fortune hawking personal computer accessories and floppy-disk software, but who was, in reality, a sex slayer hiding behind a respectable facade—a fiend who killed for fun and who had played the system like a fiddle. It was a veritable Music City scandal that drew national attention.

It was also a lurid story ginned up even further by the Unabomber public panic of the mid-1990s. With help from some less reputable publications and the Nashville rumor mill, imaginations soon started to run amok. Steeples had been a computer-store owner; some of the Unabomber's deadly letter-bomb targets included computer-store owners and computer scientists. Vanderbilt had also been where an exploding parcel had been sent by the Unabomber as far back as May of 1982. As preposterous as it seems, some people started to wonder if this local madman who owned a computer store and was causing mayhem could himself also be the Unabomber and responsible for so much more mayhem than the cops already knew about. For them, there seemed to be too many coincidences. Although the FBI task force that eventually ferreted out deranged mathematician Ted Kaczynski as the Unabomber didn't pay much if any attention to Steeples, the Nashville media certainly did. The story stayed above the fold in the *Tennessean* for days on end. There were the inevitable discussions of a TV movie of the week, former employees and customers of Steeples's computer store got their fifteen minutes of fame talking to the press, and news cameras parked outside of Steeples's home to get shaky b-roll shots of his family coming and going while hiding their faces. It was a carnival of the macabre. But it was to be short-lived.

Chapter 20

8 Ball

On July 26, 1994—a Tuesday—Steeples's wife, Tillie, wheeled their family sedan into the parking lot of the CJC on 2nd Avenue, where she rendezvoused with a newly retained lawyer named Mark McDougal, their usual juggernaut lawyer Jack Lowery being out of state at the time. She'd arranged the meet a day prior, explaining that Steeples wanted to discuss a new defense strategy. She also explained that she had a letter she first needed to get to him—to be hand delivered only. After furnishing the lawyer with the letter in the parking lot, she suggested it should be given to her husband. After all, he was being paid well enough to at least make the handoff, she reminded him.

After the two then walked into the jail entrance and went through the usual security protocols, the guards, used to seeing McDougal, greeted him with a "Hey, Mark" while at the same time greeting Tillie with awkward nods and averted eyes, and then the two went through a metal detector and were asked to empty their pockets. Past security, Tillie and McDougal sat down on one side of a typical security-glass partition in the visitors' area and waited for Steeples to be led out by a mopey and disinterested guard from a nearby sally port. As the metal door behind him slowly and loudly lurched to a close, like a medieval drawbridge, Steeples plopped himself down into a molded plastic chair at the visitors' window and was handed the envelope. Steeples looked at the envelope, looked up to Tillie, and then smiled. He knew what it was; he knew that his wife had given MacDougal the envelope rather than bring it in herself as a matter of efficiency. The contents, he knew, would be protected by privilege, and the guards wouldn't have opened and searched it as they would have if Tillie had been carrying it. That's, after all, why even the guards on duty in the visitors' area and who saw the handoff didn't think twice about it. No one but Steeples and his wife—a blue-ribbon aider and abettor—knew that McDougal had been little more than an innocent, yet pricey, Trojan horse.

An hour after Tillie and McDougal made their way out of the jail back to their respective cars, the monster Tom Steeples dropped to the floor of his cell and began writhing with convulsions and foaming at the mouth. After he was rushed to the hospital, staff there managed to save his life following what was soon revealed to be an intentional overdose of cocaine. Within a few days, his suicide solution having been thwarted, Steeples was back in lockup when another inmate, named Mike Evans, awaiting trial on some unrelated and comparatively benign misdemeanors, came to Steeples's cell on the afternoon of August 10 bearing gifts. Again it seemed there was another delivery, again from his wife, Tillie, this time couriered through Evans on the inside rather than Steeples's lawyer. Inside the package was a sweat suit, a standard matching set you'd find at any Walmart store in the state, save for one minor modification to the waistband. Within an hour of receiving the clothing, Steeples was in cardiac arrest. Less than a minute after that, he was dead.

Steeples had cheated the hangman before even a single full day in court, before he could be prosecuted for the murder of Ronnie Bingham at the Corral, much less the slaughter of the young Phillips couple in room 112 at the Econo Lodge on their first night in town. Once he became an activated psychopath the previous October, he knew he was beginning a one-way journey into the darkness. His wife knew it too. For all intents and purposes, it seems she knew about everything. That included keeping up her end of the bargain once the game was played out. It included helping her husband check out early. The "letter" she had delivered to him on July 26 hadn't been a letter at all. Inside the blank envelope was a blank piece of paper. Inside that paper was nearly four grams of powder cocaine, or an eighth of an ounce.

While Steeples had always preferred to freebase his cocaine and then smoke it, he had also been known to blast the occasional line off a bar or the dash of his car when out cavorting with prostitutes in his pre-serial-killer days. He was certainly experienced enough (and in touch with his degenerate nature) to know exactly how much cocaine—especially the good stuff the stars used—if consumed all at once, would prove fatal. An eighth of an ounce, known in the drug world dialect as an "8 ball," was the magic number. So when Tillie met a drug peddler named Fred Ross, her husband's usual supplier, on the previous evening of July 25, she figured that same amount would do the trick. Aside from enabling her murderous psychopathic husband to the very end, Tillie had 580,000 other reasons—a life insurance policy for over half a million dollars taken out on Steeples—to make sure the plan worked, assuming it all went down looking like another open-and-shut prison overdose and not a suicide. Once the delivery of the cocaine was made just as they had planned and with McDougal present, Steeples was waylaid by a couple of eager guards who wanted to pat him down and look in the envelope before closing the door to his cell. He told them the contents were privileged and that he'd sue for violating his rights, but they didn't much care. A tug-of-war ensued, and the envelope broke open. Unable to snort the whole amount, Steeples panicked and simply began shoving what he could into his mouth, attempting to swallow the entire shipment of 3.5 grams along with the envelope and the paper inside—the whole shebang. It missed the mark.

The lawyer Mark McDougal, it seemed, had been little more than a well-dressed decoy that Steeples and his wife knew could be used to facilitate the delivery of the lethal dose of cocaine. They knew he, just as superlawyer Jack Lowery before him, had the panache and profile necessary to get a client meeting inside the jail on short notice. They also sensed, given his prominence as a Nashville criminal attorney, that there would likely be no search of the envelope he himself was ostensibly delivering to his client. What Steeples and his wife hadn't counted on was the meddling of guards doing their job a little too vigorously outside of Steeples's cell, thereby foiling what was an otherwise well-executed suicide mission. Knowing that she'd never be able to manage a second similar "letter" delivery to Steeples, the revised plan was to ship a seemingly innocuous item to a seemingly innocuous inmate who could then serve as a middleman.

After meeting with Fred the coke dealer a second time in early August, Tillie had an employee of her husband's computer store go out and buy, using the store's petty-cash fund, the same sweat suit she later sent Steeples. Putting another 8 ball worth of cocaine in a latex glove and stitching the glove into the modified waistband of the track pants, she first mailed the pants to a man named

Mike Evans, a comparatively low-risk and not especially smart inmate who had fallen under Steeples's spell and would do his, and Tillie's, bidding while locked up. Missing pieces of the puzzle included how the delivery of the sweat suit was arranged and what kind of notice Evans may have had. It's also unclear how such a two-bit smuggling job managed to succeed and how the hidden compartment in the pants—the oldest contraband trick in the book—managed to get through the prison's X-ray and rigorous security-screening process. Either way, once Steeples got his hands on the clothing, he was determined not to fail a second time. Once the guards were out of view, he ripped open the waistband and then the latex glove containing his express ticket out of jail. He took a deep breath and snorted the entire 8 ball in one fell swoop. It was lights out.

After it later became clear that both McDougal and Evans had no idea how they were being used and what was in the envelope or sweat suit waistband, much less any idea about the suicide pact, staged accidental overdose and associated life insurance scam, Pat paid a visit to Tillie. Tillie's fingerprints had been found on the envelope from the July incident, and Pat had found plenty of witnesses and documents to link Tillie's preparations for the August overdose resulting in Steeples's death—from the drug dealer to the employee sent shopping for the sweat suit. Tillie was eventually sent away for five years for cocaine distribution and conspiracy. In sentencing her to serve time in the state penitentiary for women in Nashville, Davidson County judge Thomas Shriver noted that not only had Tillie Steeples been an enabler with respect to her husband's drug use and illicit liaisons that eventually paved the way for his atrocious lust murders, but that she at the same time seemed to venerate and celebrate his criminal exploits. In late April of '94, her husband facing the charges related to the murder and fire at the Corral and shortly after Steeples's arrest for the double murder of Robb and Kelli Phillips, Tillie actually had the audacity to petition the principal at the elite private school her son attended to rename the school's library in Steeples's honor. Referring to her husband as a "wonderful man," she even included a donation to the school for seventy-five thousand dollars to sweeten the deal—to effectively buy the right to rename the library. The school balked at the whole thing. In the end, Steeples's son left the school, a son who—as the second search warrant executed at the family home confirmed—seemed fixated on collecting news clippings about the murders committed by his old man.

Tillie had been a cheerleader for her murderous and psychopathic husband even after she knew how he was spending his nights and was locked up. The fact that she nonetheless tried to have a school library named in honor of a man charged with killing three people wasn't just tasteless and strange, it was indicative of its own paraphilia, one called hybristophilia. Unlike pedophilia, necrophilia, somnophilia, and the other high-risk paraphilias more commonly associated with male sex killers, hybristophilia seems more common among women. It's the same psychopathology that leads women to seek out mercilessly sadistic serial killers like Ted Bundy, Richard Ramirez, and other psychopaths as prison pen pals; it's what drives groupies to seek out these men and want to have their children. It's why couples who abduct and kill innocent strangers as a matter of foreplay, like Myra Hindley and Ian Brady in England, Karla Homolka and Paul Bernardo in Canada, and Charles Starkweather and Caril Ann Fugate in the United States—the interstate system's first serial killers and the basis for the murderous couple depicted in the films *Badlands* and *Natural Born Killers*—include women who are truly attracted to men who rape and murder. Hybristophilia, when couples are involved, is also sometimes referred to as Bonnie and Clyde Syndrome, a reference to the Texan lovers who robbed, killed, and terrorized across the country during the Great Depression.

The many dimensions of hybristophilia and the differing levels of the disorder equally do not mean that in all cases women attracted to murderous men will actually partake in crimes with them. We understand that there are other ways in which these women enable their partners—how sadism and psychopathy can often be satisfied vicariously. With hybristophilia now defined as the process in which violence is the common denominator used to form an emotional bond between two people and to sustain intimacy of any kind, it can entail any romantic or intimate bond made or strengthened through criminal violence. Sometimes this can mean simply fantasizing or bragging about a partner's violent exploits. Sometimes it can mean helping the partner escape justice, and sometimes it can mean ensuring the partner's murderous deeds form some kind of legacy—that they are elevated to the level of celebrity. In Tillie Steeples's case, it seemed to be all of the above.

Chapter 21

Good Samaritan

With Steeples dead and buried and his wife headed off to the state pen for sixty months, their children ended up pointing the finger at others. Not surprisingly, blaming the blamers is one of the most common neutralization—or avoidance—strategies used by killers and their families once the rubber hits the road. Pridemore first caught wind of it when, in searching the family home on South Mount Juliet Road the second time, he discovered that Steeples's oldest son appeared to have been compulsively collecting newspaper stories of his father's crimes and the police statements on the case—that he was following the media a little *too* closely for a teenaged kid. In the end, it turned out it was all for naught. The son, like everyone else in Nashville, was about to get a front-row seat to what Steeples had been planning as his final act—how he had planned to bring the final curtain down on himself.

The M Squad, following Steeples's last arrest, had been back to business as usual, investigating mostly domestic and drug-related murders and clearing them faster than any other agency in the state—based on the solved, or "clearance" rates seen across the US at the time—even the nation as a whole. As more and more red names were converted to black on the office whiteboard, and the clearance rate began to climb to well above the national average, it also meant Pat turned his attention back to the Trimble and Des Prez murders as his proverbial albatross.

With the somber twenty-year anniversary of the murders coming up in less than twelve months, he hoped that he might finally bring the case in from the cold to mark the tragic milestone—that he'd have something new to offer the families and media who'd been trying to keep public interest in the murders alive. Sadly, working on these cases often had to give way to the realities of the present—the urgent investigation of equally serious, current cases. Even before Steeples's arrest in May of '94 for the double slaying of the Phillips couple in March of that year, another whodunit landed on Pat's desk—a name to remain in red in perpetuity. It was also a murder that by that summer would become Pat's latest obsession to solder to the Trimble, Des Prez, and Hughes slayings. It would be the latest case of Pat chasing a man he knew had already gone serial but who was still essentially a ghost—a faceless and nameless killer who was out there somewhere.

As Pat worked a backlog of cases at the M Squad office during the day, he used his nights to scour the file of Carl Williams, a thirty-two-year-old drywall worker murdered on I-40 near Old Hickory Boulevard. The murder took place on the afternoon of April 20, 1994, and for the first three hours was wrongly investigated as a traffic fatality by Metro collision reconstruction officers. That is, until after nightfall under the portable floodlights used to illuminate the scene— in which they had assumed a person on the shoulder of the highway had been clipped by a passing car—when the cops saw the .45-caliber bullet protruding from Williams's skull. By then the scene was already contaminated and valuable time lost. The case was cold before it started.

A modest wooden cross, erected by the grieving family, marks a roadside memorial where thirty-two-year-old Carl Williams was found shot and killed execution style along I-40 near Old Hickory Boulevard. It's a case that stumped even the M Squad and which still remains unsolved—undoubtedly the work of an interstate highway serial killer or killers. Courtesy of WKRN.

Sitting at his kitchen table and studying the crime-scene photos and details of the case over the course of the summer of '94, a Hitachi television always on in the background playing either Major League Baseball or the national news as therapeutic white noise, Pat scoured the paltry official statements of uniformed officers from the afternoon of April 20. He scanned crime-scene photos of Williams's truck, dead body, and the surrounding scene for a modicum of evidence, to no avail. But as he listened one night to the details of the day's events in Los Angeles on his television in the background, with Peter Jennings riffing on the latest developments in the O. J. Simpson preliminary hearing, a thought occurred to him. The public had of course been consumed by the circus of the Simpson case, an investigation that would forever alter how police across America explained their actions and how they collected evidence. This fascination included conjecture about Simpson's intentions when, prior to his arrest that June, he hit the freeway in his Bronco with a gun on his lap, a friend driving, and led the cops on a prime-time slow-speed chase and aimless ride around LA. It dawned on Pat that whoever killed young Carl Williams was likely doing the same thing—driving aimlessly, armed with a gun, and playing it by ear. In looking closer at the photos, he realized that the murder had all the indicators of an opportunistic and random act of violence by someone who had been trolling Nashville's roads looking for a vulnerable motorist—a breakdown. A sitting duck. It was a thrill kill. The motive was that there *was* no motive.

Williams was found dead on the eastbound shoulder of I-40 of a single gunshot wound, complete with contact powder burns to the back of the head. He'd been executed at point-blank range, likely while kneeling. Driving a small pickup truck while minding his own business, he had been headed westbound when his truck broke down shortly before 5:00 p.m.; it was still broad daylight and the highway packed with commuters. Minutes later, with the hood propped and Williams looking into the guts of the engine, an empty flatbed semitruck skidded to a stop along the same stretch of highway shoulder just behind him. Williams was seen walking toward the truck, perhaps mistaking it for a tow truck that someone else, some good-natured passerby, had been kind enough to call on his behalf after seeing the breakdown.

The morning after, witnesses called Metro cops describing that the victim, Williams, had been seen waving and flailing his arms frantically at about that same time. Some said they saw Williams running *away* from the flatbed and throwing items from his pocket—keys, coins, anything he could find—at passing cars to get their attention. Some said he had a look of sheer terror on his face. Apparently no one ever saw the driver of the flatbed. No one pulled over or called 911 either. The highway didn't care—the city's social contract still dissolved by way of force majeure. Whatever happened after that truck stopped—a truck with no cargo and driven by someone mistaken as a Good Samaritan stopping to help—Williams was soon dead. Someone on board that mystery vehicle had gotten close enough to Williams to shoot him once at point-blank range without a struggle. The flatbed was then gone again in under a minute.

The only significant public attention to the slaying in the passing weeks and months had been a roadside memorial, a small cross erected at the scene by Williams's devastated family. The sheer randomness of the murder—and complete absence of leads—hadn't left the local media much to report on or the Metro cops much to work with. With the spectacle of the Tom Steeples case also overshadowing the seemingly random roadside execution of Carl Williams, Pat, as a matter of personal and professional obligation, had felt compelled to take on the file of the young man all but forgotten just months after his murder. In doing so, he at once saw the crime as part of a much larger pattern. He knew that, like Steeples, whoever did this to Williams wouldn't be able to restrict himself to just one victim. Just as Pat had done in the case of the motel murders committed by Magliolo, he was soon on the phone cold-calling neighboring police departments.

The Williams murder would be the prototype for a series of highway break-down murders across the US involving killers posing as Good Samaritans—often also the ones who had sabotaged the victim's car in the first place—and who would stop under the false pretense of offering a ride or giving the stranded motorist a boost. It was a ruse, not unlike Steeples's ruse with the Phillips couple, that was part of an elaborate death trap. Three years after the Carl Williams murder, the thriller film *Breakdown* starring Kurt Russell referenced this same MO, holding a mirror up to the American motoring public and reminding them that people of this type were out there roaming the highways. The film depicted a marauding gang of interstate psychopaths who, after tampering at highway rest steps in New Mexico with vehicles driven by tourists, would later show up to offer roadside help to the stranded couples. In the film it was a ploy to separate the man and woman so that the husband could be extorted in exchange for the life of his wife, the real intention being to kill both and then dispose of them so that they would never be found. While ostensibly motivated by greed, the gang also clearly took great pleasure in the murders they committed, keeping souvenir license plates of their victims and continuously refining their tactics.

Unlike in the film, it was unclear in the Carl Williams case what exactly caused his unexpected breakdown near Old Hickory Boulevard in Music City; whoever pulled up with the offer of assistance wasn't interested in money.

Williams was killed for pleasure, with no facade of robbery or extortion needed. Although Pat didn't have available at the time the technical terminology we now have, it was obvious from the outset that the slaying was the work of what we now understand to be a *hedonistic-thrill murderer*. Unlike the hedonistic-lust murderer such as Tom Steeples, someone who acts out of sadistic sexual impulse and maximizes violence and gore, this breed is even more unpredictable. Such murderers remain as the most poorly understood.

The hedonistic-thrill killer is a special breed of psychopath with an insatiable desire for stimulation seeking, coupled with a compulsive need for performance, attention, admiration, and being feared. These killers continuously straddle the line between being one part sadistic killer and one part theater impresario, and their MO is always inscribed with a need to shock. Forever chasing the high of their first murder, they also have an overwhelming need to continue killing. Their unabated need for attention manifests in part in their compulsive following of media reportage of their crimes. The hedonistic-thrill killer, by definition someone who murders solely for self-indulgence in the way of entertainment, is perhaps best epitomized in words used by Tommy Sells, the so-called Coast-to-Coast Killer, a train-hopping and psychopathic carnie who murdered twenty-two people between 1978 and 1999 before being arrested in January 2000 in Texas. Sells boasted: "I didn't do it for the power; I didn't do it for the sex . . . like a shot of dope, I did it for the rush!" The last such "shot" he received was, ironically, from a state needle in the arm during his execution by lethal injection in 2014.

Hedonistic-thrill murderers can operate in other ways, as well. The random attack on a seventy-four-year-old Cleveland man in April of 2017 by "Facebook Killer" Steve Stephens, a shooting streamed live on the social media site, which would shock the world, was purportedly Stephens's deranged attempt to exact revenge on his girlfriend for having ended their relationship. The breakup, of course, was merely a self-serving and feeble excuse—the tipping point—for Stephens's psychopathy to become activated, in the vein of Nashville computer entrepreneur and millionaire turned serial killer Tom Steeples. It was abundantly clear that Stephens enjoyed the whole process and that he did it for the rush, for the fun of it all. He was equally compelled to share the experience not as a matter of shaming his girlfriend on Facebook but as a matter of braggadocio.

Consider as well the 2016 case of Realtor, sex offender, and South Carolina recluse Todd Kohlhepp. In 2003, following a minor customer-service dispute at a Superbike Motorsports store in Chesnee, South Carolina, Kohlhepp later snuck into the business through the service bay to shoot and kill all four employees on-site, including the owner, the bookkeeper, and a mechanic. The massacre remained unsolved until Kohlhepp, never initially a suspect, was arrested thirteen years later in November 2016 for the murders of two missing couples lured to his farm with a promise of work. After killing the men, Kohlhepp would keep the women as slaves for weeks or months until a new couple had been lured in, the surviving captive then murdered and buried on his property. All the while, Kohlhepp, like Steve Stephens, needed to cryptically share the fun he was having on the internet, his way of intensifying and prolonging the rush of it all. Incredibly, Kohlhepp did so by posting Amazon reviews of the various murder accessories he'd bought through the online megaretailer. Separate reviews of a shovel, padlock, and knife he'd purchased and used in his crimes all contain none-too-subtle references to his dark deeds. Just like the Zodiac Killer, perhaps the most infamous hedonistic-thrill killer on record (and still officially unidentified), Kohlhepp reveled in the writings he created to maximize the spectacle and get off on the gamesmanship of it all. Again, murder as a pastime—as good sport.

Beyond solo serial killers like the Zodiac, Sells, and Kohlhepp, another form of hedonistic-thrill murderer—one of particular significance to the murder of Carl Williams—is of course the phenomenon of the freeway shooter. Mobile serial shooters who target motorists at random, recent examples including the Baseline Shooters in Arizona and the Beltway Snipers in the DC Metro area, are overwhelmingly known to work in same-sex pairs, nearly always male. There is typically, and consistently over the last twenty years, a pattern that emerges of a leader and his protégé—a serial killer in training. With 28 percent of all confirmed serial killers in US history operating in pairs, the number of dual serial shooters who now troll highways and hide among the hordes traveling them is thought to be much higher, closer to 50 percent. In most cases, as in all such partnerships and mentorships, there will be an eventual succession, the pupil one day becoming the master. Like male-female partners who kill, there is also some degree of hybristophilia at work. Whether the two males involved in this behavior have a consensually homosexual relationship that accompanies their violence or some scaled-down bromance with an emotional bond created through their acts of random violence, their murderous kinship more than meets the definition of hybristophilia.

Pat started calling various out-of-town and eventually out-of-state police departments working with high volumes of highway traffic and interstate access, in relation to the Williams file, his hunch being that one or maybe two freeway shooters were at work in tandem, and by now he also had some additional information to support his theory. It was a theory that, as usual, ran up against the prevailing Metro narrative coming from the top down as a matter of crisis management. In this case, the official version was that Williams was a victim of road rage, one of the countless and preferred public panics of the 1990s. But that convenient theory caved under the weight of eyewitness evidence once a public appeal for leads ramped up in the subsequent weeks and months while Pat worked the file hard.

Pat soon turned his mind back to how the Motel Killer of 1990–91, Michael Magliolo, had so easily toured the country searching for his victims while working as a lumper to get a free ride from truckers. Pat wondered what would have happened if Magliolo and a trucker ever struck up a conversation in which the topic of murdering for thrills might have come up, whether they'd end up joining forces. The prospect was terrifying: a chance encounter on the freeway that might have created a murderous duo no one would ever be able to connect and no one would ever even be looking for. During his cold-call telephone blitz, Pat shared this latest hunch about a murderous duo on the open road with the various out-of-town detectives and desk sergeants he spoke to. Some feigned interest, sometimes with promises to get back to him that they then broke. Others, clearly disinterested, were no doubt left shrugging their shoulders. Pat wasn't getting the same cooperation as he had with his Magliolo inquiries; the southern stars weren't aligning for him as they had back in the spring of '91. As tragic as it was, the Williams murder just didn't resonate with the out-of-state detectives. Moving forward, the case would be Pat's cross to bear, and his alone. He worked the file solo on the side as much as he could. He even posed as a broken-down motorist himself, hoping to lure the killer back out, but the killer never resurfaced.

It would be another ten years before the FBI, noticing the same pattern Pat had, went on to form the Highway Serial Killings Initiative, a task force dedicated to searching for interstate slayers, mostly turning out to be long-haul truckers and drifters who exist as anonymous strangers traveling America's freeways. In the meantime, Pat would add the case of Carl Williams to the growing pile of Music City's unsolved mayhem. The unknown duo, a pair of killers he now was convinced had killed Williams, though in another state at that same moment, would one day be back in Nashville. In the meantime, there was a solo act, with a license to drive and a loaded gun, already en route to Music City looking for his big break. There were two of them, in fact, one headed south, another headed north. One of them would redefine both serial murder and mass murder for the record books. The other would come after Pat himself.

Part IV

THE TANNING BED MURDERS

"The light of lights looks always on the motive, not the deed."

—William Butler Yeats, "The Countess Cathleen"

Chapter 22

GENTRIFIED

Nashville kicked off 1996 with a blast—a plasticized combination of TNT and RDX that leveled the tallest of the blighted apartment towers that dotted the infamous Urbandale Nations district. It was the first of a series of controlled demolitions that gave the west end neighborhood—the veritable hellscape that only a decade earlier had been clocking up to five shootings a weekend—a much-needed makeover. The new country scene that had lured Robb and Kelli Phillips to Nashville—and to their deaths—had in the nearly two years since been good to Music City. So good, in fact, by the balmy winter of '96 it seemed as though the city and region, following some shaky and inarguably tragic years, had turned a corner of sorts. It seemed a new day had dawned.

In reality the extreme makeover foretold a new era for the city's once entrenched criminal element, one that clumsily set in motion a series of changes that seemed destined to alter the composition of Nashville as traditional neighborhood borders were redrawn. Criminal empires in places such as the Nations, built to stand for generations, fell to ruin as wrecking balls and official paperwork citing eminent domain ran roughshod over those same slum tenements where Pat had, more than once, cheated death. That included in early '96 when he and Pridemore found themselves standing in the doorway of a house in the Nations when three OG Gangster Disciples rushed in with guns out, having just murdered two rival drug pushers. A Mexican standoff ensued until Pat managed to talk the three into surrendering. A total of three killings were solved that day, with cases starting to comingle as the gangs that seemed to have been taking over just two years earlier were literally running out of places to hide. Nashville was bingeing and purging real estate and planning for a new future.

But like all gentrification efforts—for better or for worse—what were once concentrated and localized social problems in Nashville soon found themselves diffused across an expanded frontier. Much like entombed asbestos that lies dormant until disrupted by renovation, their most dangerous components were no longer confined to any single cranny. Soon they were airborne, they were scattered. The remediation of the city had unintentionally created a power vacuum where there would soon be new turf to be settled and disputed zones to be claimed. In criminology, migration in and out of these transitional areas defined by precarious housing has long been thought to be a key contributor to gang activity, juvenile crime, and other structural forms of social conflict. This scenario, as it occurred in Nashville beginning in the winter of '96 as the city found itself in the throes of gentrification and drunk with rejuvenation, also creates the perfect backdrop for other types of crime. Like a type of distractionary device, it serves as an urban camouflage for more insidious offenders to move in undetected. It allows them to hide in plain sight amid the revitalization chaos.

Midtown was one of the areas of Nashville seeing the most dramatic aesthetic overhaul, and the leading beneficiary of the first of a series of progressive gentrification efforts of the nineties. A compact, bar-laden district sandwiched between the manicured Vanderbilt campus and the trendy Gulch enclave, it was the same neighborhood where footstomper George Mitchell had roamed; it was the neighborhood that also bordered the famed Music Row, where Pat first caught the case of Kevin Hughes. By February of '96, however, the name Kevin Hughes was ancient history to most people, except for Pat who was, by then, keeping detailed and even obsessive logs of all his cases, both old and new. It was this tireless and tedious documentation of every mundane detail, the minutiae that other cops might not consider germane, that ultimately would help Pat later solve the next installment in a series of macabre Midtown murders. It was another whodunit with no apparent motive and no obvious suspect. Or, perhaps, too many suspects.

The Metro M Squad had for good reason colloquially become known as the mystery-murder unit. It was an elite camp of investigators with a special kind of gumption, detectives of grit and spit who were afforded both the time and resources to investigate unusually ghastly, puzzling, or politically sensitive murders that defied open-and-shut efficiency or traditional case-management methods. Its members, under Pat's command, specialized in solving slayings that bore all the telltale indicators of possibly turning into cold cases or of the offenders going serial. By the winter of '96, its newest case proved especially puzzling and especially unsettling. It was also the first double slaying since the murders of Robb and Kelli Phillips at the hands of (now dead) Tom Steeples two years earlier. It came only a matter of months after the fiasco that was the O. J. Simpson trial and its protest verdict in Los Angeles. Over two thousand miles away in East Nashville, an eighteen-year-old Tiffany Campbell had an eerie premonition of things to come. In her diary that January, young Tiffany wrote: "I'm going to be the next Nicole Brown Simpson." She was right.

Chapter 23

MOTIVE

A few months earlier, in the fall of '95, a Houston smut entrepreneur named Keith Scott was a man on a mission. Following a spending spree that included buying out his business partners, Scott became the majority shareholder for a chain of "happy ending" massage parlors scattered across the South. Rubdown joints thinly veiled as legitimate tanning salons, his empire of discreet brothels soon stretched from Texas to Tennessee to Florida. Entrapped teenage girls worked behind papered-over windows while regulators and vice cops in all three states looked the other way. Most locations operated in decent neighborhoods but hid behind respectable facades and high-end signage as a matter of public modesty. One such location known as Exotic Tan, today a hipster hookah bar, was Scott's flagship Tennessee operation and was based in a plaza at 1805 Church Street in Midtown Nashville. While the business technically did have a tanning bed—*one* bed—a token justification for the sign out front, the usual order of business was for customers darkening the door that led to a video-monitored lobby to wait for one of the girls on duty to emerge from a locked area behind the front counter. The exchange of various euphemistic code words and pricing options would soon follow, all under the pretense of the men paying for a tanning package that might also include any number of add-ons. It was one of the worst-kept secrets in town.

Tiffany Campbell, hired by Scott to work at Exotic Tan just prior to Thanksgiving '95, soon convinced her friend Melissa Chilton, a freshman at Middle Tennessee State U in nearby Murfreesboro, to join her. Neither of their parents knew of their secret night jobs. Their regulars included downright creeps and weirdos, lonely middle-aged men, and weary travelers, any of whom by the winter of '96 could have deluded themselves into considering Tiffany or Melissa—or both—as their girlfriends. From the day she started secretly working at Exotic Tan, eighteen-year-old Tiffany was inexorably marked for death. By extension, for being in the wrong place at the wrong time, the same would hold true for her best friend Melissa.

When the winter of '96 rolled around, Tiffany had been at Exotic Tan for three months, her list of regular male callers and would-be suitors at the parlor also now including a number of local Nashville dope pushers prepared to accept an array of payment options for their product. Sadly, like so many women lured to the flesh trade and then trafficked into in-call or out-call escort work under various guises, Tiffany had come to depend on cocaine and marijuana to get through each shift, to cope with demeaning herself day after day in one of the salon's four rear studios. Some would later suggest it was used to self-medicate and to cope with something else that was also bothering her—that in the weeks leading to a Valentine's Day flashpoint, something in Tiffany's otherwise bubbly demeanor had fundamentally changed. Something—or someone—had irreparably altered her persona.

On the morning of February 22, 1996, just after 10:00 a.m., Tiffany and Melissa arrived in tandem, their usual Thursday routine, to open up shop at the salon. Within the hour, proprietor Keith Scott, calling the parlor to check on the state of business, strangely received no answer from either girl. In an era before mobile phones became permanently appended to every eighteen-year-old's body and immediate responses became a matter of expectation, Scott wasn't necessarily surprised that no one picked up the line on the first few attempts. Since the phone was located on the front counter, policy was to let the call go to the answering machine if one or both of the girls were in a back room with a client. But after over a dozen or so further attempts, with Scott finding himself consistently hearing a busy signal, he began to have some concerns. As it was now the middle of the afternoon in a busy commercial neighborhood teeming with locals, Vanderbilt students, tourists, and Metro cops, he tried to convince himself that the lack of a response was not necessarily indicative of anything sinister. Maybe, he thought, business was slow, and one of the girls was talking on the phone a little too long. On the other hand, he knew the salon subscribed to the then still comparatively new technology known as call waiting, which should have allowed him to get through. He continued to rationalize; he wondered if Tiffany, not feeling well, might have gone home without notifying him or arranging for someone to cover her shift as she should have. Perhaps even both girls had left on account of illness or for some other reason, electing to leave the phone off the hook rather than to properly notify him. But it wasn't like Tiffany to do that. It wasn't like either girl.

Best friends Melissa Chilton and Tiffany Campbell as depicted in their last known respective photographs. The two arrived for their final day at work at Exotic Tan on February 22, 1996, completely unaware of the horror that awaited them. It was a horror for which Tiffany had some vague premonitions, having previously recorded them in her diary, to be discovered upon her death. Photographers unknown.

Deciding to drive to the site himself to check things out, Scott arrived just before 2:30 that afternoon at his seedy little business, unit C in the plaza on Church near 18th Avenue, to find the front door locked. He quickly resigned himself to likely firing both girls for what appeared to be, though uncharacteristic, an unacceptable act of hooky that had also likely cost him a good half day of business. After spinning the lock, popping the door, and entering the salon proper, Scott would soon forever become a changed man. For the next sixteen years, until he died in a car wreck on a dark Louisiana highway, Scott would remain horrified by what he discovered that afternoon—the embedded visual he could never erase.

After entering Exotic Tan and finding the door leading to the rear suites from the lobby open, the music still on, Scott realized that someone was in the business after all—someone who shouldn't have been. He also discovered the reason for the endless busy signal. The landline telephone for the salon was off the hook, its handset lying precariously on the front counter. Rather than not having been properly hung up, the handset was *way* off the hook, an intentional and unsettling harbinger of discoveries to follow. Walking through the unlocked door into the parlor's rear corridor, with all the lights still on, Scott noted that the washer and dryer located in the first room on the left were both still full of clothes—some wet and some dry—still in the machines that had recently run full cycles. It had all the appearances of an outsider having been inside the business within the previous few hours, an outsider who might even still be inside.

Making his way down the hall while calling out to both Tiffany and Melissa, Scott found the first "tanning" studio—the second room on the left of the hallway—empty. Checking the third room, he found it vacant as well. The door to the fourth room on the left, the final studio off the rear corridor, was closed, a sign that would normally indicate a customer was inside with one or both of his young attendants. Leaning his left ear toward the cheap hollow-core door, Scott paused to listen, but heard nothing. He called out again and received no response. After Scott then knocked on the door, again receiving no answer, the brass latch rocked out of the strike plate in the process, the door having been haphazardly swung closed and never properly fastened. It all spelled trouble. After slowly swinging the door open the rest of the way, Scott discovered what could only be described as a massacre on the epoxied concrete floor beside the antiquated lie-down tanning bed. It was a scene wrought by terror, a scene that told a story of unimaginable depravity and cruelty. Amid a bloody mass on the floor, Scott was able to make out what he barely recognized to be the savagely mutilated bodies of his two employees, best friends Tiffany and Melissa. They'd been dead for a little more than three hours—since at least the time of his first unanswered call to the salon.

Tiffany was found fully clothed on her back amid a massive pool of crimson that almost made it to the door's threshold, a full four feet from where the body had fallen. All five or so liters of blood, it seemed, had drained out from her petite frame as she lay dead on the floor. Melissa, dressed only in a silk kimono robe—her other clothes being part of the load left in the washing machine—was far less recognizable. She had sustained sharp-force trauma from head to toe, administered with such ferocity that she was largely stabbed beyond recognition. Over the next hour, the unparalleled nature of the scene would attract an unprecedented total of over fifty cops in addition to city firefighters and paramedics. It was a number later confirmed by the crime-scene registry, the official logbook used to identify who enters a crime scene, why, and for how long. Without meaning any disrespect to the deceased, the crime scene would serve as a teaching tool, as a singular and noteworthy opportunity to put rookies through their paces, to prepare them for the frequently unsavory and violent nature of police work—to demonstrate that there are some scenes where, when it's present in sufficient quantities, you can actually *smell* blood's distinctive coppery odor before you even see it. One of these fifty-plus attendees, no rookie by a long shot, was Detective Grady Eleam. He would be the first detective; Pat would be the last.

Based on the position of the bodies, it was evident to Eleam that Tiffany had been killed first, after having been ambushed in the room and stabbed and slashed across the throat and face with overpowering force and momentum in a matter of mere seconds. The evidence in aggregate suggested to Eleam it had been an unexpected attack and she was killed almost instantaneously. The additional stab wounds were nothing less than pure overkill—a textbook lust murder committed in a fit of visceral rage. Given the sequence of the murders, Eleam had a problem with what he saw next. Slumped on top of Tiffany's body was Melissa, who, it appeared, had unexpectedly come into the room after Tiffany was already dead. Despite Tiffany having been slain first after having been ambushed in the most distant room from the lobby—and being the apparent primary target of the attack—the savagery inflicted upon her was merciful in comparison to what happened to her friend and coworker Melissa.

A number of the wounds clearly showed that the weapon used had to be something much longer and more powerful than a typical kitchen or hunting knife. The stabs and slashes to her throat were particularly telltale in nature; another twenty or so postmortem punctures essentially liquefied her heart, intestines, and other internal organs, the blade having passed through her body. Other through-and-through punctures had passed clean through both bodies with enough force to chip the coated floor underneath Tiffany, leaving fragments and flints of epoxy-coated concrete scattered throughout the blood pool that filled the room. It was all incomprehensible.

A further survey of the scene by Eleam, by then into the twilight of his career and who thought he'd seen it all, revealed that a number of items were also missing—unusual items at that. Of some note, the intruder also took the time to unfasten a bracelet from Melissa's wrist and take a key chain from her key ring, normally stored near the washer and dryer in the laundry room. Eleam was left pondering the overwhelming contradictions. The theft of otherwise valueless property inside the business looked like an investigative countermeasure used by the killer to protect his identity, precise MO, and time of the murder. The theft of the otherwise low-value items belonging to Melissa, on the other hand, at first glance appeared instead to be intrinsically motivated. That is, something the killer chose to remove from the scene, not for strategic but rather for personal reasons, prolonging his time with the bodies and taking additional big risks in the process. The purloining of the bracelet was an extraneous act that had served a symbolic rather than a functional purpose, unlike most acts of theft that have a financial motive. Despite the lack of an obvious sexual assault on either victim, one possibility was that the perpetrator was a lust killer. Like all lust killers, his crimes revealed the presence of overwhelming compulsions—violent paraphilias to which he was enslaved and which would reveal to investigators exactly what type of monster they were dealing with.

The lust killer classification describes a sadistic murderer defined by one or more of three specific paraphilic disorders, including erotophonophilia (known as bloodlust), mutilophilia (erotic interest in gore and mutilations), and piquerism (arousal from puncturing and stabbing), whereby any horrific indignities committed against a body—whether dead or alive—are in themselves surrogate sex acts that satisfy the killer's grotesquely twisted libido. The subsequent removal of the bracelet and key chain from the second and most severely mutilated victim would seem to signify the killer's additional compulsive need to collect souvenirs, a crime-scene behavior almost invariably linked with sexual homicides and lust murders. As fetish objects with horrific stories attached to them—albeit exciting and nostalgic memories for the killer—these items allow a psychopath to relive his crimes and cultivate new fantasies weeks, months, and even years after the fact. Eleam felt, however, that he had to also consider a second and more unconventional possibility. Maybe the killer was just cunning enough, knowing that the police would draw the "souvenir" inference, that he removed the bracelet as part of a decoy technique, to throw the cops a curveball. Eleam, running scenarios and flipping through visual snapshots of every murder scene he'd ever been to or seen in photographs, realized that the double murder at Exotic Tan just didn't play straight. For him, the barbarity of the Melissa Chilton murder looked like staging—like pure subterfuge intended to lead cops down a garden path and obfuscate the true motive. The removal of her bracelet was even more disingenuous. The killer was baiting him with low-hanging fruit, playing him with scorn and unspoken mistruths.

Chapter 24

SCABBARD

The posing of dead bodies, like the collection of souvenirs from victims, aside from being strongly linked with sexual homicides, is also particular to killers who invest great time in the mental rehearsal and replay of their crimes, those killers who place great fantasy value on violence. But the *staging* of bodies is something else entirely. Unlike posing, staging has an instrumental, rather than an expressive, purpose. It is strategic and cunning; it is as much a forensic countermeasure as cleaning a scene with bleach or wiping down fingerprints, perhaps more so. It is used to create an alternative story for the crime and have the police begin their investigation on the wrong foot. Contrary to what is depicted in nearly every episode of *Columbo* ever made, staging is also, with good reason, very rarely seen.

Crime-scene staging additionally describes a behavior or set of behaviors belonging almost exclusively to what are known as personal-cause murders. One of the four motivational models for homicide, it describes a scenario in which the victim is targeted for some specific reason eminently personal to the killer, including jealousy, greed, rage, and revenge. In the case of an obvious personal-cause murder, police typically, and not surprisingly, are left with a very short list of suspects based on the apparent motive and the opportunity to act on that motive. Staging is a process that in turn describes a series of calculated steps undertaken by a killer who knows full well that the victim's death will immediately implicate him or her as the most obvious suspect by default. Such killers know that they need to proactively and inventively present an alternative narrative or implied sequence of events to buy themselves time, that they need to stage a scene that suggests a different motive entirely in order to exculpate themselves. The crime scene in turn takes on the dimensions of a film set: being dressed, arranged, and even lit in some cases to tell a very specific story that the killer as both director and producer wants to tell authorities. Detective Eleam was one authority not buying the story being told at Exotic Tan. Later, neither was Pat.

After surveying the grisly scene at 1805 Church, cops concluded that the real motive in the Exotic Tan slaying wasn't sexual; rather, it was one of either anger or jealousy—maybe both—with Tiffany Campbell being the intended victim. Melissa Chilton, Pat thought, was simply in the wrong place at the time. In order to deflect suspicion that he expected to fall immediately on himself alone, the killer, Pat believed, then staged the scene to suggest that it was Melissa, rather than Tiffany, who was the intended target. With unspeakable over-the-top violence and the bogus collection of souvenirs taken to depict a faux lust murder, the killer was looking to lead the cops by the hand down another path so the real killer either couldn't or wouldn't be logically connected. Short of framing another specific person for the crime, the elusive Tanning Bed Killer, as the media and panicked massage-parlor attendants soon dubbed him, had managed to successfully create confusion that surrounded what should have otherwise been a double murder that pointed to an obvious suspect in Tiffany's life.

Pat had enough experience to know that real lust killers—especially fetish souvenir collectors—almost inevitably go or have gone serial with their crimes. There was nothing about the Exotic Tan case that read serial to him. It read as the work of someone who thought he or she was smarter than investigators. That said, the killer was certainly almost as dangerous as a serial killer, someone prepared to unpredictably and brazenly kill in the middle of a weekday morning in a busy Midtown plaza. Within hours of the brutal double murder, cops managed to catch an unlikely break. Before the bodies were removed from the scene, they managed to locate, along with the Metro forensic crime-scene techs, the one key piece of evidence that the killer, in working so hard to stage the scene and present a spurious set of circumstances, apparently managed to forget and leave behind. On the floor of the third room on the left of the rear corridor of Exotic Tan, the suite immediately beside the murder room, the evidence team recovered a black metal sheath from the cement floor near a rickety massage table. Upon closer inspection, it appeared to be a scabbard for a long tactical knife or small sword, an item clearly out of place in the tacky island-themed tanning parlor.

Again, Eleam marshaled his thoughts; he determined probabilities and estimated outcomes.

In looking at the dimensions of the scabbard—roughly eight inches in length—he knew it was consistent with the dimensions of the blade used to impale the two teen girls in the next room. To his mind the logical sequence of events likely consisted of the killer—sometime around 11:00 a.m. and after somehow sneaking through the lobby into the rear corridor while the girls were separately distracted—proceeding straight to the back tanning room. It was the same room where Tiffany was at the time, where he knew he would find her. Before swinging left into the room to ambush Tiffany with his long blade, it appeared he first removed it from the protective scabbard, tossing the sheath into the adjacent room in preparation to strike. In the picture Eleam painted in his mind, it was either the noise from the sheath hitting the cement floor or the subsequent, albeit brief, gurgling screams from Tiffany after her throat was slashed that brought Melissa out from the laundry room—a room that the killer had initially rushed past with homicidal determination and zeal to the end of the long corridor. The scenario, based on the evidence, certainly made sense. It rang true.

Despite having found a key piece of evidence, the police would unfortunately soon be stymied. After dusting the sheath—and later fuming using cyanoacrylate, or superglue—for fingerprints, the Metro forensic team came up empty. It would be another fifteen years before DNA technology would evolve to allow an offender profile to be developed from the trace skin cells of the killer's hands still lingering on the item. Until then, the M Squad would help set the standard in determining how potential samples of biological evidence—probable future exhibits at trial—should be properly stored and preserved. While many other, and often larger, law enforcement agencies in America were busy losing or contaminating such samples, the scabbard recovered from Exotic Tan would remain hermetically black-boxed for over a decade. It remained in stasis and future-proofed until science could effectively catch up. It was the one piece of usable evidence that the killer managed to leave at the scene. It also had its own long and sordid story to tell. It's a story that began back in Bexar County, Texas, at the air force police academy.

Chapter 25

BLUEGRASS

By day's end on February 22, M Squad investigators had confirmed that the scabbard for the murder weapon was US Department of Defense property. More specifically, they determined it was the sheath designed for the standard-issue bayonet used by Air Force Security Police, the so-called Blue Berets, and one of the first weapons provided when training begins at the police academy at AFB Lackland, just outside San Antonio.

The fact that the murder weapon pointed to someone who'd not only received military training but also apparently training in criminal investigation was naturally unsettling. In terms of whom cops should be looking for, it immediately made the tanning bed murders different from the hundreds of other slayings they'd worked. If the killer was indeed a cop like the M Squad investigators—an air force cop, but a cop no less—it was further indication that he'd know how to play a crime scene, that he'd know how to stage a story that would have investigators inevitably chasing their tails. The killer knew a thing or two about forensic and investigative countermeasures because he himself had been trained to look for them. The perishable first forty-eight hours of the Exotic Tan investigation had already come and gone when Detective Eleam made another startling discovery, learning that an earlier double murder in Kentucky had been unearthed and tentatively linked to the horrific scene at the Church Street salon. It was another heinous crime, one that seemed to match the same MO of the Tanning Bed Killer with remarkable precision, one that allowed the unlikely lust-killer theory to gain renewed traction. As another double murder that had the telltale signs of a rogue cop pulling the strings, it had Metro detectives soon calling it the Kentucky connection.

In accessing the FBI's still-fledgling Violent Criminal Apprehension Program (ViCAP) at the M Squad headquarters at 200 James Robertson Parkway, an imposing block-like structure across the Cumberland River from what is now Nissan Stadium, Eleam managed to secure the key particulars of an unsolved double murder in the Bluegrass State. Two years earlier, an alarmingly similar scenario to the Exotic Tan double homicide had played out in the tiny town of Oak Grove, Kentucky, with a then population of about five thousand. While technically within the boundary of Kentucky proper, the little-known town located immediately northwest of Nashville, in Christian County, was part of the census's metropolitan area of Clarksville, Tennessee. The city was then—and now—also home to Fort Campbell, a US Army base straddling the Kentucky-Tennessee border, and there were various brothels masquerading as tanning bed and masseuse joints along both sides of the Kentucky-Tennessee state line. All in all, the September '94 massacre at the New Life Massage Parlor in Oak Grove—also involving a double slaying of two female employees—was disturbingly similar to the horror that befell Tiffany Campbell and Melissa Chilton on Church Street in Midtown Nashville.

The M Squad, skeptical, in spite of the similarities, that they were chasing the same killer, proceeded cautiously as they dug into the earlier murders, soon plumbing both the Exotic Tan and New Life cases at once. In so doing, they quickly realized that there were indeed significant similarities that couldn't be dismissed outright. The most glaring similarity was that the Oak Grove murder scene also shouted cover-up. Reading like another staged murder, it was almost a textbook case study on forensic countermeasures taken by an assailant who knew his way around a crime scene and who knew how to render the scene an unwieldy mess that would spawn any number of theories, all of them wrong. By 1996, word on the street in Oak Grove was that it was actually a cop—maybe an ex-cop, and maybe more than one cop—who had been behind the 1994 slayings. It was an eerily familiar refrain.

On the night in question, the two female attendants working at New Life in Oak Grove were friends, twenty-two-year-old Candace Belt and eighteen-year-old Gloria Ross. Like Tiffany and Melissa at Exotic Tan two years later, the two young women were found dead in a gore-spattered room, this time by fellow employees. As in the Exotic Tan crime scene, it also was evident, based on the grisly crime-lab photos later reviewed by police, that the killer or killers at New Life similarly knew the ins and outs of the business's layout and the routines of its employees. The killer or killers had been able to circumvent the security protocols and stealthily navigate the confined rooms of the small parlor, also located in a commercial plaza in a perceptively safe neighborhood, without leaving any trace evidence behind. The front door of the massage parlor had also been locked from the inside, just as it had on Church Street in February of '96.

Beyond the door being locked to prevent interruption—or easy escape—the interior of New Life was otherwise undisturbed, with the exception, again, of the phone being taken off the hook. While the Christian County medical examiner was unable to determine the precise sequence of fatal events, this case had seen a bizarre and excessive combination of postmortem wounds and mutilations inflicted upon both victims. Yet, despite this plethora of similarities, there were also some marked differences between the Kentucky double murder in 1994 and the most recent Nashville whodunit growing cold. While both of the Oak Grove girls had been similarly ambushed and had their throats slashed, they had almost simultaneously been shot in the head execution style, though in which order could not be determined. This combination of killing methods suggested something of a schizophrenic MO, a collision between two normally divergent motives and methods. The one method displayed an intention to kill with expediency and efficiency while the other suggested an intention to go about matters with a more sadistic verve—a lust murder intended to conjure maximum trauma, suffering, and gore. It also suggested two different motives, one perhaps demonstrative of a personal-cause murder, the other being a sexually motivated murder once again indicative of piquerism, or some other sadistic preoccupation with the defilement of the bodies and the use of some type of blade.

The puzzling duality of the murder scene at New Life also suggested, as one possibility, two different killers. Two or more killers operating in tandem yet with divergent methods, each leaving their own individuating mark on the scene. It equally suggested the possibility of a calculating lone killer, one looking to reverse engineer a certain narrative to the crime—staging it to appear as either a lust murder or multisuspect murder when it was, in fact, a personal-cause killing committed by a single offender. Either way, the cops in Oak Grove, Kentucky, couldn't make heads or tails of it. With no leads and no suspects, the puzzling double slaying at the New Life went cold in no time. By the spring of '96 in Nashville, the Exotic Tan double slaying seemed destined for the same fate. All the while, the biggest clue still lay undiscovered—young Tiffany Campbell's diary.

The horror of the scene on Church Street inevitably threw a wrench in the rebirth of Nashville as the gentrified, inherently safe, tourist-friendly Music City people wanted. The result being, once again, mounting pressure on Metro cops to expeditiously solve the case of the elusive Tanning Bed Killer—a case that was soon running on fumes. The fact that both slain girls were working for Keith Scott in secret and leading double lives was an obstacle that made a full victim workup next to impossible. The loose ends and unanswered questions soon morphed into a roadblock that vexed Eleam as much as Pat and his partner, Billy Pridemore. With the investigation seemingly stalled in perpetuity, it was then, out of the cold there came a new lead that revealed itself when least expected. It was a break with yet another Kentucky connection.

While conducting a follow-up canvass run of the Midtown neighborhood surrounding the soon-to-be defunct Exotic Tan, investigators had managed to locate a woman hailing from some largely unknown water-tower town in Eastern Kentucky, a town situated just ten miles from the massacre in Oak Grove of two years earlier. After the double murder at the New Life Massage Parlor, the witness had coincidentally moved to Nashville, taking a basic retail job only half a block down Church Street from Exotic Tan. While working at a neighboring business just after the noon hour on February 21, this Kentucky transplant had by chance seen something odd. It was something that, until properly asked, they hadn't previously thought to divulge. The Metro uniforms going up and down the block, following the usual script during the original canvass, apparently had never coaxed it out of them, just as the witness hadn't thought to volunteer it without specific prompting. For whatever reason, as is the case with so many witnesses, they had arbitrarily assumed it wasn't important. It was.

Chapter 26

DISCHARGED

During the noon hour of February 22, the day of the Exotic Tan double murder, the witness, standing at the front counter of the store, noticed a suspicious man skulking around outside near the tanning salon. The mystery man also happened to be slinging what the newly found witness could best describe as a battered-looking khaki rucksack—a military kit bag. While the description of the armed forces gear seemed to square with the apparent DOD connection, given the sheath found at the scene, the description of the man seen leaving did not. None of the regulars at Exotic Tan checked out by Metro cops during the first forty-eight hours matched the description. Keith Scott also confirmed that the witness's description didn't match that of any known hang-around, loiterer, or other noncustomer who had ever given either Tiffany or Melissa trouble while coming or going from work. But then cops clued in to an earlier reveal; the statement taken by police from another Exotic Tan employee, someone who'd filled in for Tiffany when she called in sick on the afternoon of February 21, a day before the murders.

The frightened and reluctant young woman, interviewed by investigators the day after the bodies were found, described having covered for Tiffany on the evening of the twenty-first. While a number of men who came into the salon on that date were surprised to see that Tiffany wasn't working as normally scheduled, there was one individual she had never previously seen in the salon; she described him as a large "linebacker"-looking guy. Additional descriptors were that he was African American with a lighter complexion, about six foot two in height, and a lean and athletic 230 pounds in weight. Apart from her description squaring with the one provided by the Kentuckian at the phone store, the "linebacker" football reference was soon revealed to be a harbinger of the next lead to materialize. That would be the 1993 school yearbook from McGavock High, in East Nashville.

The McGavock yearbook would turn out to be the decoder ring needed to decipher Tiffany Campbell's diary, that exhibit uncovered by Eleam through the girl's mother around the same time the first usable suspect description was on the books—around the same time her mother first learned of Tiffany's secret job. Throughout the diary, especially in the days leading to Tiffany's ominous prediction that she would be the next Nicole Brown Simpson, references to a mysterious "he" peppered the eighteen-year-old's anxious entries and consumed her thoughts. She wrote about how "he" had arrived back in town and how she knew "he" had been continuously watching her ever since. She even described at one point how "he" had tried to kiss her, though it was unclear where or when, while talking about old times. Tiffany could never, it seemed, bring herself to actually commit his name to writing, not even in her own personal diary. But the McGavock yearbook did. It was the same year that "he" graduated at the bottom of his class and left town, it was hoped for good. "He," as Eleam soon deduced, was a local football star and inveterate O. J. Simpson fan who, as was later revealed, was equally as narcissistic as Simpson himself. Patrick Streater had also been Tiffany Campbell's high school crush.

Streater had been an all-star running back and football team MVP at McGavock High in East Nashville; his athletic skills had even come to the attention of NCAA recruiters who showed up now and again during his senior year before eventually taking a pass on him. Graduating from McGavock in June of '93, almost a year to the day before his idol O. J. Simpson was arrested for the murders of his ex-wife Nicole and her friend Ron Goldman, Streater soon found his way by default to the air force rather than college. Tiffany Campbell, also a student at McGavock, was one of several younger girls smitten by Streater's athletic exploits, popularity, and superficial jock machismo. In spite of the assortment of naïve young girls Streater had on the go at any given time during his time in the limelight, once he found himself out of luck and out of a job in the winter of '96, he returned to Nashville obsessed with reclaiming only one girl: Tiffany Campbell.

Wasting no time in picking up where he left off three years earlier, Streater made it clear that in his deranged mind Tiffany was still *his*. Within only a week of his return to Nashville, Tiffany's diary entries reveal that she, as Streater's one-time passing high school fancy, had resigned herself to a certain eventuality beyond her control. The next task was to begin piecing together the last three years of Streater's life, between the time he left Nashville and when he later returned to reclaim Tiffany. It was not long before a grim mosaic of events—and events yet to come—came into focus.

Returning to Nashville with his tail between his legs and angrier than ever, a coldly arrogant Streater had received an administrative discharge from the US Air Force Security Force—the military police for the air force—in the fall of '95 following a series of reprimands over bizarre behavior while stationed in New Mexico. After Streater was sent back to civilian life, he returned to Nashville instead of relocating to Alabama, where his new fiancée—an air force cop herself—was stationed at the time. He went home to try to reclaim the glory days of his recent past. He was also there to reclaim what he felt in his disordered and entitled mind was rightfully his property—Tiffany Campbell.

Given that his return to Music City coincided with Valentine's Day, Streater used the observance as a convenient pretext, his loyal fiancée blissfully unaware of what he was doing back in town and with whom, to rekindle his earlier romance with Tiffany, a girl three years his junior and barely out of high school. The bureaucrats back at Holloman Air Force Base in New Mexico had already been onto something when they decided to walk Streater out the door in late '95. True to form, like his man crush O. J. Simpson, Streater began to display increasingly disordered preoccupations and unfounded jealousy with his one-time romance in spite of more timely and accessible options in terms of single women. This fixation was an obsessional and domineering sense of ownership that eventually escalated to what's known as site stalking, a deliberate and high-risk form of harassment. Such a stalker—sometimes out of jealous rage, sometimes simply because he or she can, and sometimes both—begins to compulsively show up with increasing regularity at a person's home or work, often for some symbolic, irrationally nostalgic, or purely delusional reason. Mirroring what is often seen in such cases, only a week after Streater's return, Tiffany's diary entries underscored her visceral fear of the man, once her teen love interest, who had now transformed into something else entirely. He had become someone—or more accurately some*thing*—she could no longer recognize.

Assuming M Squad detectives had the motive right, all signs pointed squarely to Streater, the ex-cop with advanced knowledge of criminal investigation and forensic-evidence recovery methods in addition to a deep-seated and symbolic obsession with the primary victim. It was, however, an opinion not unanimously shared. There remained a vocal and influential minority within the M Squad and even Metro brass hats who were putting stock in the lust-murder theory—those who thought Streater, while inherently creepy, was a red herring. The two victims, so the lust-murder proponents thought, were sitting ducks for any number of equally creepy sex offenders and perverts who knew that Exotic Tan was really a misnomer. They were men who knew that in reality there was a revolving door of young and attractive female attendants, in varying states of undress, holed up alone in a business designed for privacy and a reputation for discretion. Given that the vast majority of victims of sex crimes are targeted because of their being readily and routinely visible, usually while traveling to or from work, the theory about an obsessed Exotic Tan regular gone rogue certainly had some sense to it. The salon, as the lust-murder advocates insisted, was the ideal hunting ground for a motivated sexual sadist. It was a Midtown death trap.

To muddy the waters even further, police later discovered that Melissa, the covictim, had herself been dating an air force man at the time of her death—though a regular airman stationed at Moody AFB in Valdosta, Georgia, and not a Blue Beret as Streater formerly was. Eleam, Pat, and other investigators knew that this connection to both the tanning parlor and the armed forces might well provide an alternate explanation as to why DOD property had been found at the scene. Since the boyfriend had already admitted to visiting Melissa at work, the scabbard, in theory, could have been left there in situ earlier by either of them. Even the most bumbling dime store attorney could have a field day with it in court, making hay with all kinds of theories as to its origin and itinerary.

Despite these issues, the description of the stocky black male provided by the witness from the Midtown store was not only remarkably similar to Streater's photograph in the McGavock yearbook, but also to the description provided by the Exotic Tan employee who'd covered Tiffany's shift for her on February 21, one day before her death. It also gelled with Streater's most recent air force ID card photo, which cops managed to procure on the sly from a contact back in New

Mexico. The problem was that, suspicions aside, there were still not sufficient grounds to arrest Streater, assuming he was still even in the city. Investigators also had to contend with the tenuous link to the still-unsolved New Life double murder, a reality that gave the appearance that the two incidents were somehow connected, that the staged Exotic Tan murder of Tiffany was a lust murder and not, as others believed, a personal-cause murder unconnected to the Oak Grove murders. With Streater discharged from the Blue Berets, unemployed, and not immediately locatable for any kind of questioning, it seemed the case would remain in limbo until one of two things happened. Either the New Life case in Kentucky would need to be solved, the dirty cop or cops reportedly linked to the murders ferreted out and properly connected to the case, or—even less likely—Streater would need to pop back up on police radar. He needed to strike again and get caught. By the time the infamous Tanning Bed Killer officially became Pat's case—yet another to add to the growing pile of open/unsolved horror shows that Pat absorbed into his workflow—Streater had actually made his way 2300 miles away to Sacramento. He'd come to Nashville to get in touch with his dark side; he'd since gone to California to turn pro.

Chapter 27

Festiva

By May of '96, once M Squad detectives were onto Streater and considered him the prime suspect, Pat thought Streater likely still labored under the delusion that he'd committed the perfect murder and cleverly escaped detection. If Streater was in fact the Tanning Bed Killer, he'd know that Metro cops were searching in vain for a crazed sex killer who had now attacked the employees of two separate massage parlors in two separate states. He'd be overconfident and emboldened, Pat thought.

Whether or not Streater knew how the investigation into his one-time girlfriend Tiffany Campbell's murder was progressing back in Nashville, he soon doubled back to Alabama in July of '96. Once there, he strong-armed his fiancée into requesting an official transfer with the air force police so they could push west as far and as quickly as possible. He also expedited their marriage, with vows being exchanged later that same month. Streater, conversant enough in the law by the time he was unceremoniously cashiered by the air force, knew that any statements made between husband and wife—admissions to crimes, confessions of mortal sins past—were in most jurisdictions protected by the covenant of marriage. They were sacrosanct. They were inadmissible. The new Mrs. Streater was not only a Blue Beret but also his insurance policy.

By the time he settled in the Sacramento Valley, purportedly making a second go at the straight life—which included his volunteering as a football coach at a Catholic high school in the city of Carmichael—Streater had found himself a new day job, or so he claimed. Boasting that he'd scored himself a plum security guard gig manning the desk of a swanky office tower somewhere off the Capitol Mall in downtown Sacramento, he would leave the young couple's house each morning in a guard uniform and with lunch box in hand, ostensibly heading off to work for the day. All the while, his wife bought the ruse. Something that confused her, however, was the Blue Beret–issued bayonet—government property required to be returned upon official discharge—that was still in his possession, and missing the sheath. It would be neither the first nor the last sign that Streater was not the man she thought he was. Streater, admitting that he'd pilfered the bayonet from the air force before being walked off the base in New Mexico, explained to his wife that he drove to work with it every day for "protection"—to defend himself in case of a carjacking, that new nineties crime wave he'd read about and that was especially prevalent in California.

In reality, Streater's workday was nothing short of a charade. His day consisted of waking up with the same military precision instilled in him at the academy by 6:00 each morning, then going through a recurring pretense of heading off to work. But there was no work, no swanky office tower to go and guard. Instead, he would drive to a nearby commercial plaza, where he would throw his red Festiva into park, cut the engine, and simply go back to sleep. By 4:30 p.m., he reversed the process and drove home, feigning exhaustion and offering up phony anecdotes about his long day at the office. In time, Streater found he could no longer sustain the artifice; he couldn't sleep away the day anymore. Soon he started driving around during the afternoon to kill time. As his days melted away to nothing, Streater's thoughts also soon started to wander back into dark territory.

Before long, Streater started cruising the sleepy streets of the upper-middle-class and largely retiree-dominated suburb of Roseville—at one time considered by CNN Money as both the best place to live and the "skinniest city" in America—and began dabbling in new and increasingly deviant vices. Streater's newfound home city of Sacramento was, even in the spring of '96, still a target-hardened area given the atrocities of Richard "Vampire Killer" Chase twenty years earlier. A brazen daytime killer, Chase went on a spree of terror in the late 1970s, wandering into unlocked suburban homes in broad daylight, then murdering and drinking the blood of whoever was home at the time. After killing seven women and following his 1978 arrest, Chase eerily proclaimed that his moral code legally and philosophically had justified his heinous crimes. He cautioned that if a woman was home alone with the door left unlocked, he had been technically invited to come in and drink her blood on implied consent. Chase stated that this, as he understood it, was the natural order of things—and suggested that others might follow in his wake.

When Streater started his daytime trolling in Roseville, the memory of Chase was alive in the minds of many people still haunted by his actions. Chase's chilling allocution still had local residents in the spring of '96—nearly two decades after his murders—heeding his warning and keeping their doors locked twenty-four/seven. He had taught them not to open the door to strangers, to be wary of anyone lurking on suburban streets, and not to trust male callers to the home, even in the daytime. *Especially* in the daytime.

For reasons we may never know, Streater decided to pick up where Chase left off. Streater knew the Chase investigation well; he knew the order of the day in Sacramento. He equally knew that the sedate and affluent suburb of Roseville was not Sacramento per se, or so the people there thought. It offered a remote fastness that would make the perceptively safe city's mostly stay-at-home residents soft targets by comparison—prime meat. Only he and M Squad lead investigators knew that he alone was the one who had murdered two girls in Nashville and had managed—for the time being at least—to get away with it. While Streater looked to reclaim in sunny California the rush of the kill, Pat would find himself waylaid by a dark reminder of what his friends back in New York had warned him about two decades earlier when he first voiced his desire to pursue a career in law enforcement. He also remembered the stories he first heard as a rookie working 12South patrol, stories about Nashville once being a hunting ground with open season on cops. Soon, it seemed, open season was about to return.

It was during the breezy morning of Friday, May 17, 1996, when a small contingent of Metro plainclothesmen showed up at a then derelict three-story walk-up apartment in East Nashville, near what is now a newly gentrified commercial district full of shiny things for sale; today its draws include Nashville's trendy Saturday Farmers' Market. By contrast, the building that stood in that same location in the spring of '96 was at the epicenter of a storm into which no Metro officer ever ventured without a small army of backup in tow. It was a time when spotters on porches and truant juveniles marauding around on rusty bicycles were continuously scoping for cops or any other outsider they could eyeball—anyone they could get the drop on. The staircases of the building were booby-trapped with bacon grease, the emergency exits welded shut. While the handful of law-abiding citizens left there were too terrified to object, the building had in essence been retrofitted to become a built-to-suit death trap. Whether resident or outsider, no one was exempt.

The two detectives who showed up at the building that morning had hoped that they'd arrive before the various gangs and subsidiary factions of thugs who ran the neighborhoods were able to greet the day. They arrived at the location just after 8:30 a.m. to serve an arrest warrant for aggravated assault on a known felon who, they'd learned from some paid snitches, had been hiding out in the building for at least a week. One of the uniforms the detectives brought with them as backup that morning was Officer Francis Paul Scurry, a twenty-year Metro veteran who worked Germantown patrol—a US Army veteran before that. A reasonably routine arrest that should have gone as planned did not. As Pat had learned long before, *nothing* in Music City was ever predictable. From the murderers of Girl Scouts and aspiring country stars to the so-called Tanning Bed Killer, Nashville had produced some of the most dangerous predators and serial sexual psychopaths in recent American history. The city seemed to be churning them out in record numbers and in record time.

After the police on scene initially received no answer at the unit, the lone tenant on file eventually opened up, with a claim of having been sleeping during the standard set of imperious knocks, and even an unsuccessful attempt by a maintenance man to enter with what was thought to be the right key for the door. After the tenant was placed in cuffs and passed off to one of the backup uniforms for transport to central booking—the CJC, or Davidson Center on 2nd Avenue—the remainder of the Metro cops on scene entered the apartment. Scanning the squalor of the tiny efficiency unit, Officer Scurry noted a partial footprint outlined in plasterboard dust coating the top of a broken dish shelf in the kitchen. Above the shelf, in the ceiling, Officer Scurry then noticed a push-up access door to an attic crawl space, the door appearing slightly askew. The veteran uniform cop—going above and beyond—received a boost from one of the detectives and managed to squeeze into the narrow opening. It was then he found and faced the man they'd all come to arrest, a local reprobate named Daryl Squire, at the ready in near darkness—in an improvised firing stance. Having pulled a concealed handgun from his waistband, the fugitive fired a single shot at Officer Scurry, who, in the darkness, likely saw nothing but the muzzle flash before he realized a gun was even in Squire's hand. Like so many Metro cops of the day, Scurry was not wearing his department-issued bulletproof vest and was struck with a round through the chest. Relying on his training, he still managed to unholster his own weapon, firing three rounds that hit Squire in various areas of his body. Wounded but not down, Squire then fired additional rounds at close range, effectively executing Officer Scurry as he lay prone and dying on a pile of wet insulation in the ceiling crawl space. Squire continued his rampage by firing through the opening of the attic hatch at the remaining officers in the kitchen below, all of whom were forced to retreat into the hallway, with one officer being struck in the knee before hobbling to safety beyond the doorway. For the next ten minutes, a close-quarters shootout reminiscent of an Old West gunfight unfolded.

Now cornered and looking at the electric chair for the capital murder of a Metro officer, Squire made a one-way trip out of the crawl space to die by what would be referred to in later years as suicide by cop. While people of Squire's ilk had a lifestyle not assuring any degree of longevity, he now had the opportunity to go out in a blaze of glory at the hands of Metro officers rather than, cornered with no way out, by his own hand. Running low on ammo, Squire dropped down into the kitchen and then moved square in line with the open door leading to the building's hallway. He would there face a contingent of Metro officers—uniforms and plainclothes alike—positioned behind cover in a tactical position, or what's known as the fatal funnel. Detective Sergeant Robert Moore, now also on the scene and in the corridor with a clear shot on Squire quickly sailed in a 12-gauge slug from a Remington shotgun. He gave the felon his wish, essentially tearing him in half and, in the process, ending the whole ordeal. From beginning to end, it lasted just under ten minutes and had left both cop and cop killer dead, the acrid odor of nitroglycerin and saltpeter from spent gunpowder still lingering in the building's halls.

Left: A modest grave marker denotes the final resting place of Metro officer Paul Scurry, shot and killed amid the city's renaissance, on May 17, 1996. Right: The memorial photo of Officer Scurry as it appears under glass as part of the Metro's Wall of Heroes. Gravesite photo courtesy of FindaGrave. Officer Scurry photo source unknown.

With Pat at the helm of the Metro Murder Squad and responsible for investigating all police shootings in Nashville, the Officer Scurry slaying meant, for the time being at least, less time devoted to traveling the county and state with Pridemore at his side while he checked the logbooks of every trucking company he could for leads in the Carl Williams murder. The random roadside slaying, two years later, was still haunting him. It also meant less time spent investigating the more recent double slaying at Exotic Tan—the most gory and outright horrific scene even Pat had ever seen. In the meantime it bought Patrick Streater even greater time and distance as he roamed the Sacramento area with evil intentions. As Nashville cops mourned, Scurry's personnel photo was put in a frame behind glass on the wall of honor, and he was given a hero's send-off. Meanwhile, Streater's Blue Beret bayonet still lay thousands of miles away beneath the front seat of his red Ford Festiva. The blade would remain close at hand as he reminisced about his earlier grisly crimes.

The tragic execution of Officer Scurry seemed to turn the clock back on Nashville's urban renewal but was to unexpectedly bring about a curious connection with the Tanning Bed Killer investigation. On completing his final review of his fallen Metro PD colleague's murder and logging Officer Scurry's death as "cleared" to the now dead suspect for FBI statistical purposes, Pat stumbled across an item of interest in one of the attending officers' written statements. It was something that would bring him back once more to the massacre at Exotic Tan—back to Streater as his prime suspect. Always looking for transferrable insights and commonalities that might benefit any number of the cold cases inhabiting his tortured world, Pat was soon able to cultivate new ideas for investigative avenues by drawing a nexus between the otherwise unrelated slaying of Officer Scurry and the case of the Tanning Bed Killer. It was this ability to connect these same disparate morsels of information and nurture a certain intellectual curiosity that would, in coming years, allow Pat and his colleagues to become record setters of a different kind.

A routine check using the National Crime Information Center (NCIC) database of a name associated with the cop-killer Daryl Squire—in fact, the same tenant on the lease for the dive apartment where Squire was shot—revealed an interesting rap sheet. While the Officer Scurry murder was an entirely different case, worlds away from the Exotic Tan slayings, the facts of one offense on the tenant's record had involved the use of a scientific technique that conceptually might be tweaked and applied to the Streater case. Besides aiding and abetting Squire by sheltering him, the accessory had also been previously indicted for assault with a deadly weapon and for armed robbery. The botched holdup in question, occurring at a bank in Knoxville a decade earlier, had ended up landing Squire's associate an eight-year stint at the West Tennessee State Pen in the town of Henning. But it was *how* he was caught that ultimately piqued Pat's curiosity—a discovery that in due course would help him zero in on the Tanning Bed Killer once and for all. Years before television series such as *CSI* made the term *trace evidence* a household phrase, a time when DNA testing was still a faint glimmer in the eye of crime-scene techs across America, a talented evidence team with the TBI had made a remarkable discovery.

In forensically isolating the chemical composition of the exploding blue dye in the bank's decoy pack included among the bundles of cash taken in the Knoxville holdup—packs kept in the cashier drawers of every major bank in the event of robbery—the TBI evidence team was able to track down the bandits in the absence of eyewitness testimony. While the dye pack had exploded and stained the getaway vehicle or "drop car" found abandoned near the scene of the crime, the dye's chemical signature later showed up on the carpet fibers of the floor of a car belonging to the suspect. Even though he had changed his clothes, it had been transferred by contact with his shoes, unknowingly imported from the getaway car into his own car hours later. Pat had been impressed with the investigative success achieved by going this extra forensic step. He wondered if blood typing and blood grouping—at a time long before DNA databanks allowed for precise genetic matching—might similarly allow him to either include or rule out Streater once and for all as the Tanning Bed Killer by virtue of his car having similar transfer evidence—trace amounts of the victims' blood that might allow the TBI to once again isolate any individuating characteristics to put Streater at the scene. In addition to needing some advances in forensic science, Pat would also first need to find Streater's elusive red Ford Festiva. It was no small task. It would take years, but it would be worth the wait.

Chapter 28

PREDATORS

As 1996 wound down and 1997 came into view, the ribbon was cut to unveil the new Nashville Arena—today Bridgestone Arena—the future home of an NHL expansion franchise and confirmation at last that Music City, perhaps the unlikeliest of hockey towns, was finally to host its own team. Blanketing a full block between 5th and 6th Streets in the 500 block of Broadway Avenue, the new facility had been considered the high point of the city's midnineties renaissance and an omen of good fortune to come. Its construction had all but erased the physical evidence, and for many even the bad memories, of what that same block had looked like not so long before. During its marquee opening, almost twenty thousand local taxpayers came to see what their money—in a state with no taxes of its own—had managed to bankroll, how they had effectively closed ranks to build up and move forward as a community. It was a modern-day iteration of a community barn raising that recalled Tennessee's antebellum agrarian past. A year ahead of the Nashville Predators, the city's first professional hockey team, hitting the ice for the first time, the arena's inaugural event that December was a Tennessee Christmas pageant that was packed to the rafters. People sang country-and-western renditions of holiday standards and traditional carols, held hands in prayer, and, over Bloody Marys and Jim Beam atomic eggnogs, contemplated what the following year might hold. They wondered aloud whether the Tanning Bed Killer, a blight on the city's rebirth that undercut its deserved rejuvenation and beautification, might finally be put on ice. The music played.

Within the next two months, by the winter of '97, the M Squad had a nationwide all-points want on Streater's red Ford Festiva, a stop and hold for identification, and an examination request that any cop running the vehicle's tags or Streater's name on NCIC would see and be compelled to honor. No one, it seemed, was aware Streater had already moved to California. So long as he kept police prowl cars out of his rearview mirror and stayed off the grid, the request was not urgent enough to justify a public notice to be on the lookout for the car, as one sees today in cases of an AMBER Alert or similar. The Festiva therefore remained the proverbial needle in a haystack. Its owner managed to keep an equally low profile. Despite his skulking around the city streets of Sacramento and sleeping in parking lots—perhaps on account of his wearing a security uniform, his driving an innocuous-looking economy car, or his *not* looking like Richard Chase, the city's previous bogeyman—Streater also managed to avoid police suspicion and the scrutiny of citizens of Placer County. It was his new home. It was where he'd ultimately find new prey.

Over the course of that first year living in Sacramento and trolling its affluent suburbs, Streater also managed to keep to himself his long-standing appetite for misogynistic violence and subjugation of women, choosing to find an outlet by compulsively watching sadomasochistic-bondage pornography via vintage 1990s dial-up internet. When the connection proved especially slow, he'd abandon the allurements of the early World Wide Web to instead dial 900 numbers, where he would taunt, threaten, and humiliate the female call takers. During one month alone in early 1997, he had racked up a bill of over four hundred dollars indulging himself this way, a debt that required his wife to take out a short-term loan to pay it off before Ma Bell cut off the landline service to the modest apartment of the young couple, already stretched razor-thin and living paycheck to paycheck on a single military police income. Streater insisted to his partner that the calls hadn't been placed by him—that pencil pushers at the phone company must have gotten accounts mixed up with another Streater in the Sacramento service area. Better yet, he suggested that someone must have stolen his identity and hijacked the couple's phone line. There was always some vaguely rehearsed and semiplausible excuse to be offered up; Streater's pathological lying had evolved to an alarming level of sophistication and conviction after dropping anchor in California, where he was getting daily practice with his security-guard-by-day ruse. He assured his wife that he'd look into the whole misunderstanding with the phone company—that he'd put his erstwhile police experience to good use and get to the bottom of the errant billing and have their money refunded. Rather than just stalling for time, he was in reality preparing for his next offensive.

During the first few months of 1997 and stretching through the summer, as the M Squad's all-points want lay idle on the NCIC server, waiting for the day when the Festiva's license plate would be queried in traffic—what's known as a rolling check—Streater would continue his bizarre love affair with knives, including one stowed beneath the front seat of the Festiva. By this time, he was apparently enamored with edged and deadly weapons—implements of mayhem that served to arouse him as he expanded his array of dark fetishes and paraphilias. Still poorly understood by experts in the 1990s, disordered and destructive erotic attachments to specific weapons, usually knives, have been more recently recognized in clinical and forensic literature as powerful instigators for homicidal fantasies, in some cases actually leading to violent and typically sexually driven behavior.

A number of the key case studies in this area come from outside the United States, including "the Schoolgirl Killer," serial rapist and murderer Paul Bernardo in Canada, and, more recently, Dublin architect Graham Dwyer, convicted in 2015 for the murder of a woman he met online and stabbed to death in 2012. Beginning initially with fantasies cultivated through the composition of short stories and online exchanges in BDSM chat rooms regarding acts of piquerism—the use of a blade to simulate sexual penetration—Dwyer eventually became so consumed by these fantasies that he could only become sexually aroused with both his wife and the various random lovers he met online if there was actually a knife present in the room providing visual stimulation during intercourse. His obsession later escalated to the point that he needed to use a retractable plastic stage knife to simulate stabbing his sex partners to death in order to maintain sexual performance. In the end, it was Elaine O'Hara, a depressed and convenient victim belonging to the BDSM online community, whom Dwyer would lure to a remote site that would serve as the realization of his knife's sexual power as an extension of himself. Following his conviction for O'Hara's murder, the British press estimated that Dwyer was receiving two letters a week from deranged female pen pals and *Fifty Shades* aficionados who sympathized with his methods and motive. Once again, hybristophilia in action.

Two decades prior to Graham Dwyer, however, there was Patrick Streater, a wholly American monster for which there was no known referent—no comparative case study on the books or anywhere else for the cops to draw from. While the Exotic Tan murders were clearly indicative of a personal cause, that same double slaying seemed to serve as a catalyst for Streater to, in a manner of speaking, find himself. He discovered his love for extreme violence, human suffering, and his erotic attachment to the terror of his victims—exhibiting a displaced fantasy attachment to knife work. With the tanning bed murders in many ways a rite of passage, in time the killings would transform him into the sadist he had only pretended to be back on Church Street in February of '96 in an effort to trip up the Metro cops. By the summer of '97, there was no longer a need to stage anything—he and his latest knife were intertwined as one. He had become whom he had once pretended to be. He was now whole.

Streater's first California victim was an elderly woman strolling innocently alone along a tree-lined street in the leave-your-doors-unlocked Sacramento suburb of Roseville. It was a place that was deceivingly safe and the perfect locale to unveil the new Patrick Streater and his new MO. Streater initially spotted his prey while scouring the sedate area in his Festiva before parking it a block or so away and approaching his victim from behind, half walking and half running toward her in his fake security uniform. Without so much as a word, Streater then pulverized the woman's face with a clenched fist before determinedly running off. While it appeared to be a random attack with no motive and no witnesses, there had in fact been a motive—one particularly unique to Streater. Returning to the Festiva, he presumably produced and first admired the knife. However, it wasn't quite yet time to use it again without first rehearsing other methods. He needed to switch up the approach—to modify his tactics. His MO would be to never use the same MO twice, to keep the cops guessing and present the illusion of different attackers.

A few days later, now donning dated athletic wear rather than his usual gray guard uniform, Streater came up behind another lone woman in the same area, while pretending to be jogging, and forced her to the ground. Demanding valuables but not waiting for the victim to respond or offer anything up, he snapped her arm in half with brute force before again running off unseen. A week later, he was back at it again, hunting in the same area. This time, dressed in neat casual attire, he approached the home of another senior-aged female living alone and knocked on her door. Looking through the spyhole, the home's occupant saw a sharply dressed, clean-cut, and athletic man holding a clipboard. The visual making sense to her based on the time of day, he appeared to be some type of survey taker, charity canvasser, or city functionary. The clipboard was more than a prop to help present a certain first-glance narrative. It was rather another form of staging.

After the woman opened the door in good faith, Streater forced his way inside. Beating her to the floor of the front foyer, he then pulled out from behind the wooden clipboard what it had been hiding all along—a large knife, along with a pair of heavy-duty scissors. First telling the trusting woman that he was going to rape her, and then demanding money or valuables in lieu, he almost seemed uncertain what to do with the fully compliant and terrified victim. Holding the long blade of the knife to her throat, Streater then elected to terrorize her by placing her fingers one at a time between the blades of the shears and threatening to amputate each and every one of her digits. He never followed through because he was still experimenting; the terror and violence he was inflicting were enough to excite him—to arouse him—at least for the time being.

By the end of the year, Streater, with two confirmed victims already back in Nashville, was now warming up and preparing for more in the Golden State's capital. Fortunately, his luck was about to run dry. With Pat and Grady Eleam, backed by the rest of the M Squad, doggedly working the tanning bed murders in his absence, the two-thousand-mile trek from Nashville to Sacramento wouldn't be far enough for Streater to outrun the sins of his past.

Part V

THE FAST FOOD MURDERS

"Imaginary evil is romantic and varied; real evil is gloomy, monotonous, barren, boring."

—Simone Weil, *Gravity and Grace*

Chapter 29

The Hangman

It was the summer of '95, just after the one-year anniversary of the in-custody suicide of "Dive Bar Killer" Tom Steeples, when the famed Opryland USA theme park in suburban Nashville introduced a new steel roller coaster they called the Hangman. The new attraction—an inverted looping steel coaster—replaced an earlier and comparatively tame attraction known as the Tin Lizzie, an antique car ride through Opryland's cliché-laden American West area. The swap for a more daring ride was a last-ditch move by Opryland honchos to boost declining attendance and keep the nostalgia of old Nashville alive. But it was already too late. Traditions were changing, and old institutions couldn't keep up—it was future shock in Music City.

It was that same summer when budding Nashville children's-book illustrator Janet (nee Levine) March moved to the ritzy Music City suburb of Forest Hills with her husband, Perry March. Their five-thousand-square-foot mansion nestled near the even wealthier enclave of Belle Meade—a city within Eastern Nashville boasting its own mayor and police force—was, not unlike Opryland's newest ride, little more than a costly venture to stop, or at least delay, an ongoing downward slide. Having met in their sophomore year at the University of Michigan, Janet and Perry moved to Nashville once Perry became part of the boutique law firm Bass, Berry & Sims PLC, his specialization in financial services. Perry was soon fired for sexual harassment, and as things began to unravel, he made regular visits to a psychiatrist to address what some would later refer to only as "rough edges" that needed ironing out through therapy. By August of

'96, Pat Postiglione—the tanning bed murders still open and officially unsolved with Streater MIA—would be a regular caller at the March household. He was soon immersed in the uncanny Southern-fried mystery of the vanishing young mother and illustrator. In next to no time, Pat knew full well that Janet March was dead, but he had a different problem this time around: no body.

A missing Janet March had last been seen by cabinetmakers doing warranty work at the March home on the afternoon of Tuesday, August 15. Perry March would later report to Metro PD, with an unconvincing facade of concern (in Pat's mind), that Janet, for no apparent reason, had simply up and left him and their two young children later that same day. His story later changed to indicate that his wife had mentioned something about leaving for an uncharacteristically spontaneous twelve-day vacation at a secret destination she never revealed. In the end, it was Janet's family, despite considerable resistance from Perry, who officially reported her missing to police, albeit two weeks after the fact, on August 29, and only after missing her son Samson's sixth birthday.

Finding the timeline of her disappearance and the reluctance of her husband to report her missing suspicious, Pat later had an all-points want placed on Janet's late-model Volvo with an NCIC flag of "endangered missing." The plate number also stayed on the daily hot sheets given out to Metro uniforms in every shift briefing until the vehicle was found, Pat's hunch being that the car was still in town, with or without the missing mother inside it. As expected, the car turned up, still in Nashville, three weeks later, but with no sign of thirty-three-year-old Janet. The Volvo had been found abandoned in the parking lot of the Brixworth Apartments, a residential complex only five miles from the March family home.

After the car had been located, reversed into a narrow parking space of the rental building, it struck Pat as inherently odd that someone normally lacking the confidence, as he later discovered, to drive a car backward under any circumstance—as Janet reportedly did—would do so in this one circumstance, much less at a building she had no connection to. Pat knew that a person's manner of parking was as distinct and individuating as any personality trait, with those who routinely reverse into spaces in parking lots seldom deviating from that practice. Given the cobwebs found in the wheel wells and the discovery of all Janet's credit cards and ID still in the car, all signs also suggested that not only did somebody besides Janet park the car, but that the Volvo had been abandoned at that location for weeks, likely about the time she had last been seen by the contractors on the afternoon of August 15. Following the recovery of the vehicle, Pat intuitively knew that Janet would likely never be found, alive or otherwise.

As the days melted into weeks, weeks into months, and months into years, Pat would suspect that Janet's husband, Perry, with his mercurial temper and reported "rough edges," was somehow at the center of her disappearance and inevitable death. But he also knew that murder cases, as with all criminal cases, proceed based on a body of available evidence, the corpus delicti, which even in the absence of a physical body can sometimes be considered sufficient to prove a crime as having occurred. If the case of Janet March was going to be solved, Pat knew he'd need to do it without the presence of a body or any of the available evidence that went with it. As early as January of '97, Pat was operating on the theory that she had been murdered and then buried, likely under one of the countless new residential and commercial developments springing up in Nashville and the surrounding Davidson County area, as Music City continued to bootstrap its way toward rejuvenation.

Because murder charges by necessity require that the victim actually be proven dead, proceeding to an arrest and then trial without a victim's body to corroborate the allegation is among the most speculative and high-stakes moves a cop and district attorney can make. In most no-body murder indictments, investigators will typically have some other evidence available, often evidence of blood—confirmed as that of the victim in a quantity that the consequent and only reasonable inference to draw is death of the victim. In Janet's case, however, there was not only the absence of a body but also the absence of any blood—or anything else in terms of physical evidence.

The last time Janet March was seen—alive or dead—was by contractors renovating her kitchen on August 15, 1996. Her body has never been found and is believed to most likely be buried beneath a golf course somewhere in one of Nashville's outlying counties. To lay a murder charge against the prime suspect, Janet's husband, Pat Postiglione and the M Squad would need to advance a very rare and risky "no-body" case— what's sometimes known as a case of corpus delicti. Source unknown.

It was while trying to figure out a way into the Janet March case—or at least where he might start looking for her body—that Pat began a battle with insomnia. By then married with three children, when his thoughts kept him awake at night, he took to quietly exiting the family home to participate in a new hobby: nocturnal jogging. It was a return of sorts to working the Midnight Watch—his need to be awake while the city slept. Running, sometimes for hours at a time, simply added a new dimension. He wasn't sure if it helped relieve stress, dilute horrific memories, or if he was running to get away from—or even charge toward—something in his subconscious, but soon running became more than a hobby for Pat. It became a nightly compulsion. Getting out of bed anytime between 2:00 and 4:00 a.m. every night to run ten miles at a vigorous clip, the already wiry Pat, who loved baseball and boxing, was soon even leaner. His partner, Billy Pridemore, took notice and asked him to take up a more leisurely hobby, something more civilized and that might be conducted during the daytime hours. To no one's surprise he suggested Pat take up golf—that he'd even teach him. Pat graciously declined and carried on with running. In time, Pridemore told him what he was doing was plain crazy; he even asked him if he'd spent time on the lunatic ward at Bellevue back in New York City. Within the next few months, it was a prospect that sounded reasonable given what the two would face. A new breed of monster, like a violent gale force wind, had blown into Nashville entirely undetected. Even Pat's last ten years in the M Squad had not prepared him for this latest arrival. By the time it was all over, seven of Nashville's young would be dead.

Chapter 30

It's Gotta Be D's

About the same time Janet March's Volvo turned up abandoned in the lot of the Brixworth Apartments, twenty-five-year-old Steve Hampton, a young father of three, was receiving a well-deserved promotion. After working at the Captain D's restaurant on Lebanon Road in the East Nashville suburb of Donelson for over a year, he'd finally made manager. It was a big deal for Steve, his family, and staff.

Founded in Nashville in 1969, Captain D's, with its signature fish-and-chips menu, had, within less than three decades, evolved into a fast-food empire that claimed nearly five hundred locations across the United States. By the winter of '97, it had established itself as the chief competitor to the much larger Long John Silver's, headquartered in nearby Lexington, Kentucky. But only two months into Steve's new role with the restaurant, one since branded with the remarkably unoriginal slogan "It's Gotta Be D's," the unthinkable would occur on Hampton's watch. The modest eatery would be the first in a series of Music City fast-food locations to see their staff members—part-timers and full-timers, teens and adults alike—senselessly massacred while at work. It would be a series of crimes that targeted innocent fast-food employees busting their humps for minimum wage and then paying with their lives.

It all began on Sunday, February 16, 1997, when Hampton and sixteen-year-old Sarah Jackson, a part-time employee and hard-working student at McGavock High—the same high school Tiffany Campbell of the Exotic Tan murders had attended—who'd been working at the location for only a few months, arrived at 9:00 a.m. to begin the restaurant's usual weekend routine-opening procedure.

Though Sarah should have been off that particular Sunday to attend weekly church services, she had coaxed her devout mother into letting her skip church— just this one time, she said—so she could earn some extra money toward a car she'd been diligently saving to buy. While skipping worship was something her mother frowned upon, she gave in just this one Sunday, admiring her daughter's steadfast work ethic. What would later happen that morning was something for which her mother would end up blaming herself for the rest of her life.

A conventional Captain D's franchise in Tennessee, appearing much like the casual seafood restaurant located on Lebanon Road in Nashville in February of '97 would have when the mayhem associated with the Fast Food Killer began. Courtesy of Hattiesburg Memory.

The Captain D's morning-prep routine on Sundays consisted of opening with a skeleton crew—one manager and one staff member—until the post-church and pre-Sunday-football lunch rush, when business usually picked up. On this Presidents' Day weekend, business was expected to be particularly brisk. That's why, after the regional manager on call that weekend telephoned in to check on matters—having already spoken to Hampton when he first arrived at 8:30 a.m.—he immediately became concerned when the follow-up call went unanswered. He later drove over to the restaurant to determine why, arriving just after 10:00 a.m. when the assistant manager, Hampton's second in charge, was also coming on shift. The two men immediately recognized Steve Hampton's family sedan parked in its usual space in the lot outside. Only moments later, however, the telltale signs of something sinister emerged as having transpired inside. A check of the front door revealed it was locked; a look through the windows of the restaurant revealed no signs of life. The two men had missed the first—and last—visitor to the store that day by only a matter of minutes. They'd been the lucky ones.

Following a 911 call by the regional manager who, based on instinct, knew something was inevitably wrong, two Metro PD prowl cars arrived on scene shortly after 10:30 a.m., half an hour before Steve and Sarah should have been

officially opening up shop to the Nashville public. The two uniforms, following their training, cautiously and tactically maneuvered through the restaurant
after being let in by the regional manager. They stealthily combed the eerily
quiet restaurant, moving in tight formation with department-issue .40-caliber
Glock pistols drawn, clearing the corners of empty rooms while simultaneously
scanning for any sign of the staff and potential threats. It seemed, or so the two
cops that morning thought, to be an unusual time of day, day of the week, and
location to have to apply such precise and cautious tactics—the threat of an
intruder still inside and lying in wait to attack from ambush being a very real
threat. What they—and everyone else in Music City—didn't know at the time
was that they were dealing with an equally unusual set of circumstances and with
an equally unusual offender. He was a new and rare breed of killer who'd honed
his methods elsewhere but who was now in Nashville to stay. To stake his claim.

Moving through the tacky maritime-themed restaurant, the cops, seeing
the main cash drawer open and devoid of bills—and coins—initially didn't
think much of it given that the restaurant wasn't yet open. The larger context,
however, soon became clear. Located facedown on the concrete floor of the
walk-in cooler were the bodies of Steve Hampton and young Sarah Jackson, their
company-issued royal-blue button-down uniforms spattered in blood. They had
each been shot once, execution style, in the back of the head with what was
later determined to be a .32-caliber six-shot revolver. There was no sign of a
struggle or any other injuries to the two employees; there was no sign of forced
entry, no sign that the killer had stowed away inside the restaurant overnight
and ambushed the employees on arrival. The killer hadn't gotten the drop on
his victims as much as he appeared to have simply walked them in or otherwise tricked them into entering the cooler of their own will. Once inside and
made to lie down on the floor, they likely thought they'd be spared after about
seven thousand dollars in total—what was a comparatively scant amount for a
takeover-style armed robbery—was stolen by the culprit. Yet despite appearing
to have cooperated fully and offering no resistance, it had made no difference.
Both Steve and Sarah were still killed in cold blood while cowering on the floor,
by an intruder who had somehow gained unforced access to the restaurant.
Within ten minutes of being called by the uniformed incident commander, Pat
left breakfast on the table, took a belt of warmish coffee, and headed out the
door to make his way to the scene. He observed and noted. As usual, he ran

scenarios through his head. In the meantime, the killer was already plotting his next move and his next score and set of victims. He was already reveling in the city's pain and toying with its police.

Given that the Captain D's regional manager—and later the Metro uniforms—arrived before the restaurant was set to open and the first customers of the day were due to arrive, Pat deduced, especially in the absence of forced entry, that the assailant had somehow managed to talk his way into the restaurant before the doors were open to the public. He drew the conclusion that this likely occurred not long after the two employees had arrived and locked the doors behind them to begin the opening procedure, and when Steve and Sarah could be seen, through the panoramic windows, moving around inside—could be confirmed as being the only two employees on-site. Steve Hampton, known to be a stickler for following Captain D's common-sense opening-and-closing security policies, would never, as company executives later explained, have neglected to keep the door locked during the preopening period. But despite Hampton's cautious nature, the killer had somehow convinced Steve to open the door by using some false pretext. It was the type of deadly scam that is today classified by the US Justice Department's National Center for the Analysis of Violent Crime, tasked with tracking trends in serial murder, as the ruse MO. It's a key behavioral indicator that seldom changes between a killer's crimes once it works successfully, and with variations of the same ruse being used on new victims at new locations, often with increasing frequency. With the double-murder scene at Captain D's yielding no usable forensic evidence, it was the unknown nature of the ruse used that most stumped Pat after he arrived to take charge of the scene. It's also what stood out as the clearest indicator pointing to whom he should be looking for: a ruthless killer who would have done so before at other restaurants, or at least who might do so again soon.

Another thing that stood out for Pat was that just over four years earlier, in January of '93, there had been a remarkably similar winter massacre at a Brown's Chicken restaurant in suburban Chicago. It still at that time remained an unsolved case that every homicide detective worth his salt in America had heard about and been following with great interest. Police in Palatine, Illinois, had arrived at the Brown's Chicken & Pasta on January 8 of that year after a number of employees were reported missing by their families, all overdue returning home from work at the restaurant on the West Northwest Highway in the otherwise quiet town located in Cook County. After arriving to find the rear "Employees Only" door ajar, Palatine PD officers entered to find a bloodbath, one also committed in the facility's walk-in cooler. A total of five employees plus the two franchise owners were found lying facedown on the floor of the climate-controlled and sealed room. All seven victims had been shot in the head execution style.

As had been the case in the subsequent and similarly horrific Captain D's scenario in Nashville, the employees at the Brown's Chicken had apparently cooperated fully and had gone into the cooler without resistance, but had still been summarily, coldly executed by what appeared to be two assailants. Likewise, the motive appeared to be robbery, the killer or killers somehow talking or sneaking their way into the store just after closing—a time when policy required that the doors remain locked. While the Captain D's case appeared to be the work of a lone gunman, Pat figured that the latest killer to come to Nashville might either have been complicit in the Brown's Chicken case or was at the very least emulating the MO that, in 1997, still had Illinois cops scratching their heads. It was a mass murder that, once relegated to being a cold case, also left the Brown's company in free fall, and led to its shuttering over the next few years of nearly a hundred restaurants in the wake of the massacre.

Chapter 31

Do You Believe in Magic?

In the aftermath of the Captain D's double murder, the two victims' families, their friends, the loyal customers who frequented the restaurant, and Nashvillians in general were grieving, shocked, and rightfully terrified. All the while, the killer was still planning to indulge in his new twisted pastime—he would continue to play his luck. Within a day of the murders, an elderly pensioner in East Nashville, walking along Ellington Parkway scavenging for cans, happened upon some plasticized identification strewn along the shoulder of the road, as if tossed from a car window from one of the anonymous vehicles whizzing by. Most scavengers might not have had the inclination or taken the time to stop and look more closely, particularly since there was no apparent cash value to the items. Yet this old man, with time on his hands, decided to investigate further. His decision would end up significantly advancing the investigation and changing the course of events to come.

One of the pieces of roadside scrap paper and plastic recovered that chilly morning turned out to be a video-store rental card bearing a membership identification number but no name. Two additional items located by the collector included health insurance benefits cards for two children, each with the last name Hampton, found blown against a crumbling curb near Trinity Lane. It was in fact the same Trinity Lane where "Dive Bar Killer" Tom Steeples was caught with crack cocaine in his Chevy Impala three years earlier. The man out on walkabout that morning collected the items, took them home, and then had the presence of mind to call the closest Metro PD division. A uniformed officer dutifully arrived and offered the usual platitudes about its being "the right thing to do" and "thanks for calling it in," both men entirely unaware at first of the long-term significance of the find in relation to an ongoing homicide investigation. It was only when the grizzled old can collector caught the local six o'clock news on WTVF Channel 5, and the commentator named the older of the two victims at the Captain D's job—Steve Hampton, newly minted manager, young father of three—that the possible significance of the find rang home. Hampton's documents had been recovered about eleven miles from the massacre at the restaurant and another nine miles from M Squad headquarters on James Robertson where most of the detectives' cubicles still sat empty. Pat, after all, was still at Captain D's completing day two at the crime scene—darkness having since fallen—when the desk man at Metro headquarters rang his Motorola pager about a new development in the case.

Using the restaurant's phone to call for the update, Pat immediately knew the importance of the old man's roadside discovery and its implications on the investigation. He knew that if the TBI crime lab was able to lift a partial fingerprint belonging to the killer off at least one of the cards, the identification being found wouldn't just help delineate the killer's escape route after leaving the scene, it might also just help confirm who the city's newest maniac was and where he'd been before. Sure enough, within a day, the diligent TBI techs and assistants who toiled without complaint at the lab on R.S. Gass Boulevard ended up lifting not a partial fingerprint, but a *full print* belonging to the killer. It had been successfully located and developed on the video rental card that had once been in Steve Hampton's wallet, the nameless card eventually traced to him once M Squad junior detectives brought the membership card to the store in question and made inquiries.

Knowing full well that this was the best clue yet, Pat dumped the thumbprint into the Automated Fingerprint Identification System (AFIS) network through the various police departments running their own hub databases. He sent the print to Dallas, Memphis, Mobile, Oklahoma City, Louisville, Lexington, Cincinnati, and more, and yet they all came back as negative. The returns suggested that the person who'd handled the video-store card—not Steve Hampton or the scavenger, who'd both been excluded, but the killer himself—wasn't already on file as a known felon anywhere in the United States. In fact, he had no record nearby—or nationally—whatsoever. As incredulous as he was incensed, Pat offered the same rejoinder to all the agencies that had run the print through the database, namely that they "Run it *again!*" It seemed to be the Motel Killer case all over again, Pat's hopes resting on a fingerprint and his ability to persuade cops in other states to do their jobs.

But the AFIS system operators, in many cases civilians working mostly banker's hours in each jurisdiction, didn't take kindly to the requests this time, reminding him of the integrity of the system, telling him that it was foolproof—that he must have gotten a false positive or was barking up the wrong tree. But Pat remained undeterred. The repellent crime scene at Captain D's played over and over in his mind's eye, and he knew the print had to belong to the killer of the two innocent young employees—he knew he had to lasso the killer before he hit another eatery and claimed more innocent lives. He knew other young people were already in danger. "Run it again!" he implored with vehemence each and every time. Before long, Pat's importuning became a weekly affair at AFIS terminals across the South and Midwest.

Pat spoke time and again with various law enforcement functionaries who for a living spent their time running prints through databases from the safety of a desktop computer. They never had to view the bodies of the innocent schoolgirl and her young conscientious manager, both killed by what was already shaping up to be Nashville's latest serial killer. They never, as Pat did, had to try to console their inconsolable families. They never had to make promises about catching a monster as he had promised. They would never experience nightmares about the Fast Food Killer—ones that began by the spring of '97 and would dog Pat for decades. It was why, after all, Pat had become the running man, why he ran at night. Because whether it was the Fast Food Killer, the Tanning Bed Killer, or the slayer of Trimble, Des Prez, March, or hundreds of others, it was always the *same* dream. Every time a faceless figure was finally arrested for the murders, and every time he managed to escape and kill again. It was a premonition. The recurring and intrusive nightmares were a harbinger of Pat's ever-growing awareness that he'd have only one chance to catch the killer from Captain D's. It had become personal. It always would be.

It would take only five weeks for history to repeat itself. To repeat itself, by no coincidence, on the same street in East Nashville where Captain D's was located. On the evening of March 23—once again on a Sunday—the signage hanging inside the McDonald's restaurant on Lebanon Road, just over three miles from the location of the previous fast-food massacre, read: "Do You Believe in Magic?" It was the latest in a series of new 1990s slogans for the monolithic fast-food chain. Working at the restaurant that day were Ronald Santiago, Robert Sewell, José Gonzalez, and the youngest staff member of the group, seventeen-year-old Andrea Brown. It had been an uneventful Sunday shift for the tight crew. All four were aware of what had happened the previous month just a few blocks away at Captain D's, and given that it was still an era when not all fast-food joints were necessarily expected to be open twenty-four/seven, the four employees followed the usual lockup procedure once it hit 9:00 p.m. This included, as was the McDonald's policy then and now, a requirement that all crew members clocking off after dark exit the building together, using the designated employee exit. The problem was that someone else also knew the company policy. He was waiting. A trap had been sprung.

As the McDonald's foursome walked out that night, still in their uniforms, to the rear of the building, a figure stood in the shadows patiently watching them. Emerging out of the darkness from behind the now switched-off drive-through menu board, the man produced a small .25-caliber semiautomatic pistol. It was a changeup; it was the Captain D's massacre inverted. This time he was waiting for the employees to come to him outside after closing—and all at once—rather than his having to use a ruse to gain entry before the restaurant opened. The newly adjusted MO also marked a significant diversification in terms of the steps the offender was prepared to take to achieve his grisly goals. The ambush method in this case, marking a departure from "ruse" to "surprise" as defined by the FBI, is the second of the three documented methods used by killers, usually serial killers, to acquire their victims. What happened next would ensure that the monster the local press soon started calling the Fast Food Killer would go down as a serialized mass murderer almost without equal.

By the time the Metro PD arrived to find the latest Lebanon Road restaurant massacre, it played, with one exception, like a horrific reprise of what had happened to the two helpless employees at Captain D's. Three of the four McDonald's employees were found facedown on the floor of the walk-in cooler, each shot twice in the back of the head, the exception being José Gonzalez. Since the killer's six-shot semiautomatic had apparently run out of bullets while murdering Gonzalez's three coworkers, the assailant had to change tactics as he moved in to murder him last. Improvising on the fly before Gonzalez could start to resist, the madman—hell-bent on not leaving any survivors—pulled a knife from his belt, plunging it into the young man a total of seventeen times, a frenzy that left the McDonald's stock in brown boxes on the shelves nearby all spattered in high-velocity castoff blood. The killer only stopped plunging the knife once he saw that Gonzalez was no longer moving. Assuming that his final victim of the night-shift team was dead and his latest mass murder now complete, the killer then fled the scene.

But the quick-thinking Gonzalez was only playing dead and survived the attack. It had been a shrewd move that no doubt saved his own life as well as future lives otherwise on the line. When Pat later visited him in the hospital at Vanderbilt Medical, he learned that, unlike the unsolved Brown's Chicken massacre back in Illinois from the winter of '93—a case that Pat mulled over in terms of its possible connection to the Nashville slayings—the Music City Fast Food Killer had acted alone. The police were now officially looking for one monster, not two—one who was still at large. Unable to speak while hooked up to oxygen, and touch-and-go in terms of consciousness, Gonzalez merely held up his index finger while languishing in the hospital bed to indicate a single assailant. It turned out to be a key detail.

As was the case in the Captain D's double slaying just over a month earlier, cash was again determined to have been taken—this time around three thousand dollars. Robbery, at least at first blush, appeared to be the motive. But Pat instinctively knew there had to be more to the story, given that the murders were so over the top. Not only had the killer murdered three unresisting employees, shooting them at point-blank range, he had also been carrying a knife, which he used to repeatedly stab an equally passive and defenseless store employee, seventeen times. To Pat's mind, the Fast Food Killer's acumen in acquiring access to the restaurants either by ruse or surprise, coupled with his ability to control the scene and the employees without resistance—or the use of restraints—as well as the killer's willingness to execute helpless and trusting teens and young adults, simply didn't square with any of the robbery-homicides he'd worked and closed over the years. The hauls taken from each of the robberies also amounted to what an experienced armed bandit would consider a pittance. Not only would no experienced robber consider such a sum worth the risk of the robbery alone, he would also not consider it worth the additional murders that, given all the aggravating circumstances of victim vulnerability, would be an express ticket to the Tennessee electric chair.

Pat, in considering a scenario that no one else had raised, bounced it off another Billy—in this case Billy Beaumont, his M Squad partner while Billy Pridemore was away on holiday, last seen at a best-ball tourney somewhere farther north near Myrtle Beach. The first basic knee-jerk assumption had been that the murders were likely cover-up killings, a means of eliminating witnesses to the robberies. But what if instead, Pat suggested to Beaumont, it was *the murders* themselves that were the intended crime, the money taken as an afterthought? Better yet, what if the robberies amounted to no more than staging in order to present an alternative and fictitious composite of whom the cops were actually dealing with? After Pat arranged to meet with the sole survivor of the massacre at the McDonald's on Lebanon Road in East Nashville, he realized he was right—it had never been about the money for the Fast Food Killer. For him, the kids he targeted were the equivalent of canned hunts, the restaurants they worked at little more than death boxes and fenced pens designed for trophy kills. As twisted as it seemed, the assailant was committing these murders for the thrill of it, first getting off on the mayhem he was causing and then simply tipping himself for his handiwork with any cash he could find on hand—the money more a trophy or a souvenir than any attempt to actually profit from the crimes in the traditional sense.

Pat didn't know it at the time, but his theory would, over twenty years later, align with vanguard research on the core motivations and offending pathways of two of America's most infamous criminals. The outlaw Jesse James, widely misinterpreted as a Robin Hood figure who committed brazen robberies across Missouri, Kentucky, and Tennessee in the second half of the nineteenth century until his death in 1882, was in reality little more than a war criminal with any number of paraphilias driving his crimes. As part of a ruthless gang known as Quantrill's Raiders led by a bigot and serial killer (and by all accounts a necrophile) named William Clarke Quantrill, James participated in the rape, murder, and mutilation of hundreds of civilians and Union soldiers during the Civil War as part of a guerilla campaign driven less by politics than it was by bloodlust. James's exploits after the war and following Quantrill's death, while historically reenvisioned as daring heists where there was inevitable collateral damage among civilians and lawmen, were in fact part of a protracted need to kill for thrills—executions that in many cases retreaded earlier massacres. Any money or valuables taken as part of these apparent robberies were little more than spoils of his violence and tip outs to his accessories and conspirators. The truth is that James never killed for money or property, though it certainly made for a convenient and more marketable pretext for his murders among newspapermen of the era. Nearly a century later, it seemed that flying the false flag of robbery during acts of murder—even sexual homicides with obvious serial indicators—was enough to fool even seasoned detectives.

Arguably the most infamous and dangerous serial killer in American history to never be caught, the Golden State Killer, also known as the Original Night Stalker and East Area Rapist, attacked over fifty women in their homes in the mid-1970s in the Sacramento area. His MO in every case was to conduct extensive reconnaissance on his victims and even call their homes before or after the intrusions. Once inside, he would lay his victims out prone on the floor after threatening them with a gun. He would then pile dishes on top of them as an improvised motion-detection system while he left them alone and ransacked the house, ostensibly looking for valuables. By 1978, he gave up the ruse of being a home-invasion robber, escalating to targeting sleeping couples for murder and killing at least a dozen people in their homes before he suddenly vanished in 1986. Occasionally, the attacker would revert to his earlier MO and steal jewelry or electronics, only to later discard them in the yard outside. They were valueless to him. Whether to throw off investigators or as a manner of psychological undoing, the stolen items were afterthoughts and deemed worthless. By the 1990s, catching the Golden State Killer—still at large but having placed a taunting phone call to one of his surviving victims in 1991—was the prime motivator for the creation of California's state DNA databank within the next decade.

Like the Golden State Killer, Nashville's Fast Food Killer was stealing the till cash as a secondary offense to murdering for sexual thrills. Whether the killings were committed in service to a specific paraphilia or merely to cultivate fear and grandiosity—or both—would remain to be seen. Also like the Golden State Killer, he used a gun and coerced his victims into compliance by having them lie on the floor without the use of restraints. His targets were also carefully scouted and surveilled. Pat was also sure that, despite his having not left notes near the scenes, sent letters to newspapers, or indulged in other Zodiac-like attention seeking, as the Golden State Killer had, the latest Music City serial killer was following the case in the media and monitoring the police investigation. But his need for attention and to be the star attraction of the city would also ultimately be his undoing. Pat banked on the fact that the killer's lust for fame of any kind, his quest for murderous celebrity and need for notoriety might somehow be connected to how and why he ended up in Nashville in the first place. Undoubtedly his dark and malignant narcissism would have reared its ugly head before the Captain D's murder. It would be imprinted on his earlier crimes before he began targeting fast-food restaurants and their vulnerable employees. The key would be finding an earlier crime committed by the killer—ideally his first murder—which might then be connected to the last two Nashville murders and shine a light, like the time Jesse James spent being tutored in mass murder by Quantrill, on the origins of the killer's true compulsions and where they would lead him next.

A pinch-hitting Billy Beaumont was sure his temporary partner was onto something: the idea of killings with the robbery angle played as subterfuge to lure police into an investigative tunnel with no way out, to stall investigators by having them dwell on the rap sheets of known stickup men, to have them go down the rabbit hole of the robbery-homicide theory rather than the murder for murder's sake. Beaumont agreed with Pat that the newly revised MO and improvised use of the knife might also signal yet another shift in MO in any future crimes committed by a killer quite prepared, almost effortlessly, it seemed, to adjust his methods based on the dynamics of the moment. Needing to be sure, Pat headed back to see José Gonzalez at the Vanderbilt Medical Center Trauma Unit.

Vandy Trauma, even as far back as when Pat first hit the beat with the Metro PD in the summer of 1981, was one of the main reasons why Nashville's murder rate wasn't even higher, including in that spring of '97 and still today. Over the years its skilled staff has managed to save many lives otherwise thought lost. At the same time, Pat thought to himself, if there were such things as ghosts, they no doubt roamed the corridors of that hospital after hours. For all the lives saved there, many patients also went there to die under any number of torturous or tragic circumstances. Assuming the young Mr. Gonzalez didn't end up succumbing to his injuries and being one of the spirits forever walking the floors of Vanderbilt Medical, he was still the best lead in discovering the identity of the increasingly callous and cowardly Fast Food Killer.

Like so many others seemingly destined for the next world after so many stab wounds, José Gonzalez was kept alive—and stayed alive—thanks to a remarkably skilled and committed medical team. Receiving the welcome news of Gonzalez being on the mend, and anxious to talk to the one-and-only survivor of the Fast Food Killer's crimes, Pat still had to wait nearly another week before that lone survivor started talking. Once Gonzalez was out of the woods and able to speak, and with the clock ticking until the next attack, a new complication emerged: he couldn't speak English. At the same time, Pat couldn't speak Spanish. Ditto for Billy Beaumont and the rest of the M Squad. It was an era before Nashville had become the cosmopolitan city it is now. It was an era before the skyrocketing growth, densification, and diversification of today—back before Nashville even flirted with the idea of becoming a sanctuary city. In the meantime, Pat worked the levers of the system to get a translator to the hospital on the double. Sadly, it wouldn't be fast enough to stop events already in motion.

Chapter 32

31 Flavors

The first four days in the hospital, Gonzalez, his body having swollen to nearly twice its normal diminutive 120-pound size, had been unable to talk at all. Still unsure who—or what—he was dealing with in terms of the Fast Food Killer, Pat had arranged for the patient to be moved into protective custody in his own private room with a Metro uniform posted at the door at all times. Once Gonzalez was able to speak, with the assistance of a Spanish interpreter retained by the department on the quick, he was able to describe the assailant as someone who might as well have been a reject straight out of central casting for 1990s professional wrestling villains: a towering and burly though heavily bloated-looking white male who appeared to be in his late forties but, with plenty of city miles on his face, was likely far younger, his actual age estimated as being closer to thirty. He was also sporting a thick handlebar mustache and a poufy coif of hair that looked as though it had recently been carved out of a requisite nineties mullet hairstyle—what Pat knew people in Tennessee called a Kentucky waterfall and what people in Kentucky called a Tennessee top hat. Gonzalez indicated that the killer did a lot of talking when he first got the drop on the group leaving the restaurant, calmly ushering them back inside, reassuring them all the while that it would "be okay" and that he only intended to hit the restaurant safe and be gone. Gonzalez also recalled that, once the staff members realized it was a one-way trip into the cooler, the killer seemed to take particular delight in the panic of the helpless teens, playing on that panic—even mocking it—by calmly speaking in undertones to each victim as he methodically moved around the room executing them one by one.

While Gonzalez's English wasn't strong enough to make out what the killer was saying as he spoke to each victim before shooting them, his impression was that it was some kind of taunting farewell before he put two bullets in each of their heads. That's the last thing he remembered. With a composite artist working on a sketch of the suspect based on Gonzalez's description, and a possible AFIS hit on the print from the video-store rental card still pending, Pat arranged for stakeout teams to be placed at every fast-food outlet in East Nashville in addition to loose surveillance on the few dozen other outlets—big national chains, local BBQ joints, even delis and donut shops—until the killer resurfaced. Metro cops, making rounds in shifts for each of these locations day and night while in unmarked units or in an undercover capacity, now knew what the Fast Food Killer looked like, and they knew his methods. What they didn't know was that he now had a new car and was ready to travel.

It was a month to the day, April 23, 1997, when it happened again. The Fast Food Killer's next crime would reveal him to be exactly as he had been the whole time, just as Pat had predicted, and also what was making him tick. No longer would a staged robbery be used to throw the police off his trail; no longer would the mass execution of restaurant employees inside the facility's cooler satisfy his bizarre thrill-seeking and dysfunctional sexual urges or paraphilic drives. As a textbook power-control killer, the Nashville Fast Food Killer was the type of offender whose paraphilias aren't always so clearly identified. Watching victims struggle or even beg for mercy is how power-control killers, aroused by inflicting terror in their victims, get off and simultaneously how they define themselves.

As had become apparent by the second set of murders on Lebanon Road in Nashville, the mass slaying at the McDonald's where José Gonzalez had been the lone survivor, the Fast Food Killer's paraphilias fell squarely within the realm of sadism, or enjoyment in the multifaceted suffering of others. Once his victims had achieved their purpose by arousing him after he exercised his authority, power, and supreme dominance—the ability to play God—they were slaughtered in cold blood. With news reports of the botched execution of Gonzalez leaving him as the only person capable of identifying the city's newest and strangest serial murderer, the Fast Food Killer was armed with information that Pat was confident would lead him to escalate his methods. He would have to make sure that all his future victims were dead, whether on-site or elsewhere, even if for some reason that meant taking the victims with him.

It was overnight on April 23 when the two teenage girls working at the "31 Flavors," Baskin-Robbins on Wilma Rudolph Boulevard in Clarksville, a sedate suburb about fifty miles north of Nashville, failed to return home from work. A few hours later, on the morning of April 24, Pat was at home shaving before heading to work when the story of the missing staff members hit the morning news on WTVF. Hearing the details rattled off by one of the anchors, Pat walked over to the TV thinking that it could be *him*—again. He thought it had to be him. It had to be the revised work of the Fast Food Killer, now operating outside of the city proper and out of the M Squad's official jurisdiction.

Skipping the balance of his morning routine, Pat headed straight to the M Squad office, grabbed a well-known detective named Mike Roland, whom he found staring hopelessly into a Dell monitor, and made a beeline straight to Clarksville in one of the squad's older unmarked Dodge Stratus models. It was the last set of wheels left in the motor pool lot that morning. Pegging the gas pedal and pushing the modest Chrysler Corporation engine to its limits, Pat negotiated a perilous curve off the interstate to take the shortest trek to Clarksville possible and make his way to the scene of the town's one-and-only Baskin-Robbins. As worn Goodyears chirped on the asphalt, Detective Roland white-knuckled the door grip by his side while Pat muttered to himself in a quiet rage, "Please, God, don't let that be him too." But it was already too late. Soon he'd discover his prescience was deadly accurate. It *was* him.

Once a search of the ice cream parlor for the two part-time employees, sixteen-year-old Michelle Mace and twenty-one-year-old Angela Holmes, determined that they hadn't been left on-site like the others, Pat took no pleasure in being proven right about the killer's evolving experimentations. Like the first such incident in Nashville the previous February and, as Pat was increasingly suspecting, other mass murders scattered elsewhere across the country, the killer apparently first used the Captain D's ruse MO to talk his way into the ice cream shop, convincing the girls to unlock the door when they were mopping up shortly after the last customer had been rung through. Then he hit the cash drawers and store safe as in the previous jobs, this time taking the employees with him rather than killing and leaving them on-site to be found. Whether they were taken alive or dead remained an open question—as was where he took them and why. As was what he planned to do next.

With a suspect still unidentified, a public-access all-points bulletin—the 1997 version of what's now an AMBER Alert—for the girls was drawn up and went out on the state wire by the afternoon of April 24. Before long, every law-man in Tennessee, all of them fearing the worst, was on the lookout for the two girls snatched from their workplace. With the search for the girls ramped up, Pat and detectives with both the Clarksville PD and Montgomery County Sheriff's Department were at odds over this latest robbery—now also a double kidnap-ping. The local cops, knowing (or apparently caring) little about the recent res-taurant slayings in Nashville, insisted that the scene played like two suspects were responsible. Conveniently enough, they also already had two locals—frequent flyers with the police, and known stickup men—in mind as suspects. Even once Pat brought them up to speed, the local investigators surmised that the crime was too far from Nashville for it to be the work of the Fast Food Killer. So certain, in fact, were the police of what turned out to be a myopic theory that they soon released the scene to Baskin-Robbins management, allowing the store to reopen before the girls had even been found and the true gravity of the situation was known. It was not too long after the crime-scene tape came down around the store that the bodies of Michelle and Angela were discovered.

It was inside the nearby Dunbar Cave State Park, a 110-acre geological complex peppered with Native American petroglyphs, where police found the body of Michelle Mace, her throat slit ear to ear from behind by a right-handed assailant. About two hundred feet away was the body of Angela Holmes, found facedown in Swan Lake, a man-made body of water that feeds into the mouth of the cave. Both girls were still in their Baskin-Robbins uniforms. Police believed, based on the scene, that the girls were being walked into the cave at knifepoint from behind when Angela made a run for it. It appeared that the killer, grabbing a still-compliant Michelle by the hair and cutting her throat, then set out after Angela as she tried to navigate the rough terrain in the darkness. Soon catching up to her, the killer then managed to slit her throat as well while she floundered in the shallow water.

The darkened entrance to the Dunbar Cave in the eponymous Dunbar Cave State Park in Clarksville, Tennessee, where the Fast Food Killer took his victims Angela Holmes and Michelle Mace from their part-time jobs at Baskin-Robbins in order to buy himself time. Courtesy of Lindsey Boise.

There was no question to any member of the M Squad that this latest double slaying was the work of the same killer as in the McDonald's and Captain D's cases, a killer who was becoming more brutal in his behavior. A killer now apparently opting for a knife as his first weapon of choice, following the multiple stab wounds he'd inflicted on McDonald's employee José Gonzalez. Whether he had intended on raping the girls once he had marched them into the cave or he had some other sinister plan wasn't clear. What was clear, however, was that the killer in their midst was experimenting with new and increasingly sadistic methods—that his hunting ground had expanded to an area nearly a half hour outside of Nashville. It meant that it was no longer just a Music City problem. With the newly expanded geography, Pat knew one of two things would follow in short order: either a new attack with an unprecedented level of cruelty and brutality, or a major mistake, as the killer would become increasingly arrogant, prepared to depart from his usual routine and go way off script. Maybe both.

Chapter 33

Hubris

With the intervals between his attacks becoming less predictable—the earlier pattern of on-site mass executions along the Lebanon Road corridor having already been switched up—the elusive Fast Food Killer suddenly resurfaced the night of June 1, 1997, a muggy and drizzly Sunday. That same night, a forty-something man named Mitch Roberts, the manager of a Shoney's restaurant—a Nashville original like Captain D's but more of a roadhouse-style restaurant—had been at home near Ashland City in Cheatham County, about to sit down to Sunday dinner with his wife and teenaged daughter, when the doorbell rang. The actions of the nocturnal caller and what Mitch would do next would change everything.

Roberts answered the door to find, standing in the glow of the coach light just beyond the porch, a disheveled lone male, stockily built and sporting a thick brown mustache and frizzy mound of unkempt hair. The man was no stranger to Roberts; he recognized him as a recently terminated former employee—a dishwasher—at the Shoney's location on Donelson Pike in Nashville. The man in question was one Paul Dennis Reid, a thirty-nine-year-old wannabe singer-songwriter with dreams of riding the new country wave and striking it big in Music City. Recently settling in the Nashville area by way of Texas in the fall of '96, he'd managed to get fired from Shoney's for bizarre behavior and workplace harassment on January 19, 1997, only a few weeks after being hired to work at the restaurant. Roberts remembered the date with precision because it had been the very next morning, January 20, when his comanager, Charlie Thoet, was found dead inside that same Shoney's restaurant. He'd been stabbed over thirty times in the head and face with one of the restaurant's steak knives before his assailant then cleaned out the combination safe. The robbery-homicide was still on the books as an open/unsolved case when Reid showed up at Roberts's house that night. He said that he had some key information he needed to share with Roberts—information that might help regarding the brutal slaying of his former coworker Charlie Thoet.

Sharing with Roberts that he knew of a certain unnamed kitchen employee at Shoney's who had, during Reid's own time in the kitchen, been stealing frozen steaks, he suggested that this pilferage might be related to the murder of Roberts's colleague the previous January. Reid suggested he had solid evidence to implicate this employee, evidence that he had in his car parked on the road—a newer Ford Probe that Roberts thought looked a little *too* new for an unemployed former dishwasher. Though Roberts didn't know how Reid had managed to discover his home address half an hour northwest of Nashville, this alleged new information had piqued his curiosity. With that, Roberts decided to walk outside to the parked car and into what would be Reid's final trap. Roberts would soon realize that it was his former employee Reid who was the elusive Fast Food Killer. Beginning his local reign of terror with the murder of Thoet at Shoney's, now with seven more innocent victims, he would close the circle by killing Roberts—along with his family—within his own home.

The exterior of a conventional Shoney's restaurant as it would have appeared when Paul Dennis Reid was briefly employed there in late 1996 and early 1997 before being fired. It was during his time working as a dishwasher at the Nashville-based roadhouse that he further developed a murderous MO he had begun at restaurants and bars elsewhere—back in his native Texas. Photo courtesy of Ed!/Wikipedia Commons.

It was once near the car that Reid turned to face Roberts and pulled out a .25-caliber pistol, the same gun he had used in the massacre at the McDonald's on Lebanon Road. After Reid also pulled out a set of handcuffs and told Roberts to put them on in the semidarkness of the residential street, Roberts feigned compliance in the hope, like so many previous victims, that he could appease Reid and eventually talk his way out of what seemed to be coming. Reid began walking Roberts back to the house, where the entire family was to be eliminated. After the front door was opened, one of the first things Reid noticed was Roberts's daughter playing with a newer Hi8 camcorder she'd recently received as a gift. Seeing that the lens was facing the door and that the record light was also on, Reid, the malignant narcissist obsessed with himself and his ability to play God, a wannabe country star forever consumed with his own performance, just couldn't resist hamming it up for the camera. With Reid smiling and waving as though he were stepping out of a limo at the Country Music Awards and playing to the paparazzi, Roberts—not yet fully handcuffed—bodychecked the momentarily distracted six-foot-three and 230-pound Reid off the front stoop and broke free. Then running into the house, Roberts screamed, "Get the gun!" to his wife in the kitchen ahead, while the daughter kept the camera rolling on a now dumbfounded Reid standing outside. Although Roberts didn't own a gun, that didn't matter in the grand scheme of things. For the first time during his recent spree of violence and terror, a suddenly challenged Paul Reid faced the prospect of being met with violence. As much a coward as he was anything else, Reid hightailed it back to the Ford, turned the ignition, and floored it, burning rubber while slipping into the night just as quickly as he had first materialized. He wouldn't be gone for long. Soon, things would get even stranger.

Within twenty minutes of Reid having laid a patch on the pavement in front of the Robertses' home when speeding off, leading neighbors to flick on coach lights and draw back curtains to look outside, a deputy with the Cheatham County Sheriff's Department arrived on scene. The local sheriff's department was a small police agency that consistently punched above its weight and that, in this case, was also about to give Pat Postiglione a huge and entirely unforeseen helping hand. As the deputy who arrived that night to take a report of the attempted armed home invasion was diligently filling out the usual paperwork and asking the usual questions, Mitch Roberts answered the ringing touch-tone phone on a living room end table while his wife was still speaking with the officer on scene. Incredibly, it was Paul Reid on the other end of the line. Roberts was at once utterly astounded and petrified, wondering what volley of threats would soon follow and where Reid was calling from. Perhaps, his racing mind thought, Reid was watching the house and biding his time to further intimidate while waiting for the cop in uniform to leave. "I just wanted to say I'm sorry," the gruff voice on the other end of the line muttered while at the same time implausibly chalking up the night's events to a "big misunderstanding." Paul Reid, the elusive and merciless Nashville Fast Food Killer, had just blinked.

Instinctively, Mitch swiftly handed the receiver to the officer in his house, who managed to coax Reid into returning to the home to apologize to the whole family in person. It was a feat of sheer ingenuity that played into Reid's narcissistic need to control people and situations, his misplaced sense of invincibility. The deputy, identifying himself over the phone as a police officer no less, explained to Reid that an apology could only be deemed genuine if offered in person—that Tennessee custom and Southern gentility demanded it. Incredibly, Reid, the master of ruses, took the bait—falling hard for someone else's ruse this time—and drove back to the Roberts home. He would arrive surprised to find a slew of sheriff's department officers lying in wait, their prowl cars moved out of sight around the corner. Reid wasn't even out of his new Ford Probe—purchased with money, as the seller would later confirm, stolen following the massacre at the Lebanon Road McDonald's—before he was staring down the barrels of pistols and Remington shotguns in the hands of deputies who knew in no uncertain terms that they'd just collared Nashville's Fast Food Killer. Within the next few minutes, Reid was officially in police custody, in part thanks to a quick-thinking Mitch Roberts, an equally shrewd sheriff's deputy, and—just as importantly—Reid's own hubris. It had always been his license to self-destruct.

It was shortly after this when Pat received word that Reid was in custody for the attempted murder of his former Shoney's manager and family, Mitch Roberts being the surviving supervisor at a Nashville restaurant where Reid had been employed just prior to the Captain D's double murder, and where he boasted to fellow kitchen staff that fast-food robberies with no witnesses were an easier way to make a living. With that news also came the forensic details; specifically, that the handgun in Reid's possession matched the one in the previous fast-food killings. Not waiting for Reid to be taken to central booking and officially processed and fingerprinted, Pat drove from his home in Nashville to the New Hope subdivision in Ashland City and arranged for a sheriff's print man to take ink impressions from Reid while still in custody in the back of the sheriff's squad car parked outside of Mitch Roberts's residence. It was essential to confirm that the print lifted from Steve Hampton's discarded video-store card was a match to the man who appeared to be trying to settle old accounts with the management at Shoney's. Charlie Thoet's murder there had been a nagging open/unsolved that Pat always thought might have been a dress rehearsal for the more elaborately planned fast-food slayings that came later. At long last, the Fast Food Killer had been caught. The terror he had engendered over the past few months finally seemed to be over. There remained, however, still more work to be done; there were still more answers to be sought, the biggest of which being *why*.

While Pat was busy punching out an on-the-fly but watertight search warrant on a standard-issue M Squad electric typewriter, Reid was being printed, photographed, and booked at the CJC on 2nd Avenue for the trail of destruction and the lives reduced to ruins that he'd left since arriving in Nashville with no talent, but plenty of disordered and dangerous fantasies. The mug shot snapped by the lockup staff at central booking would in due course form part of a photo array, or photographic lineup, as it's also known, of similar mug shots shown to thirty-year-old José Gonzalez, the sole survivor of the McDonald's mass murder of March 23. While still languishing in the ICU at Vanderbilt, Gonzalez would later select Reid's mug shot from that array and identify Reid as the man who'd intercepted, confined, and methodically executed his three McDonald's coworkers—and friends—before then stabbing him seventeen times. Between the match to the print on the discarded video-store card from the Captain D's murder, and the selection of Reid's photo by the survivor from the later massacre, it seemed Metro cops—and Pat in particular—had their man. If there was any lingering doubt that Reid was the Fast Food Killer, perhaps the most depraved deviant and notable forensic case study in a long line of serial killers to make their way to Music City, it was about to be discovered at Reid's East Nashville digs. It was a place of pure malevolence—what the divinity scholars at Vanderbilt and the Mount Zion Church on Old Hickory Boulevard might call "wickedness." It was pure evil.

Chapter 34

PIPE DREAMS

Armed with the search warrant he had obtained from a Tennessee judge who knew all too well about the so-called Fast Food Killer, Pat and a retinue of Metro plainclothesmen and uniforms alike descended on Reid's rented American Craftsman–style East Nashville home on Ordway Place near Gartland Avenue. Once Pat officially breached the threshold of the front door, a grim mosaic soon came into focus. It was a vista that spelled out the psychology of whom exactly Pat had been hunting and how he'd managed to elude authorities. It was a window into the mind of a madman that only intensified Pat's troubled dreams. Dreams that had more recently—and would forever—come to feature Reid as the main character. The recurring villain.

Reid's rented home, where he lived alone, quickly proved devoid of the trappings of a productive adult life of any meaning, much less his having any connection to family, friends, or anything living at all. It was in effect a home with eerie-funhouse or wax-museum qualities—one that Reid effectively turned into a distorted shrine to himself in the process. On the wall in his bedroom, police found a total of seven full mirrors he had placed at strategic angles to capture glimpses of himself while in bed. On the kitchen counter was a set of carefully staged publicity photos and head shot portraits that, though prepared by Reid to distribute to country-music agents and impresarios, managed to make it clear he'd never actually played the guitar he held—that he knew absolutely nothing about music. On the living room couch was a portfolio of random 35 mm and Polaroid exposures that Reid had taken of himself, smiling glibly and posing deliberately, it seemed, with every person he'd ever met since arriving in Nashville in early '96. Some of the photos were of him posing with Shoney's staff while looking deadly serious—a premonition of things to come—while others were pictorial catalogues that chronicled what he thought was his budding music career.

Included among the bizarre paparazzi-like images taken by Reid, in effect early versions of now common "selfies," was a solitary sticky note scratched out by Reid himself. It was a self-created artifact describing how these various images were to serve as the visual tour of his life story once he was a huge Billboard Country and Hot 100 star—when his life would one day be a point of curiosity among millions. One of the images was of a bloated-looking Reid—cruising on a distorted 1990s action movie definition of macho stereotypes—shaking hands in a sort of faux-presidential style with the man who'd leased him the same car he'd driven to Mitch Roberts's home. Another photograph depicted a public urinal that Reid had recently used, the annotation on the rear of the image describing the urinal as being the first in Nashville that he had found to relieve himself and that, as a result, it would no doubt be worth a bundle to a collector one day—one day when he reigned supreme over not only new country but the whole of Music City as a king among men.

But among this cache of disturbing souvenirs and mementos of himself, it was in the front closet of Reid's residence where the most significant piece of evidence for investigators was uncovered. Stowed in the small closet of the home, Pat found a pair of garden-variety white vinyl 1990s generic size 10 high-top shoes. After they were submitted to the tried-and-true TBI crime lab for DNA testing, Pat received confirmation within twenty-four hours that the blood of both Michelle Mace and Angela Holmes had been found on the soles of both shoes. Between the fingerprints, the Gonzalez photo ID, and now the DNA link, the noose was tightening around Reid. The earlier ballistic link to at least one of the murder weapons had been solid, but it merely confirmed that the gun had been used at the McDonald's massacre and not that Reid himself had pulled the trigger—nor that Reid had even been at the scene. On its own, it left reasonable doubt. Now, with the other evidence being cobbled from various murder scenes, and bits of evidence recovered from Reid's abode, Pat was fending off future defense arguments and proofing his case from public-defender meddling. Within another two days, Reid would be indicted and officially charged with seven murders. It turned out to be only the tip of the iceberg that was his twisted life story.

Reid's parents dived headfirst into the shallow end of the gene pool and made sure their son ended up falling backward into crime at a young age, soon dabbling in strong-arm heists, check fraud, and petty shoplifting. Reid, originally hailing from the town of Richland Hills, Texas—a WASPish three-square-mile spot on the map outside Fort Worth—finally hit the big time when he robbed at gunpoint a Houston steakhouse in the summer of '83. The stickup had involved an unusual target location and equally atypical MO—shooting and wounding one staff member and firing several rounds into the ceiling—that simultaneously spoke to Reid's unique brand of psychopathology. There had been something about the nature of the restaurant as a soft target—an otherwise low-risk and family-friendly environment—that drew him to it despite the likelihood of a comparatively small financial return. There was also something about it that would serve as an early blueprint for his horrific crimes yet to come. He knew the hapless people eating or working there were sitting ducks, that they'd never see him coming. That alone, in his mind, was the tradeoff for the small payday. Again, it was an easy concession to make, considering he was never in it for money in the first place.

After being arrested rather quickly on account of the dozen or so witnesses able to identify him, Reid was sentenced to twenty years for the violent steakhouse stickup. However, for reasons that remain unclear, he was paroled in 1990—in an otherwise no-nonsense state that builds new jails to keep its felons locked up—after serving only seven years of that sentence. His release by Texas bureaucrats would set in motion a series of calamitous events that ultimately came to an end with the slaughter of two innocent ice cream counter attendants in the cold darkness of Swan Lake at Dunbar Cave, over eight hundred miles away from the site of his first restaurant attack. As soon as he walked out of prison in 1990, Reid set his eyes on comparatively progressive and politically left-leaning Nashville as his next stopover. But before heading to Music City, he'd commit one last crime in Texas to leave his mark. It was a dress rehearsal for what would come next in Nashville—a mass slaying for which he'd watch someone else conveniently be arrested.

Chapter 35

PATSY

By April of '99, already having been in custody for two years on a slew of charges, Reid was finally the recipient of some overdue Tennessee justice. He was sentenced to seven death sentences, one for each of his victims, plus a symbolic but otherwise extraneous life sentence for the attempted murder of José Gonzalez, the McDonald's part-timer whose resilience helped break open the case of the Fast Food Killer. The attack on Roberts in Ashland City apparently came out in the wash. By the turn of the twenty-first century, Tennessee had, along with many other states across the South, moved from the electric chair to lethal injection as its primary means of capital punishment, a move that ended up stalling Reid's much-anticipated date with death almost indefinitely. His execution was ultimately stayed a total of four times—a Tennessee record—the last time being in 2003 just two hours before Reid was to be strapped to the table. In the end, Reid, eventually acquiescing to the inevitability of his execution by the state, filed no further appeals or clemency requests. In subsequent years, however, with the efficiency and morality of lethal injection itself coming on trial, Reid would benefit from bureaucratic logjams in the criminal justice system that left seven families, four business owners, and much of an entire city in limbo—feeling as though true justice had been denied. At the same time, an individual in Reid's native Texas was, for a different reason, also feeling that justice had been denied. Convicted of crimes for which Reid was actually responsible, it seemed he too was bound for the death chamber before Reid finally met his maker for what he'd done in Nashville. It was a tragic twist of fate, one that would see both men meet a remarkably similar yet unforeseen end.

In the interim, back at the M Squad office on James Robertson Parkway in Nashville, Pat was still dogged by the nagging feeling that, beyond the possible Brown's Chicken connection in Illinois, Reid had already murdered other vulnerable service-industry workers in the six years between his 1990 parole in Texas and his unfortunate 1996 relocation to Nashville. As it turned out, Pat was right, but he also found that Reid had killed en masse prior to his violent robbery of the steakhouse in 1983, the stickup that netted him his first federal sentence. The ruse MO employed in his first Nashville murder at Captain D's and used again in his final double murder at the Baskin-Robbins had somehow seemed a little too easy for him, something with the earmarks of being familiar and well-rehearsed. While Pat knew Reid would have had to cut his teeth somewhere else before coming to Nashville, a nationwide search of open/unsolved cases using Reid's MO managed to kick loose only the already familiar Brown's Chicken file from 1993. Since it was unclear at that time if Reid had ever made it as far north as Illinois, Pat then turned his attention to closed/cleared cases of a similar nature where a suspect had actually been located and arrested. His hunch was that, assuming any of Reid's earlier crimes were near the level of brutality shown in the Nashville fast-food murders, the local cops would be under significant pressure to quickly solve the cases and take someone into custody—even if it meant cutting corners.

In fact, Pat recalled that the same had nearly happened following Reid's murder of the ice cream counter attendants at the Dunbar Cave once the local police zeroed in on a local mentally delayed young man who had never even driven a car, much less had the means to carry out such a horrific double murder and leave no clues. Pat knew that if the Clarksville cops, under considerable pressure and desperate to move quickly, could almost get it so wrong, other agencies might have also. They might have even done worse. Given Reid's drifter-like, fame-seeking, and generally itinerant nature and his likely being unknown to local law enforcement in many jurisdictions, Pat figured that he would never have been one of the usual suspects rousted by investigators for any of his earlier murders. This would have especially been the case in towns with their own short list of known felons where he'd drifted in undetected and where the murders were also disguised as robberies. After Pat started his new search in Reid's native

Texas, it didn't take him long to make a match and to find Reid's fall guy for his first mass murder.

It turned out the proximity (within a month and on the same street) of the Captain D's and McDonald's restaurants hits in the winter of '97 wasn't quite as coincidental as it originally seemed. Seventeen years earlier, on July 14, 1980, when Reid was only twenty-two years old, and a full three years before the violent steakhouse holdup, Reid found his first target at the Fair Lanes Windfern Bowling Center in Houston, just over ten miles from where Reid was living at the time. It was an act of mayhem largely without precedent even for the crime-addled Houston area.

The bowling center was not only taken over but held up at gunpoint, in broad daylight, by a lone white male who had talked his way into the alley before it was due to open that Monday morning to accommodate senior league players and summer birthday parties. A witness driving by the bowling alley that same morning would later state that a man with Reid's distinct appearance was holding up a piece of paper with a message on it and that he was seen coaxing the alley's manager, much like he later did the Captain D's manager, Steve Hampton, into opening the door before the public had access. The witness in the Texas case also described the man in question as holding and repeatedly gesturing to an empty water jug he was apparently using as a prop, to convince the trusting manager at Fair Lanes to unlock the door for him so he could replenish. The inference was that the man offered a tale to the effect that his car had overheated nearby and that he needed to use the men's room faucet to refill the jug.

Once inside, the four employees on-site were forced by the intruder at gunpoint to lie facedown on the floor before each of them were methodically shot in the head one at a time, the killer sadistically whispering "goodbye" in their ears before mercilessly pulling the trigger. Fortunately, just as in the McDonald's massacre in Nashville, there was a lone survivor who managed to play dead—even with a .357-caliber round taking out his eye—and later report the details of the odd MO to police investigators. To Pat, between the whispering in the ears of the victims, the forcing of compliance and entry before opening time through the use of a ruse, the methodical execution of each employee one at a time, and what turned out to be a negligible haul in cash, it all pointed squarely to Reid, to his first cornerstone murder. Not to mention that he also lived only a short drive away from the alley at the time.

While violent takeover robberies and even mass murders at bowling alleys in America, tragically enough, aren't in themselves that rare—the methodical slaughter of four people, including a two-year-old toddler, at an alley in Las Cruces, New Mexico, in February 1990 being the most infamous—everything about the triple murder in Houston squared with Reid's methodology. There was also the fact, as Pat soon found out, that Reid not only lived close to the alley—a location actually equidistant between his home at the time and the steakhouse he would later ambush—but also that Reid had actually been seen at Fair Lanes the night before the murders. Not only seen, it turned out, but also ejected for disorderly conduct. A short time after being strong-armed out by management, Reid telephoned the front counter of the alley and warned that he would one day return to "blow heads off" and kill everyone working there.

For reasons unknown—not in 1980 and not even after the steakhouse incident three years later—Reid was never formally interviewed by police in Houston about the bowling-alley massacre. Houston in 1980 was a metro area plagued by crime, one with the dubious distinction of clocking 181 unsolved murders that year; as such, police brass certainly weren't going to let the triple slaying at the Fair Lanes bowling alley be one of them. With Reid not yet on police radar, a garden-variety down-and-outer named Max Soffar became the center of police attention. He was in due course considered a match to a composite drawing made with the assistance of the lone survivor. With composite drawings invariably being susceptible to interpretation, the machinations of the Texas justice system soon ensured that Soffar, a known felon usually cooperative with authorities, was a close enough match to the sketch to be the fall guy they needed.

In the wake of the bowling-alley massacre, with Houston PD on high alert and local citizens boycotting all things once considered innocent and family friendly, one of Soffar's criminal cronies, a man named Latt Bloomfield, managed to get popped by Houston cops once Soffar implicated him in the bowling-alley murders in a bid for the reward money. But with Bloomfield soon released due to a lack of credible evidence, Soffar ended up arrested himself while riding on a stolen motorcycle in League City, about twenty-five miles southeast of Houston. After being booked for grand theft auto and looking at some serious jail time amid the national declaration of a war on crime, Soffar doubled down and confessed to the three murders at the Fair Lanes. The "confession" couldn't have been more patently false.

Soffar ended up providing several different versions of events to detectives as he continued to string them along—from having worn a disguise to having fired a warning shot upon entering—fluctuating details that were refuted by the lone survivor of the attack. Soffar's confession was beyond inconsistent and drifted into the implausible and the absurd, not to mention that he looked little to nothing like the vague sketch, had an alibi for the morning in question, and had never previously been violent—his modest rap sheet consisting almost exclusively of nickel-dime property crime. No one is sure why he confessed and stuck with it, but even with the wildly varying and uncorroborated confession, Houston cops charged him with the three murders anyway.

It seemed that everyone needed that Fair Lanes case solved and solved quickly, and that Soffar, clearly a victim of police tunnel vision, would do despite the dubious nature of his confession. His protracted police interrogation that yielded that confession had, as was usual by that time among inexperienced or overzealous investigators, involved the use of a controversial interview tactic known as the Reid Technique. The "technique" is really an outmoded nine-step gimmick widely associated with false confessions and made infamous following the Netflix docuseries *Making a Murderer*, which depicted how it was used to extract a bogus confession to murder from a mentally delayed teenager who had no idea what he was confessing to. Houston detectives similarly obtained a sketchy and fundamentally unreliable admission that Soffar later recanted, but which was nonetheless deemed admissible at trial—and again on appeal. The unfortunate result was that Soffar, convicted of murder, would spend the rest of his life on death row, dying of liver cancer in 2016 at the age of sixty. With Soffar behind bars from late 1980 onward for the massacre at Fair Lanes, the man who was without question the real killer, Paul Reid, roamed free. He later roamed to Nashville and killed many more, the lives of seven young and innocent people being snuffed out in tragic fashion through the butterfly effect of police incompetence and judicial irresponsibility that had begun years earlier back in Texas. The family, financial, and spiritual lives of countless others were also destroyed in the process. The wrongful conviction of Soffar ensured the deaths of Reid's future victims in Music City. It would set in motion events that couldn't be undone. At Fair Lanes, Reid had mastered a ruse attack that allowed him to claim the maximum number of lives possible at one time—a mass execution disguised as a robbery gone awry. It was a coldly methodical MO that would become a referent for the fast-food murders still in the offing—a practice run for what would later happen in Nashville.

Chapter 36

Misanthropy

Even in the aftermath of Reid's arrest in Nashville and the revelations of what he'd done, Max Soffar languished on death row back in Texas. Soffar's appeal of a second conviction was rejected and, despite a petition bearing 116,000 signatures and the involvement of high-powered New York lawyers and the ACLU, nothing changed. Soffar was destined to die, it seemed, at the hands of the state of Texas while Reid would soon be executed in Tennessee.

Even though false confessions are considered to play a role in over 10 percent of wrongful convictions, juries still struggle with why someone would, as Soffar allegedly had, confess to a crime they didn't commit. In Soffar's case, without any other corroborating evidence, it was enough to seal his fate and leave him on death row. While many respected professionals were of the view that it was a clear case of wrongful conviction, and lawyers continued to work on the case looking for justice, Soffar would spend thirty-five years on death row. Though he escaped the state's needle, he would still die, while incarcerated, as a convicted murderer for crimes he did not commit.

On the other hand, Paul Dennis Reid, also escaping the state's needle three years earlier in 2013 on account of his dying of pneumonia and heart failure, went to his grave skating on additional murder charges. Apart from the Fair Lanes murders and the stabbing death of his Shoney's boss Charlie Thoet in Nashville, Pat was firmly of the view that there were also other slayings across the South bearing Reid's handiwork still waiting to be discovered. Then and now, Reid remains at the top of Pat's list of the scores of murderers—serial killers, child killers, cop killers, and more—that he took down over the course of his largely unrivaled twenty-six years in a row working nothing but the toughest of Music City homicides. Over a quarter century turning red ink into black on a whiteboard as a matter of moral and professional obligation. It has always been his calling. Going back to his time in NYC and tours with the Seabees, police work had been his destiny. Homicide, since his one-year tour on the Midnight Watch, had always been his jam.

Today, when compared from a criminological and forensic perspective to case studies of other serial killers from around the globe, Reid was unquestionably a rarity—a worthy case study for cops and academics. While it's certainly easy to hurl all kinds of epithets when describing Reid and his crimes and to label him with psychological classifications such as psychopath or sociopath, the best descriptor for him is actually what's known as a schizoid killer. Not a schizophrenic, but a *schizoid*. Less a mental condition or state of psychosis, a schizoid is someone with a type of major personality disorder—or more accurately an alloy of disorders—for which there is no known treatment, much less a cure. Schizoids don't age out of it; they don't come to terms with it—their mental state only intensifies with time until it reaches critical mass. All the while they are what's known as compos mentis; they are of sound mind and know exactly what they're doing. That's why the condition is so scary. Outsiders assume they must be insane and not know what they're doing to do the things they do. The reality is that, aside from knowing full well what they're doing and who they are, they take ownership of it. They forgive themselves for it. They make others pay for their failings.

Though there is some variance in the severity of schizoid disorder and the way experts define and diagnose it, the schizoid still ranks as one of the most dangerous and calculating offenders known, perhaps even more so than a criminal psychopath. Sometimes the result of various genetic, physiological, or chemical factors, the schizoid offender is far from insane or unaware of the criminality and wrongfulness of their actions. While severely mentally disturbed but not mentally ill, in most cases such an offender achieves some kind of satisfaction—there is an emotional, sexual, or ideological incentive to the act of murder. It is a matter of performance and grandiosity, an act of self-indulgence and even self-love. In Paul Reid's case, he loved himself to the point of autoerotic fixation—a fixation rooted in the need to play God and dominate people to satisfy his insatiable ego. Like Reid, most disordered schizoids are not only amoral and uncaring about human life but are also malignant narcissists who consider themselves superior to "regular" people. They are, in their minds, beyond classifications of good and evil.

The disorder, overwhelmingly afflicting male subjects, can generally be viewed as a combination of coldness, social withdrawal, a lack of emotional intelligence or empathy, and a general apathy toward the significance of life and death. The schizoid is reclusive and evasive yet, somewhat contradictorily, also arrogant and possessed of a strong sense of entitlement. He all but retreats from the world and constructs instead an alternate fantasy world into which he can immerse himself—like Reid ending up in Nashville with tragically laughable ambitions of country-music stardom in spite of zero experience, training, or talent. Unlike the sexually motivated serial killer, however, the schizoid's fantasies are rarely, if ever, overtly sexual, at least on the surface. Instead, their thoughts are likely to be rooted in the need to be feared and to possess power over life and death. Often obsessed with revenge but also drawing pleasure from terrifying, humiliating, and hurting others, the schizoid has dark dreams not limited to their perceived tormentors or those who draw their ire—such as managers Charlie Thoet and Mitch Roberts at Shoney's or the staff at the Fair Lanes bowling alley—but all people in general. As quintessential misanthropes, they are haters of all humanity. If they can't be king, they want to watch the world burn. There is no in-between.

Going beyond the cold brutality and senselessness of Reid's crimes, there are other killers in recent American history who fall into the same schizoid category. Consider the horrific and cowardly murders committed in July 2012 by James Holmes, an ostracized PhD-program washout at the University of Colorado who opened fire on an audience attending the premiere screening of *The Dark Knight Rises*, killing a total of twelve people and injuring over seventy. Consider also the crimes of Elliot Rodger, a deranged misogynist, racist, and involuntary celibate who spent most of his time playing *World of Warcraft* and immersing himself in a fantasy world of video games while living between England and Hollywood—all the while plotting and rationalizing the destruction of people he'd never even met.

Later wondering why women weren't falling all over him once he matriculated at the University of California at Santa Barbara in 2012, he sought his revenge against a world that he believed had stripped him of his rightful destiny as a millennial Don Juan. In May of 2014, this meant Rodger stabbed his three roommates to death while they slept, later going on a shooting rampage in the coastal town of Isla Vista, California, and targeting what he saw as stereotypical sorority girls and athletic-looking men. When it was over, he had killed a total of six people and injured fourteen others before then taking his own life. Of course, there's also Stephen Paddock, the degenerate gambler and gun nut behind the 2017 Mandalay Bay massacre in Las Vegas, a man who, in having no obvious motive for a sniper attack that left nearly sixty dead at a country-music festival, made mass murder his retirement hobby following a generally pointless and dissatisfying life of decadence and isolation.

Beyond some of these better-known cases, there also remains a disturbing and still-unexplained correlation specifically between public restaurants and schizoid mass murderers. While Reid as the Nashville Fast Food Killer is perhaps the most recent and most infamous, a key earlier case is that of the original fast-food mass murderer, the first known McDonald's slayer—a paranoid wife abuser named James Huberty. Rather than seek professional help yet fully aware that something was fundamentally wrong with how his mind worked and the fantasies he was having, Huberty instead told his battered wife on the morning of July 18, 1984, that he was going "hunting humans." Later driving to a McDonald's restaurant in San Ysidro, California, while armed with an UZI and two long guns, Huberty proceeded to walk through the restaurant firing at random, slaughtering twenty-one men, women, and children before being taken out by a SWAT team sniper. It was suicide by cop almost two decades before the turn of phrase became a household term as a new age of public mass shootings in America dawned.

Seven years after Huberty, there was also the case of George Hennard in Reid's home state of Texas. Hennard, possessed with Elliot Rodger's similarly displaced sense of grandiosity and animal magnetism, had been stalking some teenage girls near his squalid house for months to no avail. Unfulfilled with the lack of attention he was getting from the girls, on October 16, 1991, he intentionally drove his truck through the front plate-glass window of a Killeen, Texas, restaurant known as Luby's Diner. Exiting the vehicle, he then indiscriminately opened fire on the families inside, his mangled truck, broken glass, and other debris blocking their escape through the main doors. He ended up shooting and killing a total of twenty-three victims and injuring nearly thirty others before he was shot and killed by responding police officers. Though basically ignored in the annals of true crime, the massacre, at the time, ranked as one of the worst mass murders in US history.

By the early 1990s, experts ultimately recognized that a mass murderer like Hennard, much like killers in the vein of Huberty before him and Reid after, was technically not insane or even psychotic while committing his heinous crimes. With there being nothing medically wrong with him—with no malady that could be quantified or treated—the reality, something of which he was cognitively aware, was that his brain and all its constituent components simply didn't function the same way it did with other people. He was very much aware of the horror of which he was capable, and he was okay with that; those in the world he perceived as being inferior to him and human life generally counted for nothing. Deprived of achieving what his bizarre fantasies had led him to believe he was entitled to—fame, money, power, women, and admiration—he found another way to be a king among men. He found a new way to play God and wield absolute power by deciding who lived and who died. As the schizoid's hallmark, their own death often comes with the territory and provides the proverbial blaze of glory that is all part of a malevolent worldview. It's also why, after a few years of going through the motions, Reid eventually abandoned all appeals of his death sentence. He simply chose to sit and wait out the inevitable—to permanently welcome the darkness.

Part VI

The Rest Stop Murders

"Satan has his companions, fellow-devils, to admire and encourage him; but I am solitary and detested."

—Mary Wollstonecraft Shelley, *Frankenstein*

Chapter 37

VOLUNTEER STATE

It was March of 1836 when legendary hinterlander Davy Crockett, the "King of the Wild Frontier," got clipped by Santa Anna's men at the Alamo. Despite his being mortally wounded, history has it that he managed to take down about fifteen Mexican combatants with him before ultimately being claimed by the Reaper. Crockett's legendary bowie knife was also reportedly later found buried inside one of his dozen attackers; it was only discovered once the dead were finally carried out of the mangled Roman Catholic mission on the morning of March 7, after a bloody thirteen-day siege. But as stirring as his last stand was, at least according to the Tennessee public school system standardized textbooks, Crockett was and remains more than just a war hero.

Raised in East Tennessee, Crockett had served with the state militia before being elected to the Tennessee General Assembly in 1821 and eventually the US House of Representatives. His courageous death at the hands of Mexican forces, not surprisingly, soon became the stuff of legend—not only back in his native Tennessee, but also across the whole of America. It also meant that, a decade after the Alamo when the Mexican-American War erupted, President Polk's nationwide call for 2600 volunteer fighters to enlist translated into 30,000 volunteers from Tennessee alone—many chomping at the bit to avenge Crockett's death. From that point onward, Tennessee became known as the Volunteer State. The name stuck.

In the face of danger or to defend the honor of nation and state, Tennesseans have always closed ranks and stepped forward with the best of them. It was volunteers from Tennessee, after all, who had enlisted for service in 'Nam before the draft cards arrived in their mailboxes in cities like Memphis, Knoxville, Clarksville, and of course Nashville. In many cases these men had been born and raised in similar conditions to those of one-time Queens stickball champ, boxing aficionado, and self-described hoodlum Pat Postiglione. By the autumn of '71, Pat was breaking bread with these same Tennesseans in mess halls in South Vietnam and later in Guam after enlisting with the Seabees. Many of these same men hailed from water-tower towns in Tennessee no one had heard of, towns where it's said the clocks have no minute hands and no one is ever in a rush. They were towns where a certain preindustrial pace of life centered on sweet tea and soul food, camping and card games by paraffin lamp. But when push came to shove, these same men knew how to spring into action with purpose. They were not only the first to volunteer but, at the remains of the day, could out-hustle any city slicker.

It was from these same volunteers that Pat first learned, after all, about things as diverse as Southern-fried grits and Southern belles, Printers Alley, and the Grand Ole Opry. After Pat was discharged from the Seabees in the summer of '73 and released from active duty, those stories had grown on him, with Nashville and the whole state of Tennessee becoming something of a personal obsession. Following the call of Music City in the fall of '77, he took a road from NYC to Nashville, knowing full well that, in addition to Southern hospitality, there would also be new battles to be fought. Finding himself as a transplanted Yankee in Dixie—a man with a goofy-sounding name and a man without a state—he also found himself as a man with a clear idea of where he wanted to be. For the second time in his life Pat enlisted once more for a mere pittance in terms of salary, this time with the Nashville Metropolitan Police Department in the summer of '80.

Fast-forward just over twenty-two years, and by 2002, Pat had logged nearly a quarter century with Metro, all but the first seven years spent as a homicide cop. His uninterrupted stint with the Metro Murder Squad alone actually trumps the total years of service of most comparable American police careers. By the time the strangest case of his career came along, one that would ultimately put his own life in the crosshairs of one of the strangest of the numerous serial killers he would ever encounter, Pat had served more time working homicides than most cops spent working—period. This was in addition to his seven years in police purgatory from 1980 to 1987, walking and driving a raptor lair of a patrol beat in the city's veritable heart of darkness known as 12South.

He'd come to Nashville once upon a time in search of adventure but stayed for the fight. In doing so, he'd also developed one of the strangest New York Italian-Nashvillian creolized accents ever heard. Going quickly from one-time visitor to full-time resident, from civilian to sworn officer, he had eventually risen to become a record-setting detective sergeant who would manage to clear and close some of the toughest and most noteworthy cases in the annals of American crime. They were the cases once thought unsolvable, where names and associated file numbers miraculously turned from red to black on the M Squad whiteboard while Pat continuously proved that, as in the case of "the Motel Killer," Michael Magliolo, *everything* is theoretically solvable—it's often just a matter of will.

Chapter 38

Defrosted

Sliding doors were set in motion on Friday, June 14, 2002, Flag Day, when Pat, following a hunch that took him back to his days on patrol on his 12South Nashville beat, walked into Betsy's Lounge at Glenrose and Thompson looking for any known associates of one Danny Rogers. The man he was searching for was a reptilian thug from Chattanooga who'd been lurking on both the Metro and TBI's list of most-wanted fugitives for close to two weeks. The list was a proverbial Mobius strip on which the names of known felons kept turning up for new offenses year after year and which usually led back to one of a handful of family names. But Rogers was a standout, and catching him had been a priority for Pat ever since the night Rogers had killed Dedrick Havis, a local, by shooting him in the back with a Colt .380 as the victim ran for his life. That cowardly act in itself, however, wasn't enough to make Rogers a priority target. It was that while Havis was dying and writhing in agony after being shot, Rogers walked up to the victim and undid his pants.

Pat thought the additional act of unfastening the pants and spending the extra time with the dying victim before abandoning whatever he had planned was nothing if not a peculiar MO. If nothing else, it was an act that helped Pat realize the shooting hadn't been some run-of-the-mill drug hit or gangland execution. It was an MO that helped him link the murder to an earlier slaying in a neighboring county where the victim also had his pants undone, and was then castrated with a flick-knife after first being shot. It was for this reason that Rogers had catapulted so quickly to the top of a list that was normally the boringly repetitive local who's who of Metro frequent flyers. On a list that, in the past, had included the miscellaneous sex offenders spiking cocktails along Broadway with date-rape potions, the hillbilly psychopaths like Paul Dennis Reid, and various hoods and gangs terrorizing the Section 8 housing projects, the inclusion of Rogers by that summer was particularly notorious.

When Pat darkened the door of the bar just after 7:00 p.m., he found none of the Friday-night regulars as he scanned the place in search of some of his usual paid snitches. There were no criminal signs of life inside the joint to keep Pat occupied, none of the usuals to roust for valuable leads on what, by the end of that year, would be a total of twenty-three unsolved murders in Nashville. While the figure had been greater in previous years, Pat hoped Danny Rogers wouldn't be one of the ones who got away.

Pat scanned the locals filling the smoky bar that night, that frequently changing but seemingly timeless cast of characters that had always populated the place. A guy in a sullied mesh-back cap that read "Dole-Kemp '96" sipped Beam and Coke and muttered something incoherent after he made Pat for a cop. The old proprietress running the joint—a woman who looked like time standing in a pair of shoes—also made Pat for a Metro man and shot him the fisheye while grumbling under her breath. An unattended can of Pabst Blue Ribbon fizzed on the bar; the jukebox played Tim McGraw while an out-of-towner excoriated his wife for not singing along; a handwritten sign at the register read: "No Checks. No Pets. No Weapons." After Pat's pager went off in vibrate mode, he was soon reminded of the world still turning outside—that Danny Rogers would need to wait. It would in fact be another five years, almost to the day, before Pat finally caught up to Rogers. In the meantime the other killers to come to Nashville weren't about to take a day off. It was also time for Pat to settle some old accounts. A new secret society was forming, one with a very simple mantra and mission: to let Music City get right with its past. It was time to thaw out the coldest of Nashville's cold cases.

As July and August '02 summer holidays for M Squad members were being sorted out, a new plan emerged for the future of the squad. While no one was sure who first thought of the idea, the plan quickly started to take shape—a radical idea that no one was certain would work or how it might end. By that fall, Music City was clocking in with over seventy-five murders a year. While it wasn't the most dangerous city in America, it had a reputation for particularly "bad" murders, some of the most bizarre, sinister killings in the country. There was a dichotomy between the city of family fun, good music, and good manners and the more grim reality of the city of horrors that had followed in the wake of the Nashville sound and the rural purge. It was now a city home to the Tom Steeples and Michael Magliolos of the world as much as it was that of Trisha Yearwood or Kenny Chesney—and they had only composed the tip of the iceberg. The senseless slayings of Sarah Des Prez and Marcia Trimble, the thrill killing of broken-down motorist Carl Williams, and the murder of Ethel Hethcote, slain in her bathtub in 1979, were all still unsolved. They also fit a special category of crime that Pat's North-to-South sensibilities told him had to be delved into further—that there were more crimes those killers still walking the streets must have been responsible for.

After looking at his squad's salutary solve rate achieved on his watch, Pat thought it was certainly worth the risk. It was an experiment that might very well also save lives. Other cops in the Metro M Squad agreed, as did the Davidson County District Attorney's Office. It was to be Tennessee's investigative experiment—cold cases that could be divided and conquered between the police and the DA. And so was born the as yet unofficial Metro Cold Case Unit.

With its members flying by the seat of their pants and with high stakes and the possibility of total failure, Pat and his colleagues were going down a previously untrodden path. A full-time cold-case squad, even if unofficial, was a radical concept at the time, at least by standards that Pat had envisioned. By 2002 only a handful of police departments in the US, Canada, and the United Kingdom had exploited fledgling DNA technology by creating time-limited ad hoc task forces focused on very select, often single, unsolved homicides. Those departments who hadn't quick-rigged task forces of their own by 2002 soon started seeing other cops being extolled by Bill Kurtis on A&E's seminal series *Cold Case Files*, and followed suit. Typically prefaced with the word *project* followed by some optimistic, ecclesiastical, or macho-sounding code name, these task forces typically focused on only the low-hanging fruit. They focused on the cases where there had been a prime suspect, but the cops had always been one clue away from the probable cause they needed for an indictment or to empanel a grand jury to examine the evidence. It was the missing piece of evidence that DNA testing, by the turn of the millennium, now regularly provided. Many of these same task forces were driven by a top-down managerial lust for some rare good publicity. Many times they did manage—often in spite of themselves—to clear some backlogged cases with zeal. Most of these same cold-case task forces were, and remain, known as sunset positions, ones staffed by burned-out detectives simply marking time and waiting out retirement. They were staffed by cops who'd kissed the ring of someone in senior command and received a cushy sinecure in return. By making their own busywork, like moving around paper and signing courier requests for lab samples, they're known as house cats, remaining confined to a dedicated office for their last few years on the job. Few of these task forces, with some exceptions, even reinvestigate any files in earnest, and, not surprisingly, not much gets done. Innovators and go-getters need not apply.

But the M Squad never had fit the mold of the usual detective unit. It was the mystery-murder squad; it was the squad that prioritized the not easily clearable cases, often also the toughest and most tragic. It was more *Mission Impossible* than *Cold Case Files*. This new full-time cold squad would similarly follow suit. It would be a special cadre of the M Squad's already premier-league detectives—the elite of the elite—with both a natural instinct and license to color outside the lines. It was also an initiative that came at a time when few police departments sought to develop a veritable A-team of detectives working with prosecutors behind the scenes to triage, prioritize, and attack cold cases using DNA and other innovative and forward-thinking investigative methods. Pat's entreaties for the creation of a dedicated cold-case unit of this magnitude included all its participants recognizing that DNA was a leg up in making headway on a case, but it was by no means necessary to screening an open/unsolved case back in for reactivation—for defrosting. DNA was a luxury, he insisted, that not every case they'd take on would offer. Many of the cold cases would instead require old-fashioned detective work—in some cases rewinding the clock decades and starting over again from scratch. These were the precepts that were the group's guiding light from day one.

Beginning with discreet meetings every week behind closed doors at the Nashville DA's office at the CJC on 2nd Avenue, the squad included a core group of founders: Sergeant Grady Eleam, Detective Terry McElroy, Detective Billy Pridemore, and, of course, Detective Sergeant Pat Postiglione as the commanding officer. Also in the unit was the Davidson County DA, Al Gray, in addition to Deputy DA Tom Thurman, who was heavily invested in attending all the meetings. They were all about to set the history of American crime on its ear.

They also began their sleuthing exactly where they should have, with the cold cases of Trimble and Des Prez. They were, after all, near-successive sex slayings from 1975 that were the collective clarion call for the creation of a dedicated cold squad in the first place.

Chapter 39

SOLANO

In that same fall of '02, as Pat was moving detective work and cold-case innovation forward into an uncertain future, it was also time to take a trip back—a full six years back—to the winter of '96. After all, in the meantime, there were still comparatively recent and very much active cases for him to work as part of his day-to-day M Squad duties. One such duty soon meant revisiting, in addition to the Des Prez and Trimble murders, the slaughter at the Exotic Tan in Midtown, over two decades after the infamous winter of '75. While some were already calling it a cold case, for Pat it had never been cold.

During the early months following the tanning bed murders, Pat had stumbled upon a possible future method worth trying in the case of linking Patrick Streater once and for all to the gruesome scene. It was a method tangentially revealed after scouring the file of Officer Francis Scurry, the career Metro patrolman gunned down in May of '96. While the idea and methodology would eventually help bring the double slaying of Tiffany Campbell and Melissa Chilton in from the cold, Pat would need to wait for his prime suspect to officially resurface—the now repossessed Ford Festiva Streater drove from Nashville already located by Grady Eleam in new hands by the time he retired—before he could apply it. In the meantime, the fledgling Metro Cold Case Unit helmed by Pat would do its best to make sure Blue Beret washout and inveterate stalker Patrick Streater wouldn't hurt anyone else. It would be the cops out west in California, however, who would manage to box Streater in, at least for the short term.

Following his attack on the elderly victim in her own home in the fall of '97, something had apparently spooked Streater, since there then seemed to be a lull in his otherwise escalating crimes. Either that or he had changed his MO just enough to ensure that his later activities, between the time of the decoy-clipboard home invasion and when police finally managed to catch up with him in California, were still waiting to be discovered. Whatever the case, it was in April of 2002, six years after the Nashville tanning bed murders and almost five years after the Roseville home invasion, when a keen-eyed citizen noticed Streater, back once again in otherwise sedate and vulnerable Roseville, suspiciously skulking the streets. Perhaps he didn't like the looks of Streater's now *really* weathered vehicle as it prowled through the affluent area with no apparent destination. Perhaps he remembered the string of random attacks on older females five years earlier by a man who was never caught. Whatever the case, the citizen saw fit to scribble down Streater's plate number. When Placer County sheriff's detectives arrived at Streater's door within a few days to follow up, they'd already run a make on him. They'd already seen the NCIC flag on Streater's name, a flag that had remained dormant for the better part of six years. What happened next was an unexpected gift.

Having shown up to question Streater about nothing more than the Roseville suspicious-person complaint, the plainclothes officers found Streater was more than cooperative. He was, in fact, almost *too* cooperative. Within only a few hours and following a series of unforeseen and bizarre interactions, Streater was in police custody for his string of sadistic thrill attacks in 1997, having confessed after only a subtle nudge to everything they only tentatively suspected him of. The winning streak suffered its only setback after a search warrant executed at his apartment failed to turn up the signature knife used in his last confirmed assault. His soon-to-be former wife, at last wise to his proclivities, escaped the unwanted notoriety by packing up and moving out to continue her career with the Blue Berets. With that, Streater was soon left to fend for himself in what would become his new home: the infamous California State Prison in Solano.

Located in the city of Vacaville, equidistant between San Francisco and Sacramento, the prison—colloquially known as SOL—has always been an over-crowded gladiator academy. As a contemporary example of Darwin's survival of the fittest, it is populated with ruthless prison gangs ranging from the Mexican Mafia and Aryan Brotherhood to the Black Guerillas and MS-13, all of them staking their claims and controlling their operations from the inside out—and the outside in. A maximum-security penitentiary now at nearly 200 percent occupancy and with up to three prisoners to a cell at a time due to overcrowding, it is for many an unofficial death sentence. While most inmates sentenced to do their time there arrive kicking and screaming, Streater would prove to be the exception.

Within only two days of his arrest, at his first appearance in arraignment court in Placer County, Streater pleaded guilty to all charges leveled against him for his earlier attacks on the Sacramento Valley seniors. Sentenced to serve twelve years in SOL for aggravated assault and burglary, Streater had put the matter to bed and thus ensured the investigation was closed as quickly as possible. Rather than stay in a comfy county prison and play out what would likely have been up to two years of motions and wrangling before trial, followed undoubtedly by vexatious and meritless appeals to delay things further—the typical felon's playbook—Streater was instead prepared to expedite matters and make a straight shot for the big house. It was certainly preferable to having the DA or police start pulling on the frayed strings of the last few years he'd spent in California— delving into his time in Nashville and wherever else he might have been since getting kicked out of the air force, the now missing DOD bayonet, or to look more thoroughly into what he'd been up to all day while his wife, naïvely trusting to the bitter end, believed he was at work as a full-time security guard.

Back in Nashville, Pat knew that with or without the bayonet still in Streater's possession, it would be time (and science) that would close the gap and finally bring him to account for what he'd done. Pat would make sure of it. The first thing Pat did once Streater started his twelve-year prison run, and before the Exotic Tan murders would become an eighteen-year-old cold case, was to obtain a search warrant for a cheap prepaid mobile phone, or "burner" phone, he learned Streater was hiding in his prison cell. Pat had learned in a roundabout way from a snitch at SOL that Streater had reportedly bribed a dirty guard to smuggle in the device for him. Once a toss of Streater's cell kicked loose the hidden phone, it revealed nothing about any communication with the outside world. Instead, it seemed the phone had a far more bizarre and unsettling purpose.

Any number of men serving hard time keep photos or other visual materials to gaze at and help pass the time; it's one of the recurring and comparatively tolerated mainstays of prison life. For some it is as close as they will ever get to a woman for years, perhaps for the rest of their lives. It's a theme also explored in the 1982 Stephen King short story that became the acclaimed 1994 film *The Shawshank Redemption*, where pin-up girls used by the protagonist to conceal his tunnel out of the prison became the perfect cover because every inmate—even with a psychopathic warden overseeing them—is expected to have some eye candy at hand to make life tolerable. In Streater's case, the phone was not used to call anyone, but for a very different form of visual inspiration and arousal. It was a twenty-first-century take on a prison pin-up girl, and a disordered and deranged one at that.

The media folder on Streater's typical early-millennium flip phone contained only a single image. Rather than being an image of Streater's now estranged wife or of some other woman, the phone's media folder contained a photograph of a knife. A black bayonet. Whether it was *the* bayonet—the one used as the murder weapon at Exotic Tan back in the winter of '96—or some other knife could never be determined. The visual resolution offered by that vintage model of phone did not permit experts retained by Pat to conclusively say that it was an image of the murder weapon, especially with the original bayonet for comparative purposes still unaccounted for. Regardless of its provenance, it was abundantly clear that the mere image of a knife, of any knife, for that matter, was what allowed Streater to relive his crimes.

Much like "the Shoe Fetish Slayer," Jerry Brudos, was found ogling concealed catalogues for women's shoe stores while serving prison time for his four highly paraphilic murders, the cell phone image of the knife provided the one erotic visual stimulus Streater needed to cruise through his next twelve years at SOL. It was a new type of proxy crime-scene souvenir—a new take on murder porn. With the original blade no longer available or accessible behind bars, the question that remained was which crime or crimes the image was helping Streater to relive. Another question was who took the photo and when. Not surprisingly, Streater did nothing to assist cops, Pat included, in learning the answers to these disturbing questions.

Roughly three years into his sentence and after the discovery of the contraband phone had removed his one and only fantasy tool, Streater unsuccessfully tried to hang himself in his cell. He was soon transferred to the secure wing of the California Medical Facility, located on an adjacent property, to be monitored for suicidal tendencies. The California Medical Facility has its own colorful history as home to former short-term residents including Charles Manson, who was there during brief layovers while presumed to be in mental or medical distress. Whether Streater's attempt on his own life was genuine or, like the Exotic Tan crime-scene staging, pure subterfuge so that he could get some time out of SOL by himself and to gather his thoughts to plan his next move remains unclear. What was certain, however, was that Streater, one way or another—while Pat carved a compelling circumstantial case out of what had previously been a formless lump of clay—would soon be due back in Nashville. His time was running out and he would soon be headed back to Music City to face the music. It was richly ironic. For a second time Streater was coming home.

Chapter 40

Lucky Bounce

The timing of the formation of the combined Metro-DA Cold Case Unit was fortuitous for a couple of reasons. First, its advent coincided with the elusive Streater popping back up on police radar. That would be the first of what would be a record number of cold-case murders solved on Pat's watch in coming years—a record that still stands—as he and his team flipped the dial on over thirty years of serial and sexual violence that had engulfed the city. Second, it brought Pat closer with a number of high flyers in the DA's office, men who shared his Gotham City–like passion for fighting crime, and men who, like Pat, knew that pulling out the stops in an attempt to solve cold-case homicides was owed to victims, families, and the community.

One of the prosecutors Pat worked with was a no-nonsense advocate named Tom Thurman, one of the Cold Case Unit's founders. As a deputy DA, he was a brass-knuckles tough and fearless Harvey Dent–meets–Jack McCoy figure who soon affectionately became known among Pat, Pridemore, and the rest of the M Squad as "The Thurmanator." It was well deserved. It was a nickname that was coined on the heels of what would be a relic of the past that Pat and his provisional cold-case team would reactivate as the second open/unsolved tackled during their first year of operation—the murder on Music Row. This time it meant turning the clock back thirteen years to March of '89 and the unsolved shooting of Kevin Hughes from *Cash Box* magazine.

Pat didn't believe in coincidences, much less in luck. What he did believe in was the development of an underground economy in snitching and deal

making—a bull market in criminal intelligence developed through paid informers and leveraged inmates. He especially knew, as later accurately and brilliantly
depicted in the first season of HBO's groundbreaking series *True Detective*, that
murder cases—even serial-murder cases and especially cold cases—often break
through a tip or new piece of evidence gleaned from the drug world. Having
seen it all before, Pat well knew that drug dealers are the hubs to which the
spokes of a thousand other crimes are connected. Whether through the exchange
of money, information, or the drugs themselves, they are the ties that bind all
facets of the criminal underworld. They equally can serve as effective instruments
in dismantling that world if it suits them—if they can be "flipped" through the
use of a variety of incentives. A turned drug dealer who finds himself in legal
trouble can often be used to connect any number of dots once they're prepared
to make a deal to save their own skin. And they always do. That's exactly what
one pusher from Chattanooga did in order to get himself out of a pinch in the
fall of '02.

The stoolie in question was a comparatively small-time dealer, but big
enough to be collared in a joint FBI-DEA sweep, and soon found himself looking to play *Let's Make a Deal*. Facing at least a "dime"—a ten-year stretch at a
federal prison—and mentally dying a slow death within any one of the number
of concentric rings of hell at either the McCreary Penitentiary in Pine Knot,
Kentucky, or the even more odious USP Atlanta, the one-time cocaine pusher
started singing. The first person he gave up wasn't a Chattanooga drug-scene
player but instead a Nashville thug named Richard "Tony" D'Antonio, a name
that meant nothing to the federal agents putting the squeeze on their latest
catch. In time, however, the name would have currency in Music City, after the
M Squad received a courtesy email from the DEA agent in charge. It turned
out that Tony D'Antonio, the one-time right-hand man for Chuck Dixon, had
also been the muscle for *Cash Box* magazine. The informer now working for the
Feds also said he'd sold D'Antonio a gun just before a shooting on Music Row
that he heard about. The informer said he thought the gun in question he sold
D'Antonio was *the* gun.

After a check on D'Antonio's name in Metro's records came up empty, a
further check of the statewide TBI database had a few noteworthy incidents,
including possession of marijuana and some other petty crimes that linked
D'Antonio on paper to some noted underworld characters. While he also had

some listed known associates who weren't convicted felons, Chuck Dixon wasn't officially one of them. In terms of police information, the two had not been seen together under circumstances in which they might have been field interviewed, or "FI carded," through a street-level intelligence report or had their affiliation otherwise logged for tracking purposes. Pat thought the fact that they were widely known associates by virtue of being linked to *Cash Box* during the turbulent payola days but were not linked in the police database as associates was outwardly suspicious. It suggested that they had gone out of their way to avoid being seen together and that there was a reason why they wouldn't want to be cross-referenced or affiliated on paper. It also suggested that the informer might well be telling the truth and had sold the murder weapon used by D'Antonio to silence Kevin Hughes on Dixon's orders. While the lead felt genuine, Pat and the Cold Case Unit would still need much more than just the word of an incentivized drug pusher.

After a separate local, state, and federal check on Chuck Dixon came up empty, it seemed to Pat that Dixon had kept a low profile since the whole payola scheme was exposed and people started looking at him, suspicion ever lurking, for the murder on Music Row. Hedging his bets, Pat then moved to one of the handful of office terminals with an internet connection and loaded Netscape. An online search, or what cops refer to as an open source check, revealed in part why Dixon hadn't recently popped back up on police radar. He'd been dead for over a year. Whatever had happened in March of '89 and whatever his involvement had been, he'd taken the secret to his grave with him. The man who had grown up poor in Section 8s and got rich quick through payola and other rackets and schemes, cartelizing the country-charts business for many years in the process, had learned a thing or two about keeping his mouth shut from watching *The Godfather*, reportedly Chuck Dixon's favorite film and the blueprint he used for his life's work. He is said to have compulsively watched the film at least four times a week, every week of his adult life, fancying himself as the Vito Corleone of *Cash Box* and all of Nashville, for that matter. But with Dixon now out of the picture, they'd have to get more inventive to solve the Hughes murder as the next cold case to validate the new unit's existence.

Pat, after enlisting the assistance of a couple of the M Squad detectives moonlighting on the fly as cold-case investigators, headed southeast down I-24 to Chattanooga, the so-called River City. His plan was to search the property where the .38 revolver had reportedly been sold to D'Antonio and where, according to the snitch, he'd also allegedly test-fired it. Pat was taking similar ballistic steps to those used back in '96 to link Tom Steeples to the death of Ronnie Bingham, Steeples's inaugural dive-bar murder. He and his team were hoping for successful results again this time, but given the time elapsed since the murder on Music Row—now a full thirteen years—he was less than hopeful. But as much as Pat always said he didn't believe in luck, he was about to be its beneficiary for yet another time.

With the help of a TBI forensic team, an excavation of the property at the address provided by the coke pusher who'd sold D'Antonio the gun turned up a number of spent .38-caliber rounds in the ground—lots of them. It was only a matter of days before the projectiles were forensically linked to the bullets used to fell Kevin Hughes and maim rising star Sammy Sadler that fateful night on 16th Avenue. With the ballistics evidence and the testimony of the Fed informer now providing more than enough probable cause to at least arrest D'Antonio, the hope was that, like the dealer who sold him the gun and ratted him out, he would also fall on his sword. Once in custody, however, D'Antonio wasn't talking—not to Pat, not to any other cops, not to any inmates, never opening his mouth other than to enter a not guilty plea at his first arraignment. It seemed that Dixon had taught him a thing or two about remaining circumspect. The police response to his muteness was to call in the Thurmanator to prosecute the case.

Tony D'Antonio, by then fifty-six years old, went to trial in early 2003 for the nocturnal hit on Kevin Hughes that had been orchestrated, as best anyone could tell, by Chuck Dixon. The Thurmanator, with Pat at his side, had built from scratch a largely unassailable prosecution. Combining loose threads of circumstantial evidence, the dubious word of a reformed drug dealer, and the compelling ballistic evidence recovered from an out-of-town address thirteen years after the fact, he wove a logical and cogent tapestry that countered every defense argument about what they did *not* have, which was admittedly a lot. They didn't have the gun; they didn't have video, biological, or eyewitness evidence; they didn't have a confession or even a confirmed motive. As to motive, the theory advanced by the prosecution in court was that Dixon, lacking the courage to do it himself, had D'Antonio kill Hughes to stop Hughes from going public and tearing down his whole payola scheme at *Cash Box*. The further theory was that

Sadler, in the wrong place at the wrong time, had been shot either to eliminate potential witnesses or to obfuscate the real target and motive.

While fighting a seemingly uphill battle, given the limited evidence available, the prosecution marched on. It was confident, it was tenacious, it was relentless. Thurman vigorously pursued the prosecutorial theory; and the strategy, much like the investigation led by Pat that had resulted in the trigger man's arrest, remains a case study on how to proceed without, as is often the case, the proverbial smoking gun—how to conduct a solid investigation in what are so often imperfect cases. The brilliantly narrated but logically dubious true-crime podcast *Serial*, which became a breakout hit in 2015, gives the impression that murder cases are never or should never be built on imperfect timelines, the evidence of shady witnesses, and circumstantial facts. The reality is that, while imperfect, that is precisely how and why the vast majority of murder cases are solved and later successfully prosecuted. Before CCTV, DNA, and other abbreviations and initialisms became the go-to methods for solving murder cases, the challenge of credibly assembling a case was the nuts and bolts of real detective work. The willingness and fortitude to later prosecute those same tough cases is also the essence of legal advocacy, a concept that benefits victims of crime and the public interest just as much as the accused.

By November 2003 when it was all over, Dixon having managed to skate on the Hughes murder by virtue of having checked out early, D'Antonio alone paid the price. Already in declining health himself and convicted of murder and assault with intent to commit murder that same September, D'Antonio, on November 7, 2003, at the Davidson County Criminal Court building on Mainstream Drive, was sentenced to life at a lesser-known pokey in the state of Tennessee—Nashville's Lois M. DeBerry Special Needs Facility on Cockrill Bend Boulevard. It was effectively a death sentence in a maximum-security palliative-care facility for so long as he could manage to keep breathing. It would be a happier ending than the one inherited by one-time rising star Sammy Sadler—his music career ending the night he was shot as a witness to the Hughes hit. It was also a more merciful ending than that of Kevin Hughes.

Chapter 41

Heir Apparent

By the time the dust had settled on the D'Antonio trial, it was already 2004. One year later, the previously unofficial cold-case squad would come out of the shadows. With two key wins under its belt, it was time to go public and to unveil itself to the city and state. In the wake of its success in solving the 1989 Music Row murder in particular—Streater still officially California's problem and not an indictment they could yet claim as their own—the brass buttons at Metro headquarters saw an opportunity and took it. No longer an unofficial entity headquartered and meeting weekly in the DA's office, by Valentine's Day '05 the M Squad was blessed with its own officially sanctioned, officially legitimate cold squad that operated in house. It seemed natural that Pat should be in charge; it seemed natural that Pridemore should be his partner, that the Thurmanator would review and prosecute most of the charges brought forth. The more things changed, the more they stayed the same.

It was not long before the now fully accredited Metro Cold Case Unit once again showcased its vigor. In August of '05, almost nine years to the day after the mysterious disappearance of wife, mother, and respected illustrator Janet March, Pat managed to close the file once and for all—not to mention against all odds, traveling to Mexico to arrest the shifty Perry March for his wife's death. It was a rare—almost unheard of in Tennessee—indictment for murder one with the victim's body still missing. It was also a testament to Pat's verve for risk taking and pushing the toughest cases to the wall, a willingness to jump the turnstiles when and as needed.

The arrest and extradition of Perry March was a sonnet to the gumption that it takes to build a murder case without a body to work with, much less to confirm that a murder even occurred. What there was instead was Pat's meticulous assemblage of puzzle pieces accumulated over close to a decade, from the time he had headed the M Squad to when he founded and led what would later become the Metro Cold Case Unit—the elite of the elite. By the nine-year anniversary of Janet's disappearance, it was that investigative perseverance and familiarity with the case that had Pat flying Janet's husband back to Nashville from Guadalajara via Los Angeles for a much-belated court appearance, his still-missing wife's family all in attendance. Brought before a judge to face an overdue arraignment on a count of murder one—Janet having been declared legally dead for several months by that time—Perry might well have also been indicted for offering an indignity to a corpse. Whatever Perry had done to conceal his wife's remains, Pat and his colleagues figured by the time of his arrest it was bad enough that, if by some miracle she were ever found, it wouldn't be in one piece.

The case later took an unexpected turn after it was speculated that Arthur March, Perry's father, had assisted in transporting Janet's body to Kentucky, where it was believed to have been interred, whether in whole or in parts, beneath what is today an upscale golf and country club. The father had also reportedly been involved in a plot orchestrated by Perry from prison, following his arrest in Mexico and later extradition to Tennessee, to have Janet's entire family, his own former in-laws, killed en masse. In the end, through a combination of brilliantly assembled circumstantial evidence ranging from credible anecdotal reports of blood being cleaned up in the March home by Perry's father, financial evidence, and long-term behavioral indicators that now form a fledgling area of forensic expertise known as suspectology—which included Perry threatening an attorney in Mexico that he would do to him what he did to Janet—both Perry and Arthur March were ultimately convicted and sent away. Perry, convicted of first-degree murder, received life in prison while his father netted a sentence of five years of federal time for the conspiracy to commit murder and aiding and abetting his son. He died midway into his sentence due to respiratory failure in December of 2006.

While by that same holiday season of '06 it had newfound—and profound—legitimacy and had certainly yielded tangible results, the Metro Cold Case Unit had a comparatively quiet rest of the first two-plus years of official operation. As well, none of M Squad's current cases included the type of dangerous serial killers that had inexplicably often ended up in Music City during the eighties and nineties. It seemed, at least for a short while, that it was to be a period of peacetime. But Pat knew that it was too quiet, that there would be more to come. He continued to scour old files looking for cold cases whose original paperwork from the fifties, sixties, and seventies was still intact enough to make them worthy of reactivation and short-listing; he still obsessed over the Trimble, Des Prez, and Williams files; he continued to be the nocturnal running man, jogging the streets of suburban Nashville during the witching hours night after night. All the while, he waited for the other shoe to drop. It finally did on the morning of June 26, 2007. That's officially when the rules of the game changed—when Pat would, before long, find himself in a showdown with a killer whose methods had no precedent. Even in Nashville, where some of the most sick and twisted serial killers had come to roost on Pat's watch, there was nothing in the rulebook to tell him what to do when a killer chases the cops back.

Full circle: In June of 2007, while hunting the Rest Stop Killer, Pat confers with legendary forensic pathologist and "the King of Crime Scenes," Dr. Henry C. Lee, who had previously led the identification of remains found at the site of the 9/11 World Trade Center attacks. It was the same building complex where, just over three decades prior to their meeting in Nashville, a precop Pat had assisted in installing the HVAC system as a heating tech and native New Yorker. Courtesy of Pat Postiglione.

It was a muggy Monday in the early morning twilight when Pat was paged to the rear of the TravelCenters of America, locally known as TA, at 111 North 1st Street after an overnight security guard doing his rounds had discovered evidence of a most twisted murder. While precinct detectives from general homicide had been the first responders, Pat, sensing bigger trouble, had additionally sent, on behalf of the M Squad, Detective Lee Freeman. After hearing of the circumstances from Freeman, he knew that his instincts had been right, that the murder had the telltale markings—literally—of Music City's next serial killer. From that point on, Pat took charge and personally took on the case. It was a

decision that put him on a collision course with a new breed of mobile maniac—
a highway serial killer who knew no boundaries, who followed no rules. After
Pat had gone head to head with so many troubling serial killers during his career,
during which "the Fast Food Killer," Paul Reid, took his place at the top of the
list, it now seemed ten years later that there was a new heir apparent.

After Pat himself arrived at the TA rest stop early that morning, he wondered
at first if the woman, later identified as twenty-five-year-old Sara Hulbert, was
perhaps yet another "missing-missing" woman—a marginalized female taken,
trafficked, or otherwise made to vanish without anyone noticing until her body
finally turned up dead. Pat had certainly seen it before. They were the cases
indelibly seared on his subconscious for decades, and an unending number of
murder investigations later. With the day's brightening sky, the emerging natural
light allowed Pat a more detailed look at exactly what had been done to Sara.
Pat's observations suggested that rather than something done in haste or in
anger, her murder had been mentally rehearsed and done before. It spoke to a
certain degree of homicidal experience that her killer had brought with him to
Nashville. It was the work of someone who, having first cut his teeth elsewhere,
had come to Nashville to unleash hell on earth. Even before he made the first
entry in his notebook, Pat, for a number of reasons, knew the scene read "serial."
That it was the beginning of a whole new nightmare.

Discovered in the shadows of I-24 just before 1:00 a.m. at the foot of a
broken-down chain fence used as a cut-through for drug pushers and prostitutes
accessing the TA lot from the weed-laden vacant properties that lay beyond,
Sara's dead body was in a most unusual position. While Pat had seen prostitutes
and other women killed by truckers or otherwise dumped at rest stops or turning up on the shoulder of the highway, in a ditch, or along some isolated county
road, Sara Hulbert instead had been transported and *posed*. It was a distinct step
indicative of what's known as expressive violence, when a killer takes extra time
and associated risks to manipulate the body of a victim for a very specific purpose rooted in either fantasy or theatricality, sometimes both. He needs to create
a defined bloody diorama of his work for himself. He also needs to enhance the
shock value of the crime for others to discover.

In this case, the visual the killer was intent on creating had involved leaving
Sara's naked body on its back with her legs splayed but also supinated inward
so that the soles of her feet were touching, with her legs forming a symmetrical

diamond pattern, as if simulating a common groin stretch used by athletes. Pat knew in this case there had to be some far more sinister narrative purpose behind it all. He also noted a large bullet hole to the head and a contact burn indicative of having been shot at point-blank range. It was an execution-style murder and associated injury that brought Pat briefly to the still-unsolved case of Carl Williams in 1994, another casualty of the national trucking scene passing through Nashville in the night. But in Sara's case, there was, more notably, a total absence of blood at the scene. As Pat later determined, young Sara, a drug-addled and alienated prostitute, had last been seen by two "friends" just a few hours earlier as she walked off into the darkness by herself. Between the time she was seen heading from the area of the TA rest stop toward the infamous Cowan Street stroll, running adjacent to I-24, and the time when her naked corpse was found by a TA night watchman, she had met her killer. Sara, looking to turn her life around and get out of the game but having come across a bad john that night before she got her chance to start clean, had been slain somewhere else and then driven to the site as a very purposeful disposal and display location. In 2007, it was as good a spot as any in Nashville to leave a body undetected. But just dumping the body and being gone again wasn't good enough for the latest Music City killer.

Unlike the type of well-lit highway service centers most weary vacationers and business travelers might expect, the TA rest stop in 2007 was, like so many interstate rest stops along America's highways, a nether region of the long-haul trucking world where the faint of heart need not go. Affording truckers, as intended, a darkened respite from the toils of the road, a place offering basic amenities and the luxury of some private shut-eye, these places have all sorts of other secondary uses. Highway rest stops are also now classified by the FBI as "known vice areas" since they are equally places where the drug and prostitution trades flourish—where life frequently can be cheap. It's for this reason that the FBI created the Highway Serial Killings Initiative in 2009, a specialized task force dedicated to connecting—and ideally solving—some of the over three thousand unsolved serial murders believed to be connected to highway rest stops and the trucking industry.

At the time Pat inherited the Sara Hulbert case, he alone was aware of over twenty former truckers who had been incarcerated for acts of serial murder. He was also chasing another one, whom he was privately calling the Good Samaritan

Killer—identity unknown—for the murder of Carl Williams and no doubt many other broken-down motorists across the country. In Sara Hulbert's case, given the body disposal location at the TA site and the additional fact that she had last been seen headed for Cowan Street to score crack, he strongly suspected that her killer was likely a trucker who also dabbled in hard drugs. His instincts predicted there would be more victims to follow and that there were likely also existing previously claimed victims at rest stops across the South and Midwest. While the posing of the naked body as the crime-scene signature—an element unique to the offender's psychopathy and disordered fantasies—was certainly unusual for a serial-killer trucker, the modus operandi was even more so.

With most serial murderers also tending to rape their victims and to use their hands to kill them—strangulation being present as a contributing cause of death in over 90 percent of cases—the anomaly here was that Sara, showing no signs of strangulation, had been shot at close range with what was later determined to be a .22-caliber rifle—neither an easily concealed nor common murder weapon. As well, though her body was found naked, a sexual homicide by definition, she had not been raped. The evidence additionally suggested that she had been expeditiously and efficiently killed at an undetermined second location before being transported and posed at the TA site with the intention that her body be found there. With no evidence that there had been a struggle or that Sara had put up a fight, her killer, seemingly controlling the entire crime beginning to end, had been nothing short of cold and methodical in his actions, as if he had purposely hunted Sara down like game. Leaving nothing of himself behind but for a subtle running shoe impression embossed in some mud near the body, he had also managed to take something with him as an aide-mémoire of his crime.

When a large avulsion on Sara's right buttock was noted, and a chunk of flesh was found to be missing, Pat's conversations with her known associates confirmed it had been the location of a small weathered tattoo of a pair of red lips she'd gotten years earlier. It was a tattoo that her killer had carved out to keep as a memento of his crime. Unlike a souvenir taken from murder scenes, which typically consists of jewelry, clothing, or identification—much like the key chain taken in the case of the Exotic Tan murders—when living tissue is taken, it is what's instead called a trophy. It typically points to very specific and high-risk paraphilias like necrophilia and cannibalism as being the driving force behind a killer's compulsions. It also often points to there being a ritual element to the murders. If nothing else, it confirms the killer won't stop. Pat knew that whoever killed Sara Hulbert, the mystery man who would soon have all sorts of monikers—the Prostitute Shooter, the Truck Stop Slayer, and most commonly, the Rest Stop Killer—was already back on the highway. He was picking up where he left off. He was back on the hunt.

Chapter 42

LOT LIZARD

Nashville was only the latest in a series of stopovers for whoever had murdered Sara Hulbert and posed her naked body at the TA rest stop. No longer hampered as he had been in previous investigations involving serial murderers who ended up finding their way to Music City, Pat was now able to make full use of the much-improved NCIC and ViCAP databases. With a few keystrokes he was able to immediately send up a virtual flare that a killer with a very specific MO and signature appeared to have most recently struck at the TA stop on 1st Street, a place which is one of the busiest trucking interchanges in America. Not all that many years earlier, Pat would have had to make laborious written requests one at a time to neighboring agencies, or to cold-call homicide detectives in cities he figured might have also been hit by the same killer he was chasing.

By the summer of '07 it required only a couple of nationwide alerts on the servers of NCIC and ViCAP before, in what felt like record time, some other open/unsolved slayings in other jurisdictions seemed to match. Specifically, three other murders from earlier in 2007 alone popped up in Pat's email, one from another county in Tennessee and one each from Georgia and Indiana. That was soon followed by another four that trickled in and which all seemed to square with what was done in the Sara Hulbert case, one from as far away as New Mexico. The crimes shared some key commonalities since all the victims had been shot in the head, all the bodies had been found at or near highway rest stops, and all the victims had been females engaged in prostitution at or near those same rest stops. They were what the local cops and truckers who picked them up unsympathetically referred to as lot lizards.

The mere existence of these so-called lot lizards does much to dismantle the mythology of long-haul truckers as the keepers of the interstate system—the white knights of the open road. While most long-haul truckers are indeed hard-working men and women who keep food on tables and the country's economy moving, there is also a notable subculture that operates within the shadows of this arcane world. A great many also find themselves, for one reason or another, at rest stops looking for sexual favors, drugs, or both, and are prepared to pay for one with the other. Lot lizards, as rock-bottom addicts selling their emaciated and often diseased bodies for meth, crack, opioids, or all of the above, are willing to get inside the sleeper cab of an anonymous trucker, with nothing to lose. With two proverbial strangers passing in the night, things unsurprisingly often go bad.

The cover of darkness, anonymity, and the privacy of transactions afforded by America's seemingly countless highway rest stops usually prove them to be the most convenient locations for buyer and seller to meet for such purposes. This is in large part why these places are classified by the Feds as "vice areas" that pose disproportionate risks of victimization. It's because they also attract another element: those in the business for all the wrong reasons. These are the long-haul drivers whose depraved fantasies go far beyond the tacit expectations of anonymous parking-lot assignations. With long-haul trucking statistically ranking as the third-most-common semiskilled occupation among male serial killers, rest stops are little more than target-rich hunting grounds where they can troll for victims and, if need be, dispose of their victims conveniently. Following the responses Pat had received following his nationwide police alert, it was soon apparent that, just like Sara Hulbert, a number of other women working rest stops along the interstate had also found themselves in the wrong truck during their last night on earth. Pat was now almost certain it had in fact been the *same* truck.

The open/unsolved murder cases from other jurisdictions and loaded into ViCAP that had tentatively matched the Hulbert job at the TA lot in Nashville soon popped onto Pat's computer screen in short, telegram-like bursts. They were entries, each written in quintessential cop shorthand, that read as though he was reviewing the Hulbert file again and again—the same grisly details with only the names and dates changed:

01-29-2007—Suwanee, GA: Deborah Ann Glover, age 43, a known prostitute originally from the Atlanta area. Found naked from the waist down and shot through the neck with a .22-caliber rifle. Body found in a vacant lot near a Motel 6 off of I-85, a known stopover for truckers, her face covered in garbage and debris, presumably obtained from a nearby trash receptacle in the same lot.

02-02-2007—Lake Station, IN: Sherry Drinkard, age 43, an area streetwalker and sex worker hailing from the city of Gary, found at a TravelCenters of America rest stop on US Route 51 at Indiana Toll Road. Found at the rear of the lot in a dirty snowbank. While not posed, the body had been left in an "unusual" position, her arms and legs bound with black electrical tape. Victim had been shot through the head with a .22-caliber round, likely from a long gun. Estimated to have been at the site for almost a week before being found.

06-06-2007—Lebanon, TN: Symantha Winters, age 48, a known sex-trade worker with priors for solicitation. Found naked and shot through the head with a .22 rifle. Body was located stuffed in a dumpster in a Pilot truck stop parking lot.

As Pat pored over the grisly, blotter-like details of each of these murders and noted the overwhelming similarities, he followed up by directly contacting each of the detectives in charge, asking for the ballistics evidence they had in each case. Every one of the detectives told him that .22-caliber rounds are notoriously difficult to link to the same gun—an esoteric detail Pat already knew from the earlier fast-food murders, since Paul Reid used a similar type of weapon. In any event, they would still provide the ballistics evidence requested. Pat had Lee Freeman, one of his top case men, drive to each of the police departments to personally collect the evidence before then returning with the spent rounds recovered from three victims' bodies. Again, Pat was drawing on the cases of the past to inform his approach to the rest-stop slayings that had come to Nashville. He remembered in detail how the tedious but revelatory drive to Cincinnati with Billy Pridemore to see Detective Ed Zivernick during the motel murders fifteen years earlier had expedited the closure of the case and the identification and arrest of Michael Magliolo before he could kill again.

While Freeman was on his circuitous journey to collect evidence from police departments in three different states and likely more yet to be discovered, Pat turned his attention to spending what seemed like countless monotonous hours reviewing grainy and substandard surveillance footage from the TA Stop on 1st Avenue. Focusing on the June 25–26 overnight interior camera footage for both the main cash area and the exterior footage of the parking lot, he examined both sets of recordings frame by frame in the hope of catching something out of the ordinary—or perhaps something even a little *too* ordinary. The camera footage and ballistics evidence for the moment offered alternative avenues of hope in the investigation. This was in part because the partial footprint recovered from the mud at the site where Sara Hulbert's body had been posed was, it turned out, unusable. Not yielding enough detail on the shoe's make, model, and tread pattern—what are known as common characteristics—much less any individuating marks with respect to scuffs, scratches, or wear patterns—what are known as unique characteristics—the footprint was a dead end. It had offered nothing to move the case forward or justify putting out a public alert. In addition to his review of camera footage, Pat also had the well-intentioned manager at the TA methodically go through all receipts for any credit card or UltraONE membership card purchases made at the kiosk or pumps for the twenty-four-hour period leading up to the discovery of Hulbert's body. Continuing to scan with a consuming focus each and every frame of the surveillance footage from the rest stop, Pat paid particular attention to the two-hour window before the discovery of the body by the security guard—the approximate time the medical examiner said she would have been killed. It was during that review when something caught Pat's eye.

Just before midnight on the tape, a keen-eyed Pat noted something that other cops reviewing surveillance tapes might well have missed. At that very juncture, a notable mustard-yellow truck riding bobtail—deadheading somewhere with no trailer attached—was seen to pull into the lot in a rather tenuous fashion, as though the driver wasn't sure where he was going. Pat knew, given that most experienced truckers view a rest stop as something of an oasis on the horizon, that there would usually be no uncertainty about their intent and their need to pull in for fuel, some chow, a shower, or whatever. He then noted, after the truck made a loop of the lot as though looking for someone—or something—that the driver pulled nose-first into a space at the very rear of the lot, as far from the main building as possible. It was a location out of camera range for the CCTV system and just a few yards from where Sara's body was found a little over an hour later. Pat knew that pulling in nose-first, even when riding bobtail, was, in its own right, out of the ordinary since truckers normally reverse in as a matter of absolute habit, as a matter of muscle memory. The exception would be in cases where there might be a reason not to do so—an intervening factor that overrode their usual routine and led them to consciously change how they parked. Offloading a body from the passenger side and out of view of the cameras might be one of those reasons.

After a few minutes of footage, the truck was then seen to reverse into camera range before it sped out of the lot much more quickly than it entered. Unfortunately, throughout it all, the driver himself was never captured on CCTV and never was seen patronizing the main building or gas pumps. The camera had also been too far away, the artificial lighting in the lot too hazy, and the recorded images too fuzzy to obtain a license plate number. Pat's next hope was that with no trailer on the back, there might be a decipherable DOT number on the side of the tractor. While he was able to make out a partial number ending in what appeared to be "24," there could be no certainty until the frame was professionally enhanced and analyzed. It would be the next item on his investigative to-do list. In the meantime, Detective Lee Freeman had returned from his two-day trip to Indiana via Georgia. He came bearing gifts.

The three samples recovered from police evidence rooms in three other jurisdictions by Freeman and driven back to Music City, together with the .22-caliber bullet recovered from Sara Hulbert's autopsied brain by Nashville Metro forensic investigators, were all immediately sent as a rush order to the TBI crime lab in Nashville just before the weekend. The now one-week-old Sara Hulbert investigation seemed to be gaining some traction, in no small part as a result of Pat's hunches and gumption. Before he inherited the Sara Hulbert slaying, detectives from three other police departments had all unknowingly been looking—albeit not too hard—for the same man. The common connection between all four murder scenes would soon be made by lab techs when, in spite of the difficulties associated with comparisons of the stubborn .22-caliber bullet type, confirmation was received that the projectiles in the Glover, Drinkard, Winters, and Hulbert murders had all been fired from the same weapon. It was a four-way match that conclusively established that Pat and the M Squad were indeed dealing with a highway serial killer, almost certainly a long-haul trucker who knew the nation's rest-stop scene, one whose unusual calling card was to shoot his victims at close range. While that had been the calling card to date, Pat also knew that MOs can evolve, devolve, or change entirely depending on the killer's mood, level of sobriety, or the response of his victims. Within a week of the breakthrough news from the TBI lab, it seemed that the Rest Stop Killer was ready to start experimenting, unaware that police had linked four murders to his gun. By sheer coincidence it seemed that his experimentation might now include additional weapons.

Chapter 43

BUTTERFLY EFFECT

On the morning of July 11, 2007, an oppressively humid Wednesday in Music City, Pat received word via NCIC and a statewide alert of a double event on July 1, five days after the Hulbert slaying, that he sensed could only be the depraved handiwork of the Rest Stop Killer. With these open/unsolved files only just hitting the wire, no one else seemed to suspect that the latest and near-simultaneous discoveries of dead women in Alabama and Tennessee were related to the killer who had claimed Sara Hulbert and at least three other sex-trade workers at or near US interstate truck stops. All six slayings had been the work of one killer. Pat knew it had to be.

The first discovery came on the evening of July 1 when police in Birmingham, Alabama, discovered the naked body of forty-four-year-old Lucille Carter behind a trash bin outside the Conoco truck stop near the city's congested Finley Boulevard. Carter, a known transient and drug user who turned tricks when needed, was found with a plastic bag taped tightly around her head and had been slowly asphyxiated before then being shot in the head with a .22-caliber pistol while screaming inside the sack. It was a crime that recalled the murders of both Deborah Ann Glover and Sherry Drinkard earlier in the year, Deborah found with her face covered and Sherry bound with tape. The disposal of the body in a dumpster also mirrored the same disposal pathway—transported and concealed—seen in the murder of Symantha Winters, not to mention the garbage subtext present in the three other murders. Pat recognized that the killer was mixing up his MO, that he also was becoming more brazen as the intervals between his crimes were shortening. He suspected that the killer would get sloppy and soon deviate entirely from his usual routine. He was right.

Later on that same July 1, there was the additional murder of a woman named Robin Bishop at a Flying J truck stop in Fairview, Tennessee. Like the others, Bishop was a middle-aged "lot lizard" who had taken to frequenting rest stops where clients didn't discriminate based on age and where vice cops were seldom, if ever, seen making busts or running sting operations. Located about sixty miles southwest of the Winters dump site in Lebanon and about thirty miles from the Hulbert scene at the TA on North 1st Street in Nashville, the Fairview Flying J was just off I-40 where it runs parallel to the enticingly named Drag Strip Road, a place where good artificial lighting after sunset was all but nonexistent. There was sufficient light, however, for a witness, still on scene when Bishop's crushed and mutilated body was discovered in the parking lot, to describe a distinct yellowish truck he had seen trying to run Robin down after she appeared to have jumped out of the sleeper cab in a state of terror. Describing the truck as having either an ugly beige or yellow appearance under the cover of night, the witness had also been able to vaguely describe the driver. It was during the afternoon of July 11 that the description went statewide and made its way to Pat's desk.

After reading the description, it occurred to Pat that the Bishop murder bore a striking resemblance and suspect description to the murder of a woman named Belinda Cartwright at a TA rest stop in Valdosta, Georgia, on February 22, 2001. While hers was one of the victims' names initially provided by the ViCAP team in the days following the Hulbert murder when it was clear there was yet another serial killer on the loose, Pat hadn't initially given the case too much weight because of the odd cause of death, the lack of a firearm used, and the fact that Cartwright hadn't been a prostitute. She was, however, a wanderer and a hitchhiker with a history of mental illness who, like Robin Bishop, after entering the cabin of a big rig for no more than a ride, it seemed, had then tried to escape. She too had then been run down by the truck, being dragged for some distance and crushed to death beneath several of the eighteen wheels of the hulking machine. The observant witness in that case, apart from confirming that the driver was a regular at the TA stop, was able to work with a police sketch artist to build a composite drawing of the suspect. Six years later, with history seeming to repeat itself and the killer revisiting an earlier MO in the murder of Robin

Bishop, a picture was gradually coming into focus. By then, the Rest Stop Killer was already two states away and on to his next target.

During the night of July 11, the same day the description of the Fairview, Tennessee, killer had been circulated, the killer struck again. His latest victim would turn up nearly three hundred miles north of his last crime scene, this time at the Flying J rest stop on West Thompson Road off I-465 in Indianapolis. It was sometime around 8:00 p.m. when thirty-one-year-old Carmen Purpura, trying, just as Sara Hulbert had, to get her life back together for the sake of her children, made the mistake of getting into a yellow truck, towing a large trailer emblazoned with an anodyne motto about wood products, that appeared completely low risk. What, if any, words were then exchanged between Carmen and the driver hauling handcrafted family furniture remains unknown. As had happened countless times before—and will happen again elsewhere—Carmen simply entered the cab, shut the door, and unknowingly embarked on a hor-rific one-way trip. Whatever the Rest Stop Killer had been rehearsing with the uncharacteristic yet careful posing of Sara Hulbert's body and cutting out of her tattoo as a morbid trophy of his crime, he was now prepared to take to the next level with Carmen Purpura. It was a decision that, as Pat had predicted, would be as calculated as it was cruel and devious—one that would eventually bring Pat and the most nomadic serial killer to ever strike Nashville into a final showdown.

It was the next day, the morning of July 12, when the conscientious manager at the TA on North 1st Street in Nashville, having finally consolidated all the hundreds of receipts for the twenty-four-hour period surrounding the Hulbert murder, called Pat at the M Squad HQ to tell him everything was ready for pickup and analysis. With Detective Freeman having already made the lengthy trek to Illinois and Georgia for the ballistics samples, Pat decided that it was his turn, even as the boss, to get in the car and run the errand himself. He opted to head out to the TA to grab them himself also for reasons of evidentiary continuity—to see what else he might be able to glean from the scene, even weeks later, by revisiting it in broad daylight. While a prudent and pragmatic decision, a standard investigative precaution born of Pat's decades of experience being cross-examined in Tennessee courts, it was also a decision that would change the course of events to come in a way that no one could have ever predicted.

It was just before 10:00 a.m., and Pat was driving an unmarked Chevy Malibu southbound over the Jefferson Street Bridge, headed for the TA to see the manager and grab the pile of receipts, when an oncoming northbound vehicle caught his eye as it crested the hill ahead. Seeing an odd-looking yellow rig pulling a full silver trailer slowly driving in the opposite direction, Pat did a double take before, adrenaline pumping, he suddenly realized that it was *the* truck. It was the same tractor unit he'd seen on the video-surveillance tape pulling into the TA lot with no trailer attached, the same truck observed circling and then parking nose-first in the area where Hulbert's body was posed. The color of the Freightliner cab—a signature mustard yellow—was unmistakable. As his Metro-issue sedan and the truck passed each other on the bridge, Pat caught a fleeting glimpse of the DOT number on the side—a number that ended in a two and a four. There was no mistaking it; it was the truck from the tape. The Rest Stop Killer was back in town. Back for what, Pat was soon to find out.

Pat was caught unaware, completely off guard, when the killer's truck emerged, showing itself in such sudden and unexpected fashion. As Pat exited the south end of the bridge, preparing to pull a U-turn on the quick to go after the rig, he glanced in his rearview mirror to see something even more unexpected. The truck had itself used a large commercial lot on the north end of the bridge to also turn around; it was now headed back toward him—toward his position and toward the TA rest stop. It was headed back to the scene of the crime.

Pat, quickly cutting east and driving into a plaza lot, watched from a safe and discreet distance as the ominous rig headed southbound off the end of the bridge. The truck then entered the TA lot where, just as it had been seen doing in the CCTV footage, it began to circle the lot. It was then that a pair of yahoos in a murdered-out Mitsubishi Eclipse with the top up—limo tint, lacquered headlamps, bass thumping, Georgia tags—pulled in front of Pat to park their ride. In doing so they unwittingly blocked his viewpoint from the plaza and temporarily put the truck out of sight. Pat threw the Malibu back into drive and pulled to the plaza's exit, where from a new angle he could now see the rig edging in nose-first again. It appeared to be awkwardly maneuvering just as it had on the CCTV recording from the night of June 26 but with a trailer attached this time, pulling cautiously into a nondescript area that was, yet again, just out of camera range. It appeared to be preparing to park near the same spot by the same fence where the mutilated body of Sara Hulbert had been placed a little more than two weeks earlier. It was effectively, in a wide-open lot with a hundred other better options, the *same* spot. As he had previously noted, Pat knew it was a noncustomary, noninstinctive way for an experienced trucker to park a rig, unless something—or someone—needed to be surreptitiously offloaded from the passenger side, which faced away from the lot toward the empty clearing in the distance. Pat then knew that the driver was his man. It was time to finally meet and take down the elusive Rest Stop Killer. It was now or never.

After calling in his position to Metro dispatch, he rolled up on the idling rig with an Illinois tag number and a trailer that read "Quality Wood Products." The Illinois plates were registered to a company known as Carter Woodworking, based near the small city of Albion, Illinois. Detective Lee Freeman, monitoring the Metro detectives' radio band that afternoon while out in the field on other cases, radioed that he, along with a couple of uniform cars, would start making his way to the TA stop to back Pat up. Freeman knew the case well and knew that if Pat was calling in a possible match on the rig, it was legit. But Pat decided he wasn't going to wait for reinforcements—he couldn't. Whatever was about to happen was going to happen now; whoever was behind the wheel of the truck that day needed to be stopped from leaving. An unforeseen series of cause-and-effect occurrences that began with the discovery of Sara Hulbert's body had ensured that, from that day forward, the paths of Detective Sergeant Pat Postiglione and the elusive Rest Stop Killer he was chasing would refuse to diverge. "I'm making a driver-side approach," Pat barked into his portable radio, and he began the long walk to the idling big rig.

Chapter 44

JOE SCHMOE

As Pat walked up to the idling truck, the morning sun reflecting off the sleeper cabin windows obstructed his view of what was inside and who might be looking back out at him. Instinctively drawing his police-issue Glock .40 caliber from its plainclothes pancake-style holster and holding it tight to his right side, he slightly bladed his body as he moved in closer, not knowing when the driver's door might pop open or who might come out at him from an elevated position. In inching closer, Pat was back where he had been just over two weeks earlier, standing only a few paces from where Sara Hulbert's body had been found naked and posed. Once he moved in close enough to avoid the sun's glare off the auto glass, he saw that the curtains for the sleeper area of the cab were drawn across the rear windows, concealing the interior in darkness. While it was a common step to take for truckers bedding down for the night, whoever drove the rig into the TA lot this morning wasn't planning on bedding down or staying for any length of time. The curtains were closed for another reason.

Grabbing the vertical metal handle on the driver's side with his left hand while keeping his Glock down low in his right hand, Pat hoisted himself onto the box step, which quaked in unison with the rumble of the engine beneath his oxford loafers—a pair of stainless-steel Peterbilt exhaust stacks reverberated on either side of the tractor's front end. Just about anything could be going on inside the truck, he figured, since he couldn't hear a thing with the engine on. Rightfully fearing that something sinister was about to happen and that there was no time to waste, Pat rapped on the tinted driver's window with the muzzle

of his gun, facing a monochrome reflection of himself dressed in his usual summer attire of a lily-white dress shirt and muted red-and-black tie, no sports
jacket. As he quickly took note of the tired look in his eyes and the toll of this
latest serial case on his complexion, the window powered down to reveal another
face staring back at him. It was unsettling, a real-life iteration of the police sketch
of the trucker who'd run down and murdered Belinda Cartwright at the TA
lot in Valdosta, Georgia, in February of '01. The driver was a disheveled fifty-
something white male with a ruddy complexion and unkempt sandy-brown hair.
Sad brown—almost black—eyes were concealed behind the type of wide-lens,
plastic-frame drugstore glasses that, somewhat inexplicably, seem to be favored
time and again by so many serial killers.

Pulling his Metro Murder Squad shield inscribed with "Detective Sergeant"
and the badge number "27" from his belt and flashing it to the driver while
declaring "Metro PD," Pat then half asked, half ordered him to shut off the
engine. The driver, looking bewildered and doing a double take at the badge
while he adjusted his spectacles, eventually complied and slowly turned off the
truck. Once he no longer had to yell over the noise of the engine, Pat made it
clear why a plainclothes officer was standing, gun drawn, on the box step of this
truck this Thursday morning.

"We're looking into a murder that happened here or somewhere nearby a
few weeks ago," Pat said to the driver as the odor of several days on the road and
the rancid stale air of the sleeper cab finally hit him. The man behind the wheel
of the big rig, looking surprised and acting concerned, muttered something
about having heard about it on the news after Pat gave him some bare-bones
details about the victim and what the cops had found. Upon a request from Pat,
the driver fumbled with trembling hands through a faded brown leather wallet
on his lap for his ID, keeping his eyes focused on the task. He ended up turning
over an Illinois driver's license, permits for tractor and trailer, a bill of lading
from Carter Woodworking for the load on board, and lastly an expired permit
for a .22-caliber rifle. The name on the license, the permit for the tractor, and
the carry permit were all in the name of Bruce Mendenhall, born April 14, 1951.

After Pat ran an NCIC check over his portable radio, the name and plates
for the tractor all came back negative—no wants, no warrants, no criminal
record. On the surface, Mendenhall seemed like a nice enough guy, the only
thing standing out being his perhaps explainable nervousness and suspicious

presence in the lot. While the paperwork suggested, unlike many of the truckers who frequented that TA location, that he was squeaky clean, Pat of course knew that he wasn't. Quite apart from the existing linkages to the Hulbert crime scene and Mendenhall's cagey demeanor, a voice inside Pat's head, a voice that spoke to him following nearly three decades as a murder detective who'd likely chased down more serial killers than any city cop in America, told him that he could not let Mendenhall leave that lot without searching the interior of the sleeper cabin. The problem was that, suspicions aside, he still didn't have enough—nothing, in fact—to provide the probable cause necessary in law for a search of the truck, much less an arrest of the driver. Until his backup arrived, he would have to buy himself time by keeping Mendenhall talking.

Pat went on to ask Mendenhall how long he'd been trucking, to which Mendenhall replied that it was just a little over six years. It was tenure that, if true, would have put the Belinda Cartwright murder in Georgia back in 2001 as likely his first murder—at least his first committed as a trucker. After Pat asked what kind of load he was hauling and to where, Mendenhall explained that he was transporting handcrafted wood furniture to a store in Dallas. It was about 10:30 a.m. when, while the trucker was confirming his end destination, Lee Freeman finally arrived in an unmarked olive-green Impala, followed in a matter of seconds by two marked Metro prowl cars from the South Precinct, all three vehicles pulling in tight behind the laden trailer to essentially block it in. Subtly holstering his Glock, Pat then asked Mendenhall if he would do his good deed for the day to help police eliminate him as a suspect in the Sara Hulbert slaying. The requested good deed was to provide a voluntary DNA sample by way of a buccal swab, something, as Pat explained, that could be done in less than a minute since he carried a field kit in his departmental car for this very purpose. Mendenhall, not missing a beat, agreed with a "Sure, if it will help" response. Pushing further, Pat then asked Mendenhall if he would sign a consent form to allow him and Freeman to search the interior of his truck for any evidence that might help with the investigation, once again to exclude him as a suspect. Mendenhall, playing it cool, continued to play the part of law-abiding and patriotic Good Samaritan—an old-time trucker who was still the white knight of the interstate—and agreed fully. "Sure, if it will help," he exclaimed once again, voluntarily signing the standardized consent-to-search form.

Upon venturing into the mustard-yellow cabin under the authority of the signed form, Pat immediately noticed some items that struck him as germane to the now at least six slayings scattered across three states that he had managed to connect to the same killer. They were the cases he had linked in part through the forensic ballistic evidence and in part through DNA matches, plus a large dose of seasoned intuition. Items in the cabin included a roll of black electrical tape and a butcher knife, the two items curiously stowed side by side in the driver's door panel. The .22-caliber rifle listed on the expired carry permit provided by Mendenhall with his other documentation was found in the back of the cab near a repellent bed with a garbage bag of rancid takeout food containers spilling out near the mattress. Then, Pat spotted a second bag resting on the passenger seat, as though ready to be offloaded, a bag that a less-seasoned eye might have assumed was also a generic trash bag stuffed to the point of bursting. While he was snagging it and taking a full five minutes to undo the intricately tied knot that kept the bag fastened, his instinct told him that the bag itself and whatever was inside would no doubt later be scrutinized a dozen times over by experts.

Once he had the garbage bag open, a smell hit Pat's nose that overrode even the ambient stench of body odor, secondhand smoke, unwashed linens, and garbage that pervaded the whole of Mendenhall's sleeper cab. It was a metallic, acrid smell he'd absorbed before, most notably in February of '96 at the scene of the tanning bed murder case on Church Street in Nashville's Midtown. It was the distinct and unmistakable odor of human blood in copious quantities. It was also a harbinger of what Pat would discover next.

First to come to his attention was a pair of women's Crocs-brand slippers along with a Samsung cell phone and a Discover card. Beneath the credit card, however, was a pile of sullied women's clothing and a pile of blue towels found commonly at rest stops, matted in blood of a particular shade of crimson that Pat knew was indicative of exsanguination, especially the blood loss from major organs to the point of death. The signed consent-to-search form was about to become null and void as Mendenhall's jeopardy had now changed and the search turned from an attempt to confirm or deny his involvement in Hulbert's murder to searching for evidence of new murders not yet discovered. Halting the search, Pat turned to Mendenhall, who was standing outside the open driver's door of the cab with two Metro uniformed officers, and posed, point-blank, the definitive question: "Is this the truck we've been looking for?" Mendenhall, looking smug and unfazed, responded with "If you say so." Pat fired back with: "Are *you* the guy we've been looking for?" Mendenhall stayed the course by offering the same "If you say so" response. At 10:44 a.m., the Rest Stop Killer, based on the additional evidence from the halted consent search, was officially under arrest as Pat put Mendenhall in handcuffs and Mirandized him. But it was far from being over.

After the truck and its contents were seized and towed to a secure police compound, Pat obtained a search warrant for both the tractor and the trailer owned by the woodworking company. This allowed him and the evidence team to more thoroughly search the contents of the bag beyond the cursory inspection at the TA stop that had turned up the bloodied towels and women's clothing. The credit card found before Mendenhall was arrested turned out to be in the name of Carmen Purpura; the number on the cell phone was a 317 area code, one of two for the metro Indianapolis region. Figuring that both items likely belonged to the same person, Pat called the Indy detective in missing persons and learned that no one by the name of Carmen Purpura had been reported missing to police—not yet anyway. Just like Sara Hulbert, Carmen, like so many women who eventually turn to prostitution, was in a subgroup of people on the margins who represent the missing missing. She was missing, but not yet on paper and not officially reported to police because no one was looking for her or had noticed she was gone. After some good local detective work managed to turn up a security-camera screengrab from an ATM in Indianapolis two days before the bag of her bloodied belongings turned up in Mendenhall's truck, this last known image of Carmen showed her wearing the same clothes later found in the truck along with her cell phone and credit card.

In the end, Carmen Purpura, forever to remain missing, was declared legally dead by the court. The murder indictment that later followed against Mendenhall was a replay of the Janet March case, when her husband had been successfully prosecuted for murder without her body ever having been found. The preponderance of all the other evidence, especially the quantity of blood, was sufficient, it was believed, to leave Carmen's death as the only reasonable conclusion to draw, even in the absence of her body having been found. Whatever happened between the time Carmen was last seen on the bank ATM camera and when her belongings turned up in a garbage bag saturated with blood at the same TA rest stop where Sara Hulbert's body had been found posed weeks earlier remains unknown. She was and sadly remains one of a still-undetermined number of women who mistook Mendenhall's innocuous, plain appearance as evidence of his being a low-risk client. Serial killers, with rare exceptions, usually evince this same generic Joe Schmoe facade, one that hides a sinister undergrowth. It enables them to convince people to open their doors at night, to enter a car on a deserted highway, or to accompany them somewhere unfamiliar. It's one of the reasons why serial killers like Mendenhall simultaneously fascinate and horrify us; they are our coworkers, our next-door neighbors, and even our blood relatives—wickedness hiding in plain sight. Even when they're caught, there is something strikingly plain and ordinary about their demeanor that makes the horrific scale of their crimes seem strangely out of character. They never seem to look the part. It was a pretense that Mendenhall would try to use to his advantage once he was behind bars while Pat and his team of investigators began to piece together the trail of carnage he had left along the nation's highways.

Chapter 45

Dead Time

Carmen Purpura wasn't the only one of Mendenhall's victims whose body was never to be found. Beyond the seven victims across three states already attributed to him—Belinda Cartwright, Deborah Ann Glover, Sherry Drinkard, Symantha Winters, Robin Bishop, Sara Hulbert, and Carmen Purpura—three other female DNA samples were found on the sullied mattress inside Mendenhall's Freightliner cabin. While two samples belonged to women yet to be identified, a third was found by September of '08 to be from a timeworn woman named Latisha Milliken, who disappeared from Nashville in the summer of '07. A crack addict with no fixed abode, Milliken was last seen in a homeless encampment known as Tent City off Hermitage Avenue and was reported missing by her family on the afternoon of June 26, 2007. Known to have frequented the TravelCenters of America rest stop off I-24, Milliken disappeared roughly a month prior to the murder of Sara Hulbert, and almost certainly constitutes Mendenhall's first confirmed Nashville victim. Her case remains in the open/unsolved category—her name lingering in red erasable ink on the Metro Cold Case Unit's whiteboard.

When Mendenhall, in custody at the old Nashville lockup at 200 James Robertson Parkway in the city's downtown, was formally interviewed by Pat, he never denied that the murders occurred—he admitted that he knew full well that the girls were dead and who had killed them. The simple fact, he asserted, was that he was not the murderer. Mendenhall claimed that two other Tennessee-based men whom he named, the purported masterminds behind the murders, had forced Mendenhall, a comparatively meek and easily manipulated trucker, to dispose of the evidence after the fact. The bag of Carmen Purpura's property and blood found in his truck was simply the latest example, so the story went, of his doing their bidding. The scenario as Mendenhall described it, while technically a confession as to his knowledge of all the murders, was used as an attempt to deny his involvement in the actual acts of killing, an attempt to deflect the heinous acts themselves, including the mutilation and trophy taking in the Hulbert case, to others. It's a compensating behavior, one known as neutralization, often seen across the board among various types of offenders, even hardened criminals. Its usual purpose is to downplay the harm of their actions to give them some false peace of mind about the gravity of their conduct. Its purpose in Mendenhall's case was to additionally sow confusion among the police and to buy himself what he hoped would be reasonable doubt at trial.

Mendenhall's story, however implausible, would still need to be checked out to clear the two other truckers named. Involving a series of steps requiring significant manpower, it would delay inquiries and probing into whatever else Mendenhall had done or what he may have been planning next. His tall tales of an interstate cult targeting sex-trade workers at rest stops—lot lizards, as he also called them—was a convenient, somewhat similar retread of another case. A comparable story had been offered up by infamous serial sex killer Henry Lee Lucas, "the Highway Stalker," after his arrest in June '83 for a series of murders committed with his dull-witted but sadistic accomplice Ottis Toole. Linked to the murders of three people while he nomadically wandered the highway system, Lucas would later falsely confess to killing over three thousand victims while part of a secret murder cult he claimed was called the Hand of Death, a Satanic society with highly placed people everywhere across America that was compelling them to participate. The very idea of such a group, whether fact or fiction, was itself a retread of the plot in a 1978 novel titled *Fair Game*, the later inspiration for the campy 1986 film *Cobra*, starring Sylvester Stallone.

The Lucas story was just believable enough that cops from far and wide came for months on end to meet with him, to listen to his stories, and to obtain confessions to open/unsolved murders, which he would inevitably provide for them as he looked to become known as the most prolific killer in history. Lucas had of course been lying and simply playing the authorities as a means to gain attention and notoriety. Mendenhall, by falsely accusing two others for the rest-stop killings, was doing the opposite as he sought to minimize his own involvement but also to sow seeds of doubt and muddy the waters. In due course Pat was able to rule out the two men named, through a combination of alibi, eyewitness, and DNA evidence. Mendenhall's fanciful story had even at one point included a third "suspect" who wasn't a trucker at all but a severely disabled man who had never so much as driven a car in his life. After the investigation of the red herrings offered by Mendenhall finally wrapped up, a full picture of the killer the police had in custody came into focus.

Mendenhall, before the early 2000s when he started driving a big rig and women began dying at his hand, had led a relatively normal life in comparison to most serial killers. Assuming his first semiconfirmed victim was Belinda Cartwright in February '01, he would have begun killing just shy of his fiftieth birthday, the only known American serial killer to have begun so late in life. In most cases, serial killers "age out" once their sex drive wanes and the disordered fantasies and eroticism of violence no longer occupy so much of their time and energy. Mendenhall, on the other hand, seems to have curiously "aged in" unless, as is likely, earlier victims are yet to be identified. In Mendenhall's case, there seems little doubt that there are other victims waiting to be identified from his earlier life back in Albion, Illinois. Pat's theory is that it was only the .22-caliber rifle, as the unusual weapon of choice for such a sadistic, trophy-taking, body-posing serial killer, that changed as Mendenhall grew older. That, and his transitioning into long-haul trucking to more easily acquire his victims. Having been diagnosed with Type 2 diabetes and having become insulin-dependent, Mendenhall by 2001 no longer had the strength or stamina, Pat theorized, to subdue, strangle, and prolong the deaths of his victims as he likely had during any still-unidentified murders committed while he was a younger man. The decoder ring that may link the rest-stop murders to any earlier crimes likely remains the case of Sara Hulbert, the first murder that put his serial crimes on the M Squad's radar. While the MO used by a killer can of course change, a killer's signature tends to remain stable across an entire criminal career. It's likely that Mendenhall's earlier victims also showed some indication of posing or of expressive mutilations that either had a ritual or trophy-taking objective, but that, like so many serial killers' victims, had these telltale behavioral indicators misread—or overlooked entirely. What the pose means—the legs splayed and soles of the feet pressed together—no one but Mendenhall knows. It remains an open question.

For unknown reasons, a switch seems to have been thrown in Mendenhall's brain in the late 1990s, beginning with an incident that people who know him say changed him—an event that, as Pat figured it, either lured Mendenhall into killing, like the belatedly activated psychopath Tom Steeples, or simply reawakened otherwise dormant homicidal impulses from his earlier years. After unsuccessfully running for mayor in his hometown of Albion, Illinois, Mendenhall later became strangely obsessed with a female hitchhiker he had picked up who, at the end of the ride, reportedly rebuffed his sexual advances. There was something about that incident—one most well-adjusted people would otherwise shrug off—which led to a period of extraordinary decompensation and an identity disturbance before Mendenhall took up his long-haul trucking career. This was about the time Mendenhall's wife of several years and the mother of his two children had herself acquired Type 2 diabetes and was suffering from progressive blindness and immobility. It was a perfect storm of factors that seemed to awaken whatever Mendenhall had been keeping at bay, the deviant impulses that had otherwise burned out with age.

Once Mendenhall's wife, Linda, finally succumbed to the disease and died in 2009, Mendenhall—by then indicted for a total of five murders, including the two Tennessee women—came into a modest inheritance by way of a life insurance policy taken out years earlier, with him as sole beneficiary. It was then that he began to plan his next murders. He'd begin with the man who was first to put it all together and who, by no coincidence, was also the man to bust him. Detective Sergeant Pat Postiglione was the first on Mendenhall's new hit list, after being suddenly flush with cash. If Mendenhall couldn't do it himself, he'd contract it out. Money, he knew, was a powerful motivator—especially among other inmates. And so, Mendenhall set his sights on finding a gun for hire. He became consumed with fantasies of revenge.

While serving what's known as dead time at the Music City lockup, denied bail while awaiting trial for the Sara Hulbert murder at the TA stop, Mendenhall made the acquaintance of another inmate awaiting trial on his felony charge of assault with a deadly. With the unusual nickname of C-4, the man, as the name implied, was an expert in high explosives. A former US Army demolitions engineer, he was a man who had fallen into a dark place and was soon dabbling in mercenary work for organized crime and street gangs following his discharge, mostly by blowing up cars and buildings between Nashville and Memphis for money. But unlike Mendenhall, who would be doing dead time until trial and then likely getting life with no parole, thus never getting out, C-4 was soon out on bail and roaming free until trial. He'd be the Rest Stop Killer's ace in the hole.

Mendenhall, with fifteen thousand dollars in life insurance proceeds burning a hole in his pocket and nowhere to spend it—his two children estranged from him after the spate of murder charges—saw an opportunity to put his new jail-house friend C-4 to good use following his pending release from jail. The bizarre plan was to blow up Pat, his partner Lee Freeman, and three civilian witnesses so they could not testify against him. Without any of them around to appear in court, Mendenhall's flawed thinking went, he might stand a chance of beating at least the two murder raps in Tennessee and the slaying of Carmen Purpura. He was especially interested in having the three civilian material witnesses, who knew something of his background in Albion, permanently silenced before the cops started to ask them more about his earlier years. It was their testimony he especially didn't want aired in a court of law on public record; it was their recol-lections of the past that Mendenhall saw as potentially the most dangerous to him in the long term. They were by no coincidence also the same men he had tried to implicate as being involved in the murders, the same purported gang of killers who'd coerced him into disposing of the evidence and who'd implicated him. Either way, whether in service to preventing the inclusion of inculpatory evidence or preserving phony exculpatory evidence, they all needed to die.

What Mendenhall didn't know about the man he knew as C-4 was that, though he was in a dark place in his life, he had standards, so to speak. C-4 was also nothing short of insulted by the notion that he was desperate enough to commit five capital murders-for-hire—including two well-known police officers—for a mere pittance of fifteen thousand dollars. C-4, knowing he would get more bang for his buck by putting on his snitch jacket and diming Mendenhall out to his lawyer, wanted to see what kind of consideration he might receive from the state of Tennessee in exchange for his full cooperation. Working with Metro and the TBI to corroborate just how serious Mendenhall was about eliminating both the police and the civilian witnesses, C-4 wore a wire while he and Mendenhall walked along the rooftop yard of the old jail. The Rest Stop Killer told the man he viewed as his own private hit man exactly how it all needed to go down and when Pat, Lee, and the witnesses would all need to be eliminated. Medenhall's bizarre logic was that it would then appear to police that the "real" Rest Stop Killer was still at large and that they had arrested the wrong man.

But the man known as C-4 was no dummy; he had been around long enough that he knew this information was worth far more than the usual snitch money. He went straight to his lawyer and parlayed the offer from Mendenhall into a sweeter deal from the DA. Once some carefully orchestrated recordings of Mendenhall asking C-4 to carry out the five murders were played for the judge at trial, everyone in Nashville soon realized just how twisted Mendenhall, despite his innocuous and frumpy exterior, really was. As predicted, for his cooperation, C-4 skated on all his outstanding charges and walked free. Mendenhall, on the other hand, got slapped with an additional five felony indictments, three for conspiracy to commit murder and two for solicitation of capital murder, all of them federal charges.

As of the spring of 2017, a full decade after the Mendenhall serial murders came to a close, he has been convicted of the murders of six of the eight women whose DNA he was forensically linked to, from samples found inside his truck. The murders of Belinda Cartwright at a TA truck stop in Valdosta, Georgia, and Robin Bishop at the Flying J outside Fairview, Tennessee, both run down by a mustard-yellow rig in 2007, the same year as the .22-caliber slayings, remain officially open/unsolved and the investigations still active.

Unofficially, most people in the know are convinced beyond a shred of doubt that Mendenhall is good for those murders as well. He also remains a suspect in at least five other slayings across four other states involving a similar MO and suspect description, as well as a priority subject for the FBI's Highway Serial Killings Initiative. For his attempt to have the man known only as C-4 eliminate five people, including Pat Postiglione as the man who brought him down, Mendenhall, after pleading guilty to three of the five additional charges, had a total of thirty years added on to the six consecutive life sentences he's currently serving at the Turney Center Industrial Complex, or TCIX, a mixed-security-level prison located in Only, Tennessee.

For all the carnage he wrought, Mendenhall is unfortunately just a drop in the ocean. Since the FBI currently has a total of over sixty offender profiles in its Highway Serial Killings Initiative databases, it means that there are at least sixty other Mendenhalls still out driving the interstate under the pretense of lawful employment, still trolling highway rest stops and on-ramps hunting for victims, whether hitchhikers, lot lizards, or others. They do so confident in their knowledge that by the time anyone misses the victims, or their bodies turn up, they themselves will already be out of state. Out of state and back on the road again. And the rate is accelerating.

Epilogue

THE BENEDICTION

"Beware the fury of a patient man."

—John Dryden, "Absalom and Achitophel"

When the eerie and archaic-looking Tennessee State Prison finally closed in 1992, the nearly fifteen hundred inmates housed there were moved to Riverbend Maximum Security on Cockrill Bend Boulevard in Nashville, the same expansive property where Music Row killer Tony D'Antonio would spend the remainder of his days in palliative care a decade later. One of the inmates being moved as part of the relocation was one Jerome Barrett, the Berry Hill and Belmont rapist who'd once spontaneously confessed to killing "four blue-eyed bitches" during a prison fight years earlier. The same Jerome Barrett who'd also ordered at least one murder on another inmate during his four-decade stint there. That same year, Pat Postiglione arranged for the delivery of a moving-in present for Barrett at his new cell at Riverbend: a hidden voice recorder.

Under the auspices of a wiretap affidavit authorized by a Tennessee judge, Pat had Barrett's cell under audio surveillance—or "gizzed up," as the slang goes—at varying intervals between 1992 and when he was paroled to the city of Memphis in 2006 after serving forty-one years of his forty-four-year sentence. In the meantime, DNA had come of age and the Metro Cold Case Unit had materialized, parsed off from the already stellar and highly specialized M Squad. By 2001, Pat on his own had also already confirmed his rookie hunch—from his time in Session 7 at the academy to his days working 12South—through the state DNA database that the murders of Marcia Trimble and Sarah Des Prez in the spring of '75 were indeed connected. A scene-to-scene DNA hit that year had confirmed that the semen found on both victims belonged to a common offender—a high-risk but unknown offender not yet in the state or federal system. A sex slayer, targeting both children and adults, who'd been off the grid for the last forty years.

With the cryptic statements made to himself or as part of his bravado in front of other inmates and guards captured on the hidden wire, as well as the fact that the Belmont U student Barrett was convicted of raping had happened to be living with her family just a block from Marcia Trimble's house in 1975, it was collectively seen as more than enough to swear out a warrant for Barrett's DNA the moment he was released back into society. On a summer afternoon in 2006, Pat did just that. He then drove to Memphis and met some local detectives and uniforms parked outside Barrett's cousin's house, where he was visiting at the time. Outside at the curb was parked a crass canary-yellow Hummer that Barrett, apparently immediately following his release from Riverbend only weeks earlier, had managed to lease with the help of his dying mother. He told her that he needed the truck for a landscaping company he was going to start and that it was all part of a fresh start. It would turn out to be the first job Barrett held since the winter of '75 when he volunteered at the Nashville mosque, handing out flyers near the Belmont and Vanderbilt campuses—the perfect cover for his stalking activities. Whoever had called the Trimble home anonymously while the Feds and local task force were listening over forty years earlier had been right. The cops should have checked the mosque and its volunteers. To this day no one knows who made the call or how they made the connection to Barrett—or who else knew of the connection. As the adage says, someone always knows something. It usually pays to listen.

After a court-ordered buccal swab was taken from Barrett's mouth in the rear of a Memphis prowl car that afternoon, it was simply a matter of time before the historical record was finally set straight and justice was done. Justice delayed, justice overdue—but justice nonetheless. As one part crime fighter and one part time traveler, Pat, by the end of 2006, was an open/unsolved luminary on a national level, leading the charge in thawing out cold cases and setting the example for the rest of America. Within a week he had a DNA match to both crime scenes from 1975, and by 2007 he had Jerome Barrett in custody and charged with the murders of Trimble and Des Prez, arguably Nashville's most infamous unsolved murders—two murders forever soldered together and the apotheosis of innocence lost. Pat's theory all along had been that Barrett had been simultaneously stalking Sarah Des Prez and the Belmont student he later raped but let live. His theory was that Barrett, regretting that oversight, had then returned to the Belmont victim's Green Hills neighborhood where she lived with her family to finish her off on the mild afternoon of February 25, 1975. That was when, by pure circumstance, he encountered young Marcia Trimble out delivering her Girl Scout cookies. It was then and there that the monster decided to take her instead.

Barrett, an inveterate coward to the end, would never cop to these crimes nor confirm or deny this theorized series of events. In fact, he wouldn't talk to anybody or admit to anything and even later turned his back on the judge upon being sentenced in July 2009 to serve life plus forty-four years for the murders committed that fateful winter some thirty-four years earlier. It took thirty-three days to find Marcia's body and another thirty-four years to convict her killer, but Pat, like M Squad captain Mickey Miller before him—the original lead investigator in the Vandyland murders—never gave up. In the meantime, Sarah Des Prez's father lived just long enough to see justice realized, dying within weeks of Barrett being convicted and sentenced for the murder of the daughter he discovered dead in her third-floor apartment back on February 2, 1975. One of Sarah's brothers, Walter, checked out even earlier, having separately chosen to take his own life rather than continue to live in a world where those types of unspeakable crimes go unpunished. If only he had waited a little longer.

In February 2013, four years after Barrett was sent back to Riverbend to live the rest of his pointless and pollutant existence, Patrick Streater was at long last indicted for the tanning bed murders, just as Pat had always hoped he would be. By August of 2015, having completed the prison sentence he was serving for the attacks on seniors in Roseville, Streater was extradited from California and returned to Nashville. He was brought back almost twenty years after the day when it all started, Valentine's Day. He was charged with two counts of first-degree murder for the double slaying at Exotic Tan. It was the air force–issue scabbard that ended up doing him in, as Pat had first predicted back in February of '96. While the printing and fuming of the sheath found at the scene on

Church Street had yielded no concrete results during the original investigation, DNA forensics had grown in leaps and bounds over the intervening years. It had evolved even further since it was used to snag Jerome Barrett for the most infamous cold cases in Music City history.

Forensic advances made during the first decade of the new millennium meant that "touch" DNA—the recovery of an offender sample through epithelials, or errant skin cells, left after the simple handling of an item—now permitted a latter-day definitive match on the scabbard to Streater's DNA on file in California following his later felony convictions there. It had been the sweat from his hands left on the scabbard when removing the blade that had left a distinct profile now suitable for DNA comparison. It was evidence that had remained intact and in sufficient quantity, even with that same sheath having been tested annually for nearly a decade, as DNA technology progressed and finally caught up with Pat's intuition. To this day, Streater's stolen air force–issued bayonet remains unaccounted for. The Exotic Tan case is still before the courts awaiting disposition while Streater also remains a person of interest in the now reopened September 1994 Oak Grove double murders of Candace Belt and Gloria Ross. With a trio of disgraced Kentucky cops having been charged and acquitted in that case—including the original detective leading the investigation—in the fall of 2016, Streater has once again landed on police radar. Between Oak Grove and Exotic Tan, it no doubt explains why he kept his head down and pleaded out as soon as he could, once collared by the Pacer County cops back in California. He'd done horrific things he didn't want the cops in California to ever know about. In the meantime, he remains out on bail awaiting trial—back home in Nashville living with his mother.

Jerald Gregory, the killer of Candy Moulton on Father's Day '89, is now out on parole for the twisted sex slaying that ended with four wooden spoons inserted in the vagina of the bound and gagged young housewife as she bled to death on her bed. Gregory has apparently tried to put that grisly and unspeakable crime behind him in a most unusual way: by becoming a gangbanger, now veiling his need to hurt people—his sexual attachment to violence—as being part of a well-rehearsed OG street thug persona and bona fide member of the Nashville Gangster Disciples. It's unlikely that his gang buddies and felon associates know the real story about why he ended up in Music City in the first place. It's doubtful they know the real backstory of how he ended up doing hard time in Tennessee as an eighteen-year-old cretin from Mississippi. Maybe now they will.

On the other end of the spectrum, fallen attorney Perry March is still serving a life sentence for the murder of his wife, Janet, whose body has still not been found. As a real lawyer turned vexatious prison lawyer, he now spends his days filing frivolous and equally vexatious complaints about the quality of the kosher food in the Tennessee prison system and how his rights are being violated.

Meanwhile, Paul Dennis Reid—arguably the worst of the worst—after finally resigning himself to the death sentence he was to eventually receive, instead died in prison of medical causes on November 1, 2013. It was a day for glad tidings.

In the end, Pat and his Cold Case Unit cronies would end up solving and closing a remarkable total of *fifty-five* open/unsolved murders between the squad's founding in 2005 and his retirement in 2013. It's a state, national, and as best anyone can tell, an international record for cold cases solved—usually through solid arrests, indictments, and subsequent convictions—that successfully drew on a variety of innovative old-school and new-school methods. It's a record that isn't likely to be topped anytime soon anywhere. Yet, to the end, Pat remains remarkably modest and self-effacing about it all. Maybe it's because he still feels he has unfinished business. And he does.

Of all the otherwise dormant cases he and his talented team would bring in from the cold and against all odds, the tragic case of Carl Williams, murdered execution style along I-40 in April of '94, is one that continues to haunt Pat into retirement. It's the one case that still nags at him, that keeps him up at night, that ensures he's still now and forever the running man. Maybe it'll be while he's out on one of his late-night asphalt odysseys that the break in the case will reveal itself, when a new investigative avenue previously unexplored will dawn on him. Maybe it'll be by his ensuring that he stays in touch with the living members of the Williams family—as he has with all the victims' families—that something elusive will reveal itself to him. Maybe it'll be by making certain that the case stays in the public eye almost twenty-five years later that a once reluctant witness or tipster will come forward and avail him or herself to the police so many years on. As Pat knows, whoever killed Williams has done the same thing elsewhere since then. The FBI also knows it, and that's in part why they invite Pat to present that case—and more recently the Mendenhall murders and attempted hit on Pat himself—at their highway serial killer conferences and workshops several times a year. The detectives, both Metro M Squad and FBI, now tasked with tracking homicidal truckers recognize full well that the Plains and the South are where these maniacs have always honed their skills. It's where they still do. The question that remains is what they do when they're not on the road. The question remains where and how they kill during their R&R time. It's a missing link that Pat's lifetime of work—and this book—can help shore up.

Maybe that's why, Pat being Pat, when it was time to hang it up in the spring of 2013, his idea of enjoying retirement meant going to work full-time back where his cold squad first achieved lift-off: the Davidson County DA's office. By the time he retired in 2013, he'd already been a golf widow since 2008, when Billy Pridemore packed it in to play the links full-time. Pridemore later got elected as a Nashville city councilor and offered tremendous support to his former colleagues once it was confirmed that his interim replacement, Lee Freeman, had been greenlit for execution along with Pat in the aftermath of the Mendenhall trial. In the wake of that turbulent rest-stop-murders saga, Freeman quit the force and went to work as a fraud investigator for the state of Tennessee. Not knowing what could possibly come next, Freeman hung up being a cop as soon as he could after being marked for death by a serial killer hell-bent on revenge. No one blamed him. He now has a good gig chasing hospital-bill cheats, insurance shysters, and other health care parasites bleeding the public coffers, for roughly the same salary and none of the headaches. It's a path countless good detectives have taken and will again.

All the while, Pat soldiers on, working a forty-hour week plus occasional overtime. The county now pays him to do police work from a different office but looking at many of the same cases. But the truth is, he'd do it for nothing. By conservative estimates, Pat's thirty-three-year career included nearly five years' worth of unpaid overtime as he took cases home with him and carried them everywhere he went, day and night. But Pat was, going back to his first application to the NYPD, never in it for the money. Always a runner and sports fan, he's more concerned with stats. Fifty-five cold cases solved in eight years just wasn't enough. Even though he has singlehandedly caught more serial killers, as best anyone can tell, than any detective either living or dead on record in America, a record unlikely to be broken anytime soon, he feels it still isn't enough. There's still more to be done.

There are still the cases of not only Carl Williams but also the disappearance of thirteen-year-old Tabitha Tuders, last seen walking to her school bus stop on 14th Street in April of 2003. Like Janet March, she's presumed dead, and her body has never been found. Going back ever further—back even before Marcia Trimble and Sarah Des Prez—there was the case of twelve-year-old Kathy Jones, found dead in November of '69 after disappearing en route to the skating rink near her home, her skates with laces intertwined found next to her tiny frozen body dumped in the woods. Bound and gagged, she choked to death on a sweat sock stuffed down her throat. It was an unsolved murder prefaced by the equally heinous murder of fourteen-year-old Reba "Kay" Green, inexplicably stabbed to death in her own bed while her twin sister beside her remained untouched on a cold night in January 1966. Then there's Wanda June Anderson, age eleven, found dead in her backyard on 16th Avenue South, raped and bludgeoned to death in July '65 while babysitting her six nieces and nephews. Like in the case of Reba Green the following year, the other children remained untouched—Wanda having somehow been lured out of the home before being attacked with a pipe. It is all the stuff of nightmares. It is also the crux of Pat's career—his raison d'être. He was and forever remains a Yankee in Dixie. Forever the running man.

ACKNOWLEDGMENTS

This was an ambitious, albeit overdue book. It is a book that is one part true crime and one part human interest story—the untold social history of a city that for most visitors is their happy place. Like Pat Postiglione in 1977, Nashville is their bucket-list vacation destination. It's an experience, whether real or imagined, that for most visitors usually ends up being reverse engineered as being happy by necessity. It's also an experience usually limited to only a half-dozen manicured and largely surreal city blocks where no one has ever heard of the horrors that happened in Nashville once upon a time. If by fluke they have heard of them, they're not willing to discuss them. Not then and certainly not now.

This book by extension also represents a scholarly and intrepid research project that would have never come to fruition absent the assistance of some earnest and learned colleagues. Beginning with my own time on the ground in Nashville spent as a visiting scholar at Vanderbilt, I'd like to thank my host, Dr. Bob Barsky, and the faculty's dean, Dr. Martin Rapisadra, for their wonderful collegiality, professional support, and, in the tradition of academic freedom, permission to explore—and lecture on—this project and my other books to the great interest of students, faculty, and staff. To this same end, I'd like to thank Brad Hector and the rest of the senior staff at Fulbright Canada in Ottawa, along with the US Department of State, for making my time at Vanderbilt as a graciously invited visiting scholar possible in the first place.

On the topic of my brief time in Music City—too brief, in fact—in addition to the overwhelming debt of gratitude owed to this book's real-life protagonist, Pat Postiglione, for his unwavering assistance and for trusting me with his life's story, I'd also like to offer thanks to some of Pat's erstwhile colleagues and ongoing friends within the ranks of the Nashville Metro PD. These include but are not limited to public information officer Don Aaron for arranging my ride-alongs and Officer Austin Kendrick, who took me out on patrol to see the Nashville not seen on MTV, CMT, or any TV, for that matter—much less in any brochure or on any website. Thanks are also due to the rest of the officers I met and broke bread with during my time there. The department—still effectively known only as Metro—remains among the most professional, tolerant, and progressive I've had the honor of seeing in action. That includes not only within the United States but also in my native Canada and beyond. That alone merits mentioning.

In terms of Canadian law enforcement, I've offered thanks in previous books to those who stand out as progressivists in a profession often known for the opposite. I restate my thanks here to those same committed men and women who are often faced with extraordinary challenges from both the inside and out, and who sometimes question their calling. Special thanks are additionally due in this case to Constables Grant Worral and Eddie Earl of the Waterloo Regional Police, Sergeant Ryan Fairful and Staff Sergeant Kim Reynolds of the Western University Community Police, as well as retired deputy chief Brent Shea, Staff Sergeant Ryan Scrivens, and Constables Omar Hassan and Andy Michalski, all of the London Police Service.

I also owe a special debt to my colleagues, the academic leaders and luminaries spearheading the three think tanks where a great deal of the original research in the book originated. Specifically, I owe a boatload of gratitude to Tom Hargrove and Eric Witzig of the Murder Accountability Project, Dallas Drake of the Center for Homicide Research in Minneapolis, and Enzo Yakzic of the Atypical Homicide Research Group in Boston. Special thanks also to the various members of these groups, all of which I am proud to be a part, for their shared wisdom and experience, including retired police detective Steve Daniels in Wisconsin, professor and criminologist DJ Williams at Idaho State University, and psychiatrist Dr. Michael Welner of the Forensic Panel. Credit also goes to Dr. Welner for the reference to Lady Macbeth as the first murderous "undoer" on record, used earlier in this book. My two research assistants at Western University, Jackie Reed and Jeremy Fairfall, also deserve special mention, as do Professors Christopher Keep, Jan Plug, James Johnston, Michael Fox, Tim Freeborn, Kathleen Fraser, and Brock Eayrs. While on the topic of Western, I'd also like to thank—as usual—the volunteers with my Cold Case Society, especially recent standouts Maryam Khan, Emily Kingsmill, and Stacy Van Acker, emeritus members Lance Freer, Brikena Qamili, and Mack Boudreau, as well as my 2IC, Professor Neisha Cushing.

Lastly, a special heartfelt thanks to the very gracious and prescient Vivian Lee and the entire editorial team at Little A Books; my literary agent Grace Freedson; my television agent Sohrab Merchant; and my lawyer, Danny Webber in Toronto. In this industry as much as policing—perhaps strangely more so—it's important to always have backup.

With gratitude,

Michael Arntfield, PhD

NOTE FROM THE AUTHOR

As we go to publication, Patrick Streater appears to have withdrawn from plea negotiations and is publicly challenging the DNA evidence in the defense of an otherwise circumstantial case. His guilt or innocence in the tanning salon murders of Tiffany Campbell and Melissa Chilton remains unresolved at this time.

SELECTED BIBLIOGRAPHY

Aamodt, Mike G. "Serial Killer Statistics." Radford University/FGCU Serial Killer Database (last modified November 23, 2015). http://maamodt.asp .radford.edu/serial killer information center/project description.htm.

Adams, David. *Why Do They Kill? Men Who Murder Their Intimate Partners.* Nashville, TN: Vanderbilt University Press, 2007.

Aggrawal, Anil. *Forensic and Medico-legal Aspects of Sexual Crimes and Unusual Sexual Practices.* Boca Raton, FL: CRC Press, 2009.

———. *Necrophilia: Forensic and Medico-legal Aspects.* Boca Raton, FL: CRC Press, 2010.

American Psychiatric Association. *The Diagnostic and Statistical Manual of Mental Disorders,* 2nd ed. Arlington, VA: American Psychiatric Publishing, 1968.

———. *The Diagnostic and Statistical Manual of Mental Disorders,* 5th ed. Arlington, VA: American Psychiatric Publishing, 2013.

Anderson, Benedict. *Imagined Communities: Reflections on the Origin and Spread of Nationalism.* London: Verso, 1983.

Arntfield, Michael. "Cybercrime & Cyberdeviance." In *Criminology: A Canadian Perspective,* 8th ed. Toronto: Nelson Education, 2017.

————. *Gothic Forensics: Criminal Investigative Procedure in Victorian Horror and Mystery*. New York: Palgrave-Macmillan, 2016.

————. *Mad City: The True Story of the Campus Murders That America Forgot*. New York: Little A Books, 2017.

————. *Murder City: The Untold Story of Canada's Serial Killer Capital*. Victoria: Friesen Press, 2015.

————. "Necrophilia in Literature, Poetry and Narrative Prose." In *Understanding Necrophilia: A Global Multidisciplinary Approach*, 109–20. San Diego: Cognella Academic Publishing, 2016.

————. "New Media and Necrophilia." In *Understanding Necrophilia: A Global Multidisciplinary Approach*, 161–72. San Diego: Cognella Academic Publishing, 2016.

————. "Towards a Cybervictimology: Digital Predation, Routine Activity Theory and the Anti-Sociality of Social Media." *Canadian Journal of Communication* 40, no. 3 (2015): 371–88.

Arntfield, Michael, and Marcel Danesi. *Murder in Plain English: From Manifestos to Memes—Looking at Murder through the Words of Killers*. Amherst, NY: Prometheus Books, 2017.

Arntfield, Michael, and Joan Swart. "The X-Factor: Corporate and Occupational Psychopathy in Law Enforcement Management and the Operational Impact on Cold Case Homicides." *Journal of Cold Case Review* 1, no. 2 (2015): 50–68.

————. *Social Media and Mental Health: Depression, Predators and Personality Disorders*. San Diego: Cognella Academic Publishing, 2018.

Bauman, Zygmunt. *Liquid Love: On the Frailty of Human Bonds*. Cambridge: Polity, 2003.

Beauregard, Eric, Matt DeLisi, and Ashley Hewitt. "Sexual Murderers: Sex Offender, Murderer, or Both?" *Sexual Abuse: A Journal of Research and Treatment* 00, no. 0 (2017): 1–19. https://doi.org/10.1177/1079063217711446.

Beauregard, Eric, D. Kim Rossmo, and Jean Proulx. "A Descriptive Model of the Hunting Process of Serial Sex Offenders: A Rational Choice Perspective." *Journal of Family Violence* 22, no. 1 (2007): 449–63.

Ben-Ze'ev, Aharon, and Ruhama Goussinsky. *In the Name of Love: Romantic Ideology and Its Victims*. Oxford: Oxford University Press, 2008.

Bouchard, Martin, and Patrick Lussier. "Estimating the Size of the Sexual Aggressor Population." In *Sex Offenders: A Criminal Career Approach*, 351–71. Edited by Arjan Blokland and Patrick Lussier. Malden, MA: Wiley-Blackwell, 2015.

Brenner, Charles. *An Elementary Textbook of Psychoanalysis*. Garden City, NY: Doubleday, 1974.

Bugliosi, Vincent. *Helter Skelter: The True Story of the Manson Murders*. New York: W. W. Norton, 2001.

Burgess, Ann W., Cheryl Regehr, and Albert R. Roberts. *Victimology: Theories and Applications*. Burlington, MA: Jones & Bartlett, 2013.

Bursik, R. J. "Social Disorganization and Theories of Crime and Delinquency: Problems and Prospects." *Criminology* 26, no. 4 (1988): 519–51.

Butler, Samuel. *The Way of All Flesh*. Reprint, North Chelmsford, MA: Courier, 2004. First published in 1903.

Canter, David. *Criminal Shadows: Inside the Mind of the Serial Killer*. New York: HarperCollins, 1994.

Canter, David, and Donna Youngs. *Investigative Psychology: Offender Profiling and the Analysis of Criminal Action*. Hoboken, NJ: Wiley, 2009.

Chalmers, Phil. *Inside the Mind of a Teen Killer*. New York: Nelson, 2010.

Chan, Aris C. Y., Philip S. L. Beh, and Roderic G. Broadhurst. "To Flee or Not: Postkilling Responses Among Intimate Partner Homicide Offenders in Hong Kong." *Homicide Studies* 14, no. 4 (2010): 400–418.

Chan, H. C., and K. M. Heide. "Sexual Homicide: A Synthesis of the Literature." *Trauma, Violence, & Abuse* 10, no. 1 (2009): 31–54.

Cleckley, Hervey. *The Mask of Sanity: An Attempt to Clarify Some Issues about the So-Called Psychopathic Personality*. Maryland Heights, MO: Mosby, 1941. Fifth edition facsimile reprinted in 1988 by Emily Cleckley.

Crowley, Kieran. *Sleep My Little Dead: The True Story of the Zodiac Killer*. New York: St. Martin's, 1997.

Cullen, Dave. *Columbine*. New York: Hachette Book Group, 2009.

Danesi, Marcel. *The "Dexter Syndrome": The Role of the Serial Killer in Popular Culture*. New York: Peter Lang, 2016.

———. *Signs of Crime: Introducing Forensic Semiotics*. Berlin: Mouton de Gruyter, 2013.

Dawkins, Richard. *River out of Eden: A Darwinian View of Life*. New York: Basic, 1995.

———. *The Selfish Gene*. Oxford: Oxford University Press, 1976.

DeLisi, Matt. "An Empirical Study of Rape in the Context of Multiple Murder." *Journal of Forensic Sciences* 59, no. 2 (2014): 420–24.

———. "Extreme Career Criminals." *American Journal of Criminal Justice* 25, no. 2 (2001): 239–52.

de Sade, Marquis. *Philosophy in the Bedroom*. Reprint, New York: Grove, 1994. First published in 1795.

Dickie, John. *Cosa Nostra: A History of the Sicilian Mafia*. London: Hodder and Stoughton, 2004.

Dobash, Rebecca, and Russell Dobash. *When Men Murder Women (Interpersonal Violence)*. Oxford: Oxford University Press, 2015.

Douglas, John E., Anne W. Burgess, Allen G. Burgess, and Robert K. Ressler. *Crime Classification Manual: A Standard System for Investigating and Classifying Violent Crime*. New York: Lexington Books, 1992.

Durkheim, Emile. *The Elementary Forms of Religious Life*. New York: Macmillan, 1912.

Ellroy, James. *My Dark Places*. New York: Vintage, 1997.

Fox, James A., and Jack Levin. *Extreme Killing: Understanding Serial and Mass Murder*, 3rd ed. Thousand Oaks, CA: Sage, 2015.

Freud, Sigmund. *Civilization and Its Discontents*. Reprint, London: Hogarth, 1963. First published in 1931.

———. "Instincts and Their Vicissitudes." In *The Standard Edition of the Complete Psychological Works of Sigmund Freud*, Vol. 14, *1914–1916: On the History of the Psycho-Analytic Movement, Papers on Metapsychology and Other Works*. London: Hogarth, 1957.

———. *The Interpretation of Dreams*. New York: Avon 1901.

Girard, René. *Violence and the Sacred*. Baltimore: Hopkins, 1979.

Glasgow, Michael, and Phyllis Gobbell. *An Unfinished Canvas: A True Story of Love, Family and Murder in Nashville*. New York: Berkley Books. 2007.

Grotjahn, Martin. *Beyond Laughter: Humor and the Subconscious*. New York: McGraw-Hill, 1966.

Hare, Robert. *The Hare Psychopathy Checklist—Revised*. Toronto: Multi-Health Systems, 1991.

———. *Psychopathy: Theory and Research*. New York: Wiley, 1970.

———. *Without Conscience: The Disturbing World of Psychopaths Among Us*. New York: Guilford, 1998.

Hentig, Hans von. *The Criminal and His Victim: Studies in the Sociobiology of Crime*. New York: Schocken, 1948.

Hickey, Eric W. *Serial Murderers and Their Victims*, 7th ed. Boston: Cengage, 2016.

Hinsie, Leland E., and Robert Jean Campbell. *Psychiatric Dictionary*. New York: Oxford University Press, 1970.

Hobbes, Thomas. *Leviathan*. London: Andrew Crooke, 1651.

Holmes, Ronald M., and Steven T. Holmes. *Profiling Violent Crimes: An Investigative Tool*, 4th ed. Thousand Oaks, CA: Sage, 2008.

———. "Understanding Mass Murder: A Starting Point." *Federal Probation* 56, no. 1 (1992): 53–61.

Jackson, Christine A. *The Tell-Tale Art: Poe in Modern Popular Culture*. Jefferson, NC: McFarland, 2012.

James, Bill. *Popular Crime: Reflections on the Celebration of Violence*. New York: Scribner, 2011.

Jones, Douglas, and Phyllis Gobbell. *A Season of Darkness: It Began with the Murder of Pure Innocence*. New York: Berkley, 2010.

Jung, Carl. *The Portable Jung*. Harmondsworth, UK: Penguin, 1971.

Keppel, Robert, and Richard Walter. "Profiling Killers: A Revised Classification Model for Understanding Sexual Murder." *International Journal of Offender Therapy and Comparative Criminology* 43, no. 4 (1999): 417–37.

Kosir, Travis, and Dallas Drake. "Tracking Sex-Related Burglaries as a Means of Identifying Sexual Homicide Offenders." Policy paper, Center for Homicide Research, 2012.

Lachman, Gary. *Turn Off Your Mind: The Mystic Sixties and the Dark Side of the Age of Aquarius*. New York: Disinformation Books, 2001.

Largo, Michael. *Final Exits: The Illustrated Encyclopedia of How We Die*. New York: HarperCollins, 2006.

Larson, Erik. *The Devil in the White City: Murder, Magic, and Madness at the Fair That Changed America*. New York: Crown, 2002.

Lasseter, Don. *Die for Me: The Terrifying True Story of the Charles Ng and Leonard Lake Torture Murders*. New York: Pinnacle Books, 2000.

Lesser, Simon. *Fiction and the Unconscious*. Boston: Beacon, 1957.

Lim, Sun. S., Shobha Vadrevu, Yoke Chan, and Iccha Basnyat. "Facework on Facebook: The Online Publicness of Delinquents and Youths-at-Risk." *Journal of Broadcasting & Electronic Media* 56, no. 3 (2012).

Lunde, Paul. *Organized Crime: An Inside Guide to the World's Most Successful Industry*. London: Dorling Kindersley, 2004.

McGee, James P., and Caren R. DeBernardo. "The Classroom Avenger: A Behavioral Profile of School Based Shootings." *Forensic Examiner* 8, no. 5–6 (1999): 16–18.

McNab, Chris. *Serial Killer Timelines*. Berkeley: Ulysses, 2010.

Mellor, Lee. *Cold North Killers: Canadian Serial Murder*. Toronto: Dundurn, 2012.

Millon, Theodore. *Disorders of Personality: DSM IV and Beyond*, 3rd ed. Hoboken, NJ: Wiley, 2011.

Millon, Theodore, and Roger Davis. *Disorders of Personality: DSM IV and Beyond*, 1st ed. Hoboken, NJ: Wiley, 1996.

Money, John. *Lovemaps*. New York: Irvington Publishers, 1986.

———. *Lovemaps: Clinical Concepts of Sexual/Erotic Health and Pathology*. New York: Prometheus Books, 1993.

Neuman, Yair, Dan Assaf, Yochai Cohen, and James Knoll. "Profiling School Shooters: Automatic Text-Based Analysis." *Frontiers in Psychiatry* 6, no. 86 (2015). http://www.ncbi.nlm.nih.gov/pmc/articles/PMC4453266/.

Newton, Michael. *Hunting Humans: An Encyclopedia of Modern Serial Killers*. New York: Breakout Productions, 1990.

Nicaso, Antonio, and Marcel Danesi. *Made Men: Mafia Culture and the Power of Symbols, Rituals, and Myth*. Lanham, MD: Rowman & Littlefield, 2013.

Oakley, Barbara A. *Evil Genes*. Amherst, NY: Prometheus Books, 2008.

Olsson, John. *Forensic Linguistics: An Introduction to Language, Crime and the Law*, 2nd ed. London: Continuum, 2008.

———. *Word Crime: Solving Crime through Forensic Linguistics*. London: Continuum, 2009.

O'Toole, Mary E. *The School Shooter: A Threat Assessment Perspective*. Quantico, VA: Critical Incident Response Group, National Center for the Analysis of Violent Crime, FBI Academy, 2000.

Pantaleo, Katherine. "Gendered Violence: An Analysis of the Maquiladora Murders." *International Criminal Justice Review* 20, no. 4 (2010): 349–65.

Petherick, Wayne. *Serial Crime: Theoretical and Practical Issues in Behavioral Profiling*, 2nd ed. Burlington, MA: Elsevier, 2009.

Philbin, Tom. *I, Monster: Serial Killers in Their Own Chilling Words*. Amherst, NY: Prometheus Books, 2011.

Reade, W. Winwood. *The Martyrdom of Man*. Reprint, Grove, OR: University Press of the Pacific, 2004. First published in 1872.

Rossmo, D. Kim. *Geographic Profiling*. Boca Raton, FL: CRC, 2000.

Schmid, David. *Natural Born Celebrities: Serial Killers in American Culture*. Chicago: University of Chicago Press, 2005.

Simpson, Philip. *Psycho Paths: Tracking the Serial Killer through Contemporary American Film and Fiction*. Chicago: Southern Illinois University Press, 2000.

Slotkin, Richard. *Gunfighter Nation: The Myth of the Frontier in Twentieth-Century America*. New York: Macmillan, 1998.

Stewart, Gary. *The Most Dangerous Animal of All*. New York: Harper, 2015.

Strand, Ginger. *Killer on the Road: Violence and the American Interstate*. Austin: University of Texas Press, 2012.

Sutherland, Edwin H., and David R. Cressey. *Principles of Criminology*, 10th ed. Philadelphia: Lippincott, 1978.

Thomas, Ronald R. *Detective Fiction and the Rise of Forensic Science*. Cambridge: Cambridge University Press, 1999.

Turner, Allan. "Twice-Convicted Houston Killer Max Soffar Dies Days Before Federal Appeals Argument." *Houston Chronicle*, May 4, 2016. http://www.houstonchronicle.com/news/houston-texas/houston/article/Twice-convicted-Houston-killer-Max-Soffar-dies-7349787.php#photo-9897525.

U.S. Department of Justice. Federal Bureau of Investigation, Behavioral Analysis Unit. *Serial Murder: Pathways for Investigation*. A Report from the National Center for the Analysis of Violent Crime. Quantico, VA, 2014.

van Ornum, William. "The Secret Service on Preventing School Violence." *National Review*, December 17, 2012. http://www.nationalreview.com/corner/335825/secret-service-preventing-school-violence-william-van-ornum.

von Krafft-Ebing, Richard. *Psychopathia Sexualis*. Stuttgart: Ferdinand Enke, 1886.

Vronsky, Peter. *Female Serial Killers: How and Why Women Become Monsters*. New York: Berkley, 2007.

Websdale, Neil. *Policing the Poor: From Slave Plantation to Public Housing*. Boston: Northeastern University Press, 2001.

Wiggins, Bradley E., and G. Bret Bowers. "Memes as Genre: A Structurational Analysis of the Memescape." *New Media & Society* 17, no. 11 (2015): 1886–1906.

Williams, DJ. "Mephitic Projects: A Forensic Leisure Science Analysis of the BTK Serial Murders." *The Journal of Forensic Psychiatry & Psychology* 28, no. 1 (2016): 24–37.

Williams, DJ, Jeremy N. Thomas, and Michael Arntfield. "An Empirical Exploration of Leisure-Related Themes and Possible Constraints Across Descriptions of Serial Homicide Cases." *Leisure Sciences*, 2018 (in press).

Wortley, Richard, and Lorraine Mazerolle, eds. *Environmental Criminology and Crime Analysis*. Portland, OR: Willan, 2008.

Wraight, Christopher D. *Rousseau's "The Social Contract": A Reader's Guide*. New York: Bloomsbury Academic, 2008.

Yates, Judith A. *When Nashville Bled: The Untold Stories of Serial Killer Paul Dennis Reid*. CreateSpace, 2014.

Youngs, Donna, David Canter, and Nikki Carthy. "The Offender's Narrative: Unresolved Dissonance in Life as a Film (LAAF) Responses." *Legal and Criminological Psychology* 21, no. 2 (2016): 251–65.

Zasky, Jason. "Arch Enemy: The Strange Addiction of the Footstomper." *Failure.* July 1, 2002. http://failuremag.com/feature/article/arch_enemy/.

INDEX

ABOUT THE AUTHOR

Bestselling true-crime author Michael Arntfield spent more than fifteen years as a police officer and detective in Canada before going on to become a globally noted homicide scholar and criminologist, including a year spent as a visiting professor at Vanderbilt University in Nashville. There, he met retired Metro Nashville detective sergeant Pat Postiglione, and the vision for *Monster City* took shape. An industry-leading consultant on crime trends and emerging forensic methodologies, Arntfield is the author of more than a dozen books, including *Mad City*; he is also the host and producer of a true-crime series airing on both the Oxygen Network and the Oprah Winfrey Network, while he remains a professor of criminology at Western University in Canada. He lives with his family, who split their time between Canada and Florida. For more about the author, visit his website, http://michaelarntfield.com.